A Modern Treatise on the Principle of Legality in Criminal Law

Gabriel Hallevy

A Modern Treatise on the Principle of Legality in Criminal Law

Springer

Assoc.Prof. Gabriel Hallevy

ISBN 978-3-642-13713-6 e-ISBN 978-3-642-13714-3
DOI 10.1007/978-3-642-13714-3
Springer Heidelberg Dordrecht London New York

Library of Congress Control Number: 2010935595

Cover design: WMXDesign GmbH, Heidelberg, Germany

Printed on acid-free paper

Springer is part of Springer Science+Business Media (www.springer.com)

To my wife and daughters.

But the Lord saw that the wickedness of humankind had become great on the earth. Every inclination of the thoughts of their minds was only evil all the time. The Lord regretted that he had made humankind on the earth, and he was highly offended. So the Lord said, "I will wipe humankind, whom I have created, from the face of the earth – everything from humankind to animals, including creatures that move on the ground and birds of the air, for I regret that I have made them".

Genesis 6:5-7

Preface

The present book is based on the lectures delivered by the author in the past few years as part of the Criminal Law course of the Faculty of Law at the Ono Academic College. There has been little research on the principle of legality in modern criminal law, although this is one of the most ancient legal principles of human society. In recent generations there have been several attempts to define the principle conclusively, but only with regard to some of its aspects. No comprehensive definition of the principle of legality has been attempted to date.

A conclusive definition of the principle of legality in criminal law requires both an accurate inward-looking definition of the principle itself, and an outward-looking treatment of its relation with criminal law theory. Only a coherent theory that includes the principle of legality as an integral part of criminal law theory can do justice to the principle of legality. This view is consistent with the scientific concept of law, which regards the law as part of science.

A Modern Treatise on the Principle of Legality in Criminal Law is therefore a scientific treatise on one of the four principles of the criminal law. The present treatise is divided into six parts, according to the scientific understanding of the principle of legality in criminal law. Chapter 1 explores the relation between the principle of legality and the general theory of criminal law in the context of the structure and the development of the principle of legality in human society. This chapter outlines the four secondary principles of the principle of legality, and describes them in general terms.

Chapters 2–5 discuss in detail each of the four secondary principles of the principle of legality. Chapter 2 discusses the legitimate sources of the criminal norm, Chap. 3 discusses the applicability of the criminal norm in time, Chap. 4 discusses the applicability of the criminal norm in place and Chap. 5 discusses the interpretation of the criminal norm. Each of the four chapters concludes with a discussion of the conflict of laws issues relevant to the secondary principle under investigation. Finally, Chap. 6 addresses the problem of the conflict of laws *within* the conflicts of laws and rounds out the discussion.

I wish to thank Ono Academic College for supporting this project, and especially Dean of the faculty of law and vice chairman Dudi Schwartz for his staunch support on so many important occasions. I thank Gabriel Lanyi for his comments and Anke Seyfried of Springer Heidelberg for guiding the publication of the book from its inception to its conclusion. Finally, I wish to thank my wife and daughters for the helpful discussions and support they offered along the way.

Kiryat Ono, June 2010 Gabriel Hallevy

Contents

List of Figures

List of Tables

Chapter 1
The Meaning and Structure of the Principle of Legality in Criminal Law

Contents

1.1 The Role of the Principle of Legality in the Criminal Law Theory

1.1.1 The Basic Structure of Criminal Law Theory

Criminal law is part of the scientific sphere called "law," or the legal science. Therefore, criminal law is a scientific sphere. In the past, in the Anglo-American legal systems, there was a conceptual difficulty in classifying law as a science because of its development through case-laws, which made use of the praxis of binding precedents (*stare decisis*). This attitude matched the general scientific development in Anglo-American countries, which was casuistic. By contrast, the European-Continental legal systems considered law to be a science,[1] and therefore in Europe it was necessary to study at the university to become a jurist. In the first university in Europe, the University of Bologna, law was one of the scientific

[1]For the development of the law as science in the Middle Ages and afterwards in Europe see Harold J. Berman and Charles J. Reid Jr., *Roman Law in Europe and the Jus Commune: A Historical Overview with Emphasis on the New Legal Science of the Sixteenth Century*, 20 SYRACUSE J. INT'L L. & COM. 1 (1994).

G. Hallevy, *A Modern Treatise on the Principle of Legality in Criminal Law*,
DOI 10.1007/978-3-642-13714-3_1, © Springer-Verlag Berlin Heidelberg 2010

subjects being studied.[2] The Faculty of Law of Bologna played a crucial role in the development of law in the Middle Ages (*jus commune*).[3]

In the modern era there seems to be no controversy that the law represents indeed a scientific sphere.[4] The law should therefore develop through legal research, using the relevant research methodologies, some of which are unique to this particular scientific sphere. This is also the reason for placing the legal studies in the academia.[5] If the law is as science and requires a scientific methodology, it is necessary to create a single scientific theory that governs the law. This is a fundamental endeavor in every science, including the law. Such a theory must meet two requirements: it must describe accurately all relevant events without using any random elements and it must predict accurately all relevant future events.[6]

The emergence of such a new theory is not always simple. The primary theory appears to be inconclusive after some time, and exceptions arise that the theory cannot explain. As a result, amendments or changes are introduced in the primary theory to account for the exceptions. When the theory can no longer explain the exceptions, it is replaced by a new one. The new theory may also turn out to be inconclusive, and must therefore be amended, changed, or replaced.[7]

Legal theory is developing in the same way. A single legal theory that would clarify all relevant legal issues would not be restricted to specific legal areas. In the context of this book, however, the theory is restricted to criminal law, therefore the theory under consideration is **Criminal Law Theory**. The need for such a theory in criminal law is crucial. The large number of doctrines, legal norms, exceptions, and exceptions to the exceptions muddied the waters of criminal law, which have become vague and unclear. The single theory of criminal law, which organizes all of criminal law and speaks with one coherent voice, is about **legal social control**. Society controls the individuals through criminal law, and therefore the

---

[2]University of Bologna was established in 1088 AD, and it is considered as the first university in Europe. For the development of the law as science in the European universities see HASTINGS RASHDALL, THE UNIVERSITIES OF EUROPE IN THE MIDDLE AGES 135 (1935).

[3]JOHN HENRY MERRYMAN, THE CIVIL LAW TRADITION: AN INTRODUCTION TO THE LEGAL SYSTEMS OF WESTERN EUROPE AND LATIN AMERICA 7–14, 27–34 (1969).

[4]W. D. Lewis, *The Law of England Considered as a Science*, 10 L. REV. & Q. J. BRIT. & FOREIGN JURISPRUDENCE 23 (1849); George W. Goble, *Law as a Science*, 9 IND. L. J. 294 (1934); John D. Appel, *Law as a Social Science in the Undergraduate Curriculum*, 10 J. LEGAL EDUC. 485 (1958); John J. Bonsignore, *Law as a Hard Science: On the Madness in Method*, 2 ALSA F. 49 (1977); Marcia Speziale, *Langdell's Concept of Law as Science: The Beginning of Anti-Formalism in American Legal Theory*, 5 VT. L. REV. 1 (1980); Lynn R. Campbell, *Law as a Social Science*, 9 DALHOUSIE L. J. 404 (1984); David L. Faigman, *To Have and Have Not: Assessing the Value of Social Science to the Law as Science and Policy*, 38 EMORY L. J. 1005 (1989).

[5]George L. Priest, *Social Science: Theory and Legal Education: The Law School As University*, 33 J. LEGAL EDUC. 437 (1983); Mark Warren Bailey, *Early Legal Education in the United States: Natural Law Theory and Law as a Moral Science*, 48 J. LEGAL EDUC. 311 (1998).

[6]STEPHEN W. HAWKING, A BRIEF HISTORY OF TIME 18 (1989).

[7]Ibid, at pp. 19–22, 147–160.

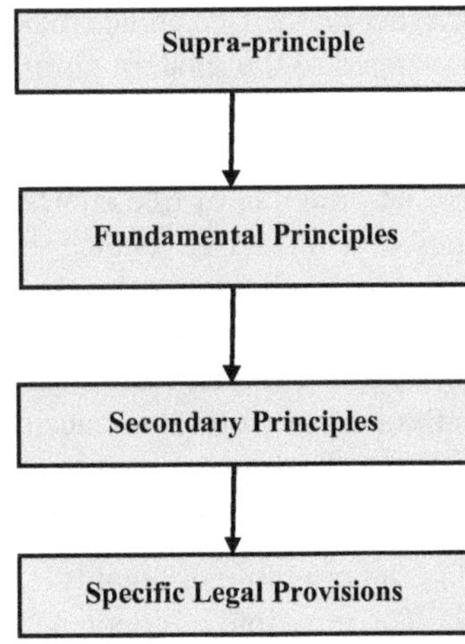

Fig. 1.1 The structure of scientific legal theory

justifications of criminal law theory must be based on social approaches and explanations.

A scientific theory has various levels of application. The levels are hierarchical, with lower levels subordinated to the higher ones. The highest level represents the essence of the theory, generalized into a supra-principle. This supra-principle is the core of the theory, and all other levels are subordinated to it. Exceptions at this level require replacing the entire theory. From the supra-principle derive the fundamental principles that break down the supra-principle into basic legal principles, which in turn guide the application of the supra-principle. From each fundamental principle derive secondary principles. It is the secondary principles that create the legal form of the concrete application of the fundamental principles. From each secondary principle derive specific legal provisions that make the secondary principles applicable to specific events.

Figure 1.1 shows a schematic description of this four-level structure.

According to this structure, specific legal provisions cannot contradict secondary principles, secondary principles cannot contradict fundamental principles, and fundamental principles cannot contradict the supra-principle. This structure functions as a template, which is then filled with content relevant to criminal law theory.

The **supra-principle** of criminal law theory is the **principle of free choice**. According to the supra-principle, no criminal liability can be imposed on an individual unless the individual has chosen to commit a criminal offense. When an individual is compelled to commit an offense, imposing criminal liability is not considered to be justified. The individual autonomy of the human being is the social concept behind the supra-principle.[8] To function as the supra-principle of criminal

[8] ANDREW ASHWORTH, PRINCIPLES OF CRIMINAL LAW 25–28 (5th ed., 2006); ANTHONY JOHN PATRICK KENNY, FREEWILL AND RESPONSIBILITY (1978); HERBERT L. A. HART, PUNISHMENT AND RESPONSIBILITY: ESSAYS IN THE PHILOSOPHY OF LAW ch. 6 (1968).

law theory, the free choice must be well defined. Although free choice may seem to be related to the modern political philosophy of the eighteenth century, its origins reach back to the dawn of humanity.[9] When certain regimes rejected the free choice concept, they were considered to be illegitimate.

The principle of free choice negates determinism. The basic assumption of free choice is that free choice is possible. Deterministic concepts, which regard individual behavior to be dominated by external forces, negate the principle of free choice.[10] Determinism may be relative. Under certain circumstances, when an object falls from an individual's hand, the path of the object may not be under the individual's control, but causing the object fall may be.

From the supra-principle derive the **fundamental principles**. In criminal law theory there are four fundamental principles:

(1) The principle of legality
(2) The principle of conduct
(3) The principle of culpability
(4) The principle of personal liability

The supra-principle of free choice refers to the individual's choice between permitted and forbidden behavior. To enable free choice it is necessary to draw accurately the borderline between "permitted" and "forbidden." The rules of formation of what is "permitted" and "forbidden" are embodied in the first fundamental principle of criminal law theory, **the principle of legality**. When an individual chooses to commit a forbidden act, the act must be physically carried out to duly enable the imposition of criminal liability.

The rules of formation of the physical appearance of free choice are embodied in the second fundamental principle of criminal law theory, **the principle of conduct**, the objective expression of free choice.

Exercise of an individual's free choice requires certain mental positions in the individual's mind, including both positive and negative aspects. The positive aspects are embodied in the mental elements of the offense, the negative aspects in the general defenses.[11] Thus, an offense may require specific intent in order to impose criminal liability — a positive aspect (mental element). When the

---

[9] RONALD DWORKIN, TAKING RIGHTS SERIOUSLY 180 (1977); JOSEPH RAZ, THE MORALITY OF FREEDOM 425 (1986); Barbara Hudson, *Pushing the Poor: a Critique of the Dominance of Legal Reasoning in Penal Policy and Practice*, PENAL THEORY AND PRACTICE 302 (Robin Antony Duff ed., 1994); RONALD DWORKIN, A MATTER OF PRINCIPLE 181–204 (1985).

[10] Paul R. Dimond and Gene Sperling, *Of Cultural Determinism and the Limits of Law*, 83 MICH. L. REV. 1065 (1985); Morris D. Forkosch, *Determinism and the Law*, 60 KY. L. J. 350 (1952); John L. Hill, *Freedom, Determinism, and the Externalization of Responsibility in the Law: A Philosophical Analysis*, 76 GEO. L. J. 2045 (1988); Ian Shrank, *Determinism and the Law of Consent – A Reformulation of Individual Accountability for Choices Made without Free Will*, 12 SUFFOLK U. L. REV. 796 (1978); Jos Andenaes, *Determinism and Criminal Law*, 47 J. CRIM. L. CRIMINOLOGY & POLICE SCI. 406 (1957); Michele Cotton. *A Foolish Consistency: Keeping Determinism out of the Criminal Law*, 15 B. U. PUB. INT. L. J. 5 (2006).

[11] ANDREW ASHWORTH, PRINCIPLES OF CRIMINAL LAW 157–248 (5th ed., 2006).

individual is incapable to form culpability (*doli incapax*), owing to mental disease, infancy, lack of self-control, uncontrollable intoxication, etc., the possibility of imposing criminal liability is negated because of subjective reasons related to the negative aspects.

The rules of formation of the mental appearance of free choice are embodied in the third fundamental principle of the criminal law theory, **the principle of culpability**, the subjective expression of free choice. Because the imposition of criminal liability requires free choice on the part of the individual, it is necessary that the free choice be the individual's own and personal free choice. One individual is not criminally liable for the free choice of another.[12] Free choice and criminal liability are embodied in the same legal entity.

The rules of formation of the personal appearance of free choice are embodied in the fourth fundamental principle of criminal law theory, **the principle of personal liability**. The four fundamental principles are the outcome of the supra-principle of free choice and derive from it.

From the four fundamental principles derive **secondary principles**. From each of the four fundamental principles derive four secondary principles. The secondary principles form a concrete and specific template for the application of the fundamental principles. From each of the secondary principles derive **specific legal provisions**, the specific applications of secondary principles. The specific legal provisions represent concrete rules of imposition of criminal liability upon the individual. Figure 1.2 illustrates schematically the four-level structure of criminal law theory.

There are no exceptions to criminal law theory, not in its structure and not in its content.

1.1.2 The Basic Structure of the Principle of Legality in Criminal Law

The supra-principle of free choice requires that the individual have a real possibility to choose between what is "permitted" and "forbidden," i.e., between committing a specific offense and not committing it. This possibility can exist only if exact borderlines are drawn between what is "permitted" and "forbidden." In a context that lacks a clear borderline, there is no meaning to free choice. The borderlines are part of the definitions of specific offenses, which forbid certain behaviors. The

[12] See 2 Kings 14:6: "But he did not execute the sons of the assassins. He obeyed the Lord's commandment as recorded in the law scroll of Moses, Fathers must not be put to death for what their sons do, and sons must not be put to death for what their fathers do. A man must be put to death only for his own sin"; Ezekiel 18:20: "The person who sins is the one who will die. A son will not suffer for his father's iniquity, and a father will not suffer for his son's iniquity; the righteous person will be judged according to his righteousness, and the wicked person according to his wickedness".

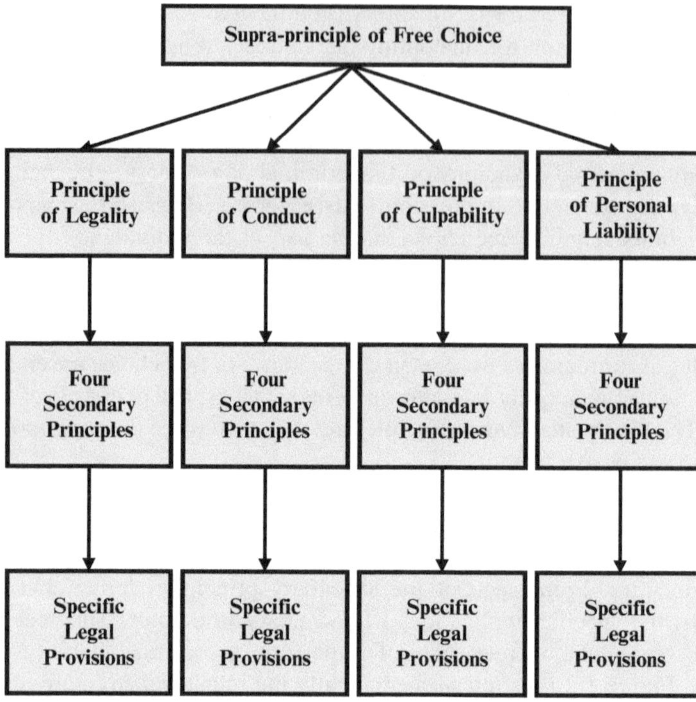

Fig. 1.2 The structure of criminal law theory

principle of legality shapes the general rules by which the criminal norm applies to individuals.[13]

Because the principle of legality has to do with the applicability of the criminal norm, it relates to criminality *in abstracto*, not *in concreto*. Criminality *in abstracto* means analyzing the criminal norm in abstract terms, irrespective of individual events. Criminality *in concreto* is generally the domain of the courts, where the imposition of criminal liability on an individual in given circumstances is analyzed in specific terms. The principle of legality relates to the criminal norm and not to the criminal event. Figure 1.3 describes the basic structure of the principle of legality in criminal law.

According to its basic scientific structure in criminal law, the principle of legality has four main aspects, expressed by its four secondary principles. The first secondary principle relates to the sources of the criminal norm, and asks the question: What are the legitimate sources of the criminal norm. For example, can an international covenant form a criminal norm applicable to individuals? Can the constitution? Can judicial decisions?

---

[13]See e.g. Gabriel Hallevy, *The Impact of Defense Arguments Based on the Cultural Difference of the Accused in the Criminal Law of Immigrant Countries and Societies*, 5 J. OF MIGRATION & REFUGEE ISSUES 13 (2009).

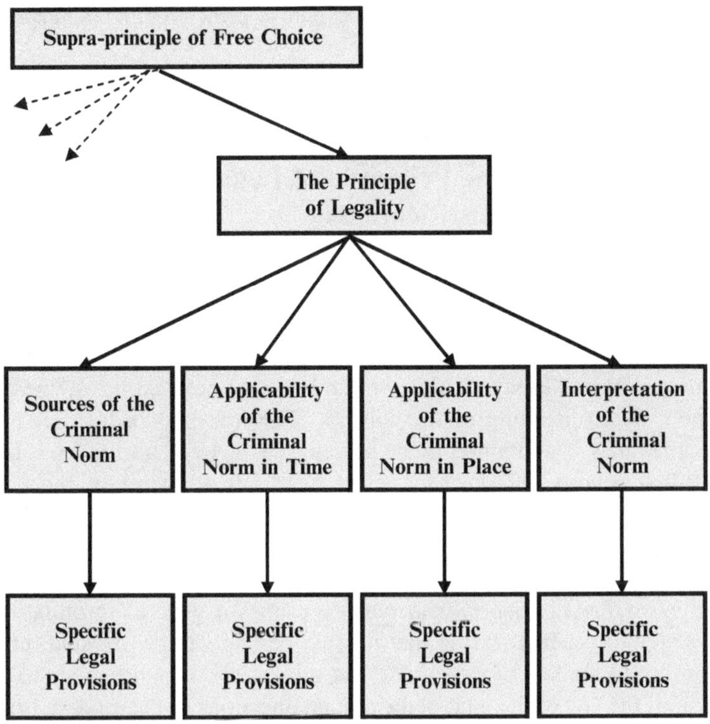

Fig. 1.3 The basic structure of the principle of legality in criminal law

The second secondary principle relates to the applicability of the criminal norm in time, and asks the question: How should the criminal norm be applied with relation to time? For example, can the criminal norm be applicable retroactively, or prospectively, or both?

The third secondary principle relates to the applicability of the criminal norm in place, and asks the question: How should the criminal norm be applied with relation to place? For example, can the criminal norm be applied territorially, or extra-territorially, or both?

The fourth secondary principle relates to the interpretation of the criminal norm, and asks the question: How should the criminal norm be interpreted? For example, must the criminal norm be interpreted strictly, or purposively, or leniently toward the individual? Some aspects of this question relate to the formation of the criminal norm *ex ante* (how should the criminal norm be formulated), others to the application of the existing criminal norm *ex post* (how should the criminal norm be interpreted). The four secondary principles are discussed in four subsequent chapters.[14] Finally, the book

[14]The first secondary principle is discussed hereinafter at Chap. 2; The second secondary principle is discussed hereinafter at Chap. 3; The third secondary principle is discussed hereinafter at Chap. 4; The fourth secondary principle is discussed hereinafter at Chap. 5.

addresses the possible conflict between the secondary principles and their specific legal provisions as it applies to individual laws.[15]

1.2 Development of the Principle of Legality in Criminal Law and Its Modern Justifications

Despite the Latin maxim *nullum crimen sine lege* (there is no crime without a law),[16] the origin of the principle of legality in its modern meaning is not in Roman law but in the age of Enlightenment in the eighteenth century.[17] Although there are some rigorous formulations of this principle in ancient cultures, these do not include the modern meaning of the concept. The first known formulation of the principle of legality is contained in the second law of Ur-Nammu, from the end of the twenty-first century BC, in the Ancient East.[18] In Roman law, there are some legal provisions that may relate to the principle of legality and that lasted for a long period.[19] These provisions, however, were not considered to be binding in an absolute manner.

Article 39 of the English *magna carta* provides a general formulation of the principle of legality when stating that no free person can be arrested, unless it is done according to the law of the land.[20] But this article does not relate to the exact formulation of the law of the land in the crucial questions of the modern principle of legality. Although Article 39 played a significant role in strengthening the rule of law in England, it was not adequate to establish the principle of legality in criminal law.[21]

The modern principle of legality originates in the insights of the European Enlightenment, in the eighteenth century, where first industrial revolution, created a new socio-economic middle class within the old absolutist regime. The new middle class then pressured the regimes to create the legal frames that would

---

[15]Hereinafter at Chap. 6.

[16]Another Latin maxim in that theme is *Nulla Poena sine Lege*.

[17]Schottlaender, *Die Geschichtliche Entwicklung des Satzes: Nulla Poena sine Lege*, 132 STRAFRECHTLICHE ABHANDLUNGEN 1 (1911).

[18]RUSS VERSTEEG, EARLY MESOPOTAMIAN LAW 21, 108 (2000). The translation of this second law is: "If a man acts lawlessly, they shall kill him".

[19]Digesta, 42.48.19.155(2); Digesta, 50.16.131: "Poena non irrogatur, nisi quae quaque lege vel quo alio jure specialiter huic delicto imposita est".

[20]Article 39 of the Magna Carta provides: "Nullus liber homo capiatur, vel imprisonetur, aut disseisiatur, aut utlagetur, aut exuletur, aut aliquo modo destruatur, nec super cum ibimus, nec super cum mittemus, nisi per legale judicium parium suorum vel per legem terre".

[21]SIR JOHN FORTESCUE, DE LAUDIBUS LEGUM ANGLIAE 93 (1470, trans. Gregor, 1874): "In such a Constitution, under such humane laws, every man may live safely and securely"..."Indeed, one would much rather that twenty guilty persons should escape the punishment of death, than that one innocent person should be condemned and suffer capitally".

protect their economic interests in the course of the social changes taking place at the time. The middle class, based economically on the industrial production in the cities, had new social needs, different from those of the nobility and farm dwellers outside the cities, which were based upon land.[22]

For example, it was necessary to define a new and specific offense to prohibit smuggling. An offense of this type, irrelevant in earlier times, became necessary to the new socio-economic middle class, which was been based on industry.[23] Moreover, because of the high rates of conviction and harsh punishments meted out for property offenses, the courts tended to avoid convicting poor offenders by using a wide legal interpretation. As many property offenders were exonerated, not to impose severe penalties on the poor, the middle classes were left defenseless against property crime and pressured the regimes to create new offenses, with moderate and proportional penalties.[24] The new offenses were aimed at producing a credible social deterrence.

At the same time, the ideas of the Enlightenment spread throughout Europe and contributed to the formation of a new political philosophy of liberalism. Liberalism focused on the individual and contrasted the individual with society.[25] Importing the liberal philosophy into the law created a liberal concept of law, or the liberal legal concept.[26] According to this concept, two principal social powers confront each other in the context of criminal law. The *first* is the power of the sovereign to impose social control. This power exists in all parts of the socialization process. In the context of criminal law, it is manifest as *legal social control*, i.e., the societal control of the individual through legal means.[27]

The direct outcome of legal social control is that society can direct the behavior of individuals. This power is a significant characteristic of every regime in all human societies, democratic or totalitarian, ancient or modern. The difference between various societies lies in the result of the balance between this power (legal social control) and the second one.

The *second* power is individualism. In the context of criminal law, it is *legal individualism*,[28] manifest in the fundamental freedoms of the individual, for example, the freedom to own property and the freedom of speech.[29] Legal individualism emerged out of the political struggles against the absolutist regimes in Europe of the

[22]MICHEL FOUCAULT, DISCIPLINE AND PUNISH 87 (1979).

[23]Cal Winslow, *Sussex Smugglers*, ALBION'S FATAL TREE: CRIME AND SOCIETY IN EIGHTEENTH-CENTURY ENGLAND (1975).

[24]JEREMY BENTHAM, THEORY OF LEGISLATION 179, 207, 217 (1975).

[25]See e.g. in JOHN HENRY MERRYMAN, THE CIVIL LAW TRADITION: AN INTRODUCTION TO THE LEGAL SYSTEMS OF WESTERN EUROPE AND LATIN AMERICA 27–34, 40–49 (1969); J. M. KELLY, A SHORT HISTORY OF WESTERN LEGAL THEORY 258–277 (1992).

[26]RONALD DWORKIN, A MATTER OF PRINCIPLE 181–204 (1985).

[27]VOLKER KREY, DEUTSCHES STRAFRECHT ALLGEMEINER TEIL, TEIL I: GRUNDLAGEN 2–7 (2002).

[28]JOHN BREWER AND JOHN STYLES, AN UNGOVERNABLE PEOPLE: THE ENGLISH AND THEIR LAW IN THE SEVENTEENTH AND EIGHTEENTH CENTURIES 14 (1980).

[29]JOSEPH VINING, LEGAL IDENTITY 2 (1978).

eighteenth and nineteenth centuries, which used their powers to create criminal norms to control the individuals.[30] The individuals, in turn, identified the criminal law with the absolutist regime. The political struggles against the absolutist regimes brought about the recognition of the legal individualism and created a new balance between legal social control and legal individualism.[31]

Since the eighteenth century, legal individualism has become a major restraining force on the power of the state to apply legal social control. During the nineteenth and twentieth centuries, the power of legal individualism increased, and in the modern state legal individualism is considered to be the basis of modern society, with legal social control deemed as the necessary restraint on legal individualism to enable human existence in organized society.[32] This arrangement is consistent with the modern liberal concept, in which the people are the basis of sovereignty in the modern state, and the state reflects legal individualism in its reign. The only restraints permitted on legal individualism are those restraints that enable social life. Intervention of the state in the individual's life is an exception that requires valid and explicit justification.[33] Thus, the concept of the night watchman state was born.[34]

The application of legal individualism became a major part of the rule of law in the liberal state, in which the criminal norm is created only by the elected representatives of the society, not appointed (by gods or people).[35] This concept matured after the First World War, and became crucial after the second. Deviation from this concept is considered to be a characteristic of tyrannical regimes.[36] One of the outcomes of this concept is the supremacy of the parliament over other organs of the state, because parliament represents society and reflects it.

---

[30] LINDSAY FARMER, CRIMINAL LAW, TRADITION AND LEGAL ORDER 6 (1997).

[31] FRANCO VENTURI, UTOPIA AND REFORM IN THE ENLIGHTENMENT (1971); E. P. THOMPSON, WHIGS AND HUNTERS 259–265 (1975); Douglas Hay, Property, *Authority and the Criminal Law*, ALBION'S FATAL TREE (1977); ALAN NORRIE, CRIME, REASON AND HISTORY – A CRITICAL INTRODUCTION TO CRIMINAL LAW 16–19 (2nd ed., 2006).

[32] Ian Dennis, *The Critical Condition of Criminal Law*, 50 CURRENT LEGAL PROBLEMS 213 (1997).

[33] HERBERT L. A. HART, PUNISHMENT AND RESPONSIBILITY: ESSAYS IN THE PHILOSOPHY OF LAW 181 (1968): "...the simple idea that unless a man has the capacity and a fair opportunity or chance to adjust his behaviour to the law its penalties ought not be applied to him".

[34] ROBERT NOZICK, ANARCHY, STATE, AND UTOPIA (1974); JONATHAN WOLFF, ROBERT NOZICK: PROPERTY, JUSTICE AND MINIMAL STATE (1981).

[35] Norrie, *supra* note 31, at p. 19: "Change of the law is for the legislators. The proper and logical solution to the problem of law is a comprehensive legal **code**, which in one coherent, logical, concise document establishes the law, its penalties, and the duties of free citizen" (emphasis in original).

[36] On June 28, 1935 the German penal code has been amended and provided: "Irgendeine Person wird bestraft werden, der eine Handlung einsetzt, die das Gesetz erklärt, strafbar zu sein, oder, der von Strafe gemäß grundlegenden Ideen von Strafgesetz und der gesunden Empfindung der Leute verdient. Wenn kein bestimmtes Strafgesetz direkt zutreffend zur Handlung ist, wird es gemäß dem Gesetz, die grundlegende Idee bestraft werden, von dem ihm am besten passt". The Soviet used this approach within articles 6 and 10 of the Soviet penal code of 1926.

There are two main differences between Anglo-American and European-Continental legal systems in applying this concept. The European-Continental legal systems tended not to accept the praxis of binding precedent (*stare decisis*), which enables courts to "legislate" through judicial decisions. Judges are not elected by the public, and therefore are not allowed to enact laws. As a result, only codification (legislation of the parliament) has the legitimate power to enact laws.[37] In the Anglo-American legal systems, following the English tradition, the binding precedent praxis has been accepted to preserve the power of the courts. In criminal law the courts exercise this power very strictly.[38]

The second difference has to do with the functionality of the principle of legality in criminal law. In Anglo-American legal systems the principle of legality is considered as a protecting "shield" from unjustified application of legal social control through criminal law. Thus, the individual exercises the principle of legality as a defense argument.[39] In European-Continental legal systems, the principle of legality can also function as an offensive weapon.[40] In these legal systems, equality is a value that cannot be easily disregarded, and whenever the criminal law is applied to an individual, the principle of legality requires the same application to other individuals in the same circumstances.[41]

Since the eighteenth century criminal codes have emerged all over Europe, partially or fully embracing the principle of legality in its liberal interpretation. Before the French Revolution, it was manifest in the Prussian criminal code of 1721, the Bayern criminal code of 1751, and the Austrian criminal code of 1769.[42] The first criminal code that restrained criminal legislation was the Austrian criminal code of 1787, embraced by Joseph II.[43] Under the French Revolution, Article 8 of the Declaration of Rights of the Man and of the Citizen (La Déclaration des droits de l'homme et du citoyen), of August 26, 1789, embraced the principle of legality as an integral part of the French social order.[44] It was restated in the 1791

---

[37]Norrie, *supra* note 31, at p. 19: "The code both guards individual liberty against the State and safeguards individual property and security through deterrence. It provides the ideal text for the individual to read and calculate by, as well as maximum protection and respect for his liberty".

[38]Morgan, [1976] A.C. 182, [1975] 2 W.L.R. 913, [1975] 2 All E.R. 347; Abbott, [1977] A.C. 755; NEIL MACCORMICK, LEGAL REASONING AND LEGAL THEORY 15, 227 (1978); NICOLA LACEY, CELIA WELLS AND OLIVER QUICK, RECONSTRUCTING CRIMINAL LAW 17–23 (3rd ed., 2003, 2006).

[39]United States v. Batchelder, 442 U.S. 114, 99 S.Ct. 2198, 60 L.Ed.2d 755 (1979); Romer v. Evans, 517 U.S. 620, 116 S.Ct. 1620, 134 L.Ed.2d 855 (1996); Vacco v. Quill, 521 U.S. 793, 117 S.Ct. 2293, 138 L.Ed.2d 834 (1997).

[40]GEORGE P. FLETCHER, BASIC CONCEPTS OF CRIMINAL LAW 206–211 (1998).

[41]Ibid. Krey, *supra* note 27, at pp. 2–19.

[42]JEROME HALL, GENERAL PRINCIPLES OF CRIMINAL LAW 32 (2nd ed., 1960, 2005).

[43]Ibid at p. 33.

[44]Article 8 of the declaration of rights of the man and the citizen (La Déclaration des droits de l'homme et du citoyen) from August 26, 1789 provides: "Nul ne peut être puni qu'en vertu d'une loi établie et promulguée anterieurement au délit et légalement appliquée".

Constitution and in Article 4 of Code Napoléon, in 1810.[45] Code Napoléon served as the legal basis for many other criminal codes in the nineteenth century, including the Bayern criminal code of 1813, the Prussian criminal code of 1851, and the German penal code of 1870.[46]

In Germany, the principle of legality (Gesetzlichkeitsprinzip) was codified in Article 1 of the German penal code (Strafgesetzbuch),[47] and it is considered to be part of the constitutional concept in Germany because it has been included in the constitutional Basic Law as well.[48] The principle of legality in Germany bans courts from creating offenses (only parliament is authorized to enact criminal norms), prohibits aggravating retroactive criminal norms, and bans analogy as a legitimate method of interpretation of the criminal norm.[49]

German criminal law embraced two additional applications of the principle of legality. First is the secondary principle of subsidiarity (Subsidiaritätsprinzip), whereby criminal law is exercised only as a last resort (*ultima ratio*), when all other options are not relevant in a given case.[50] Second is the secondary principle of protection of legal rights (Rechtsgüterschutzprinzip), whereby the criminal law can be applied legitimately only when legal rights have been infringed by the offender. Moral values are not considered as legal rights and cannot justify exercising the criminal law.[51]

English common law regards the principle of legality as part of the concept of the rule of law, whereby subjects can be controlled criminal norms that are not arbitrary, hidden, or vague.[52] English common law applies the principle of legality in criminal law through four secondary principles: (a) non-retroactivity,[53]

---

[45]Article 4 of the Code Napoléon of 1810 provided: "Nulle contravention, nul délit, nul crime, ne peuvent être punis de peines qui n'étaient pas prononcées par la loi avant qu'ils fussent commis".

[46]Hall, *supra* note 42, at p. 34.

[47]Article 1 of the German penal code provides: "Eine Tat kann nur bestraft werden, wenn die Strafbarkeit gesetzlich bestimmt war, bevor die Tat begangen wurde".

[48]Grundgesetz, art. 103 (II) provides: "Eine Tat kann nur bestraft werden, wenn die Strafbarkeit gesetzlich bestimmt war, bevor die Tat begangen wurde".

[49]Most of the provisions of the principle of legality in criminal law of the German law are concentrated in articles 1-10 of the German penal code. See more in HANS-HEINRICH JESCHECK UND THOMAS WEIGEND, LEHRBUCH DES STRAFRECHTS – ALLGEMEINER TEIL 128–137 (5 Auf., 1996); Heribert Schumann, *Criminal Law*, INTRODUCTION TO GERMAN LAW 387, 388–389 (2nd ed., Mathias Reimann and Joachim Zekoll eds., 2005); NIGEL FOSTER, GERMAN LEGAL SYSTEM & LAWS 203 (2nd ed., 1996).

[50]Arthur Kaufmann, *Subsidiaritätsprinzip und Strafrecht*, GRUNDFRAGEN DER GESAMTEN STRAFRECHTS-WISSENSCHAFT, FESTSCHRIFT FüR HENKEL 89 (1974).

[51]Albin Eser, *The Principle of 'Harm' in the Concept of Crime – A Comparative Analysis of the Criminally Protected Legal Interests*, 4 DUQ. U. L. R. 345 (1966); BVerfGE 45, 187.

[52]JOSEPH RAZ, THE AUTHORITY OF LAW 214–215 (1979).

[53]Shaw v. Director of Public Prosecutions, [1962] A.C. 220, [1961] 2 All E.R. 446, [1961] 2 W.L. R. 897, 45 Cr. App. Rep. 113, 125 J.P. 437; Knuller (Publishing, Printing and Promotions) Ltd., [1973] A.C. 435, [1972] 2 All E.R. 898, [1972] 3 W.L.R. 143; Tan, [1983] Q.B. 1053.

(b) maximum certainty,[54] (c) strict construction,[55] and (d) the presumption of innocence.[56] The Human Rights Act of 1998 added the dimension of human rights to the principle of legality,[57] but English legal tradition could not comply with such a principle of recent European vintage, and English courts refused to accept it. This traditional judicial policy made use of the thin ice principle,[58] the social protection policy,[59] the extremely wide purposive interpretation technique,[60] and policy of easing the burden of proof.[61]

In American law the principle of legality is considered to be one of the basic foundations of criminal law. At the heart of the principle of legality in U.S. criminal law is the linkage between the courts and the legislator through application of the criminal law. One of the basic rules of the principle of legality in American law is that a vague criminal norm is void ("void for vagueness").[62] Initially, this rule was inspired by constitutional standards, in which any norm that does not meet the requirements of the Sixth Amendment to the United States Constitution is void.[63]

---

[54]Hughes v. Holley, (1988) 86 Cr. App. R. 130; Pattni, [2001] Crim. L.R. 570; Cotter, [2002] Crim. L.R. 824; Clark, [2003] 2 Cr. App. R. 363.

[55]Taylor, [1950] 2 K.B. 368; Gomez, [1993] A.C. 442, [1993] 1 All E.R. 1, [1992] 3 W.L.R. 1067; Pepper v. Hart, [1993] A.C. 593; Hinks, [2001] 2 A.C. 241, [2000] 3 W.L.R. 1590, [2000] 4 All E. R. 833; Andrew Ashworth, *Interpreting Criminal Statutes: A Crisis of Legality?*, 107 L.Q.R. 419 (1991).

[56]Woolmington v. Director of Public Prosecutions, [1935] All E.R. 1, [1935] A.C. 462, [1935] 104 L.J.K.B. 433, [1935] 153 L.T. 232, [1935] 51 T.L.R. 446, [1935] 79 Sol. Jo. 401, [1935] 25 Cr. App. Rep. 72, [1935] 30 Cox C.C. 234; Lambert, [2002] 2 A.C. 545, [2001] 3 W.L.R. 206, [2002] 1 All E.R. 2; Sheldrake, [2005] 1 A.C. 264, [2005] 1 All E.R. 237, [2005] 1 Cr. App. R. 28.

[57]Article 3(1) of the Human Rights Act, 1998, c.42 provides: "So far as it is possible to do so, primary legislation and subordinate legislation must be read and given effect in a way which is compatible with the Convention rights"; See more in Percy, [2002] Crim. L.R. 835, [2002] A.C.D. 24; A. v. The Secretary of State for the Home Department, [2005] 2 W.L.R. 87, [2004] U.K.H.L. 56; ANDREW ASHWORTH, HUMAN RIGHTS, SERIOUS CRIME AND CRIMINAL PROCEDURE (2002).

[58]Chan Chi-hung, [1996] A.C. 442; ANDREW ASHWORTH, PRINCIPLES OF CRIMINAL LAW 73–74 (5th ed., 2006).

[59]Lim Chin Aik, [1963] A.C. 160, [1963] 1 All E.R. 223, [1963] 2 W.L.R. 42; Cambridge and Isle of Ely County Council v. Rust, [1972] 2 Q.B. 426, [1972] 3 All E.R. 232, [1972] 3 W.L.R. 226.

[60]Charles, (1976) 63 Cr. App. R. 252; Oxford v. Moss, (1978) 68 Cr. App. R. 183, [1979] Crim. L. R. 119; Gold, [1987] Q.B. 1116, [1987] 3 All E.R. 618, [1987] 3 W.L.R. 803, [1988] A.C. 1063; Preddy, [1996] A.C. 815, [1996] 3 All E.R. 481, [1996] 3 W.L.R. 255.

[61]Hunt, [1987] A.C. 352, [1987] 1 All E.R. 1, [1986] 3 W.L.R. 1115, 84 Cr. App. R. 163; Carass, [2002] 2 Cr. App. R. 77; Andrew Ashworth and Meredith Blake, *The Presumption of Innocence in English Criminal Law*, [1996] CRIM. L. R. 306 (1996).

[62]United States v. Brewer, 139 U.S. 278, 11 S.Ct. 538, 35 L.Ed. 190 (1891); James v. Bowman, 190 U.S. 127, 23 S.Ct. 678, 47 L.Ed. 979 (1903); United States v. Evans, 333 U.S. 483, 68 S.Ct. 634, 92 L.Ed. 823 (1948).

[63]The sixth amendment of the United States constitution provides: "In all criminal prosecutions, the accused shall enjoy the right to a speedy and public trial, by an impartial jury of the state and district wherein the crime shall have been committed, which district shall have been previously ascertained by law, and to be informed of the nature and cause of the accusation; to be confronted with the witnesses against him; to have compulsory process for obtaining witnesses in his favor,

Currently, the United States Constitution exerts its influence over the principle of legality in criminal law through the Fifth and Fourteenth amendments.[64]

Under the influence of constitutional insights,[65] American criminal law also embraced rules of strict construction in the interpretation of the criminal norm in favor of the defendant.[66] The ban on retroactive criminal norms is considered to derive directly from the United States Constitution, and it applies both at the federal and the state levels.[67] This ban concerns the relations between the courts and the legislator, prohibiting the courts from applying a legislation retroactively.[68] American law regards the applicability of the criminal norm in place, by contrast, to fall under the jurisdiction of the courts.[69]

---

and to have the assistance of counsel for his defense"; See more in United States v. L. Cohen Grocery Co., 255 U.S. 81, 41 S.Ct. 298, 65 L.Ed. 516 (1921); Yu Cong Eng. V. Trinidad, 271 U.S. 500, 46 S.Ct. 619, 70 L.Ed. 1059 (1926).

[64]The fifth amendment of the United States constitution provides: "No person shall be held to answer for a capital, or otherwise infamous crime, unless on a presentment or indictment of a grand jury, except in cases arising in the land or naval forces, or in the militia, when in actual service in time of war or public danger; nor shall any person be subject for the same offense to be twice put in jeopardy of life or limb; nor shall be compelled in any criminal case to be a witness against himself, nor be deprived of life, liberty, or property, without due process of law; nor shall private property be taken for public use, without just compensation"; and the first section of the fourteenth amendment of the United States constitution provides: "All persons born or naturalized in the United States, and subject to the jurisdiction thereof, are citizens of the United States and of the state wherein they reside. No state shall make or enforce any law which shall abridge the privileges or immunities of citizens of the United States; nor shall any state deprive any person of life, liberty, or property, without due process of law; nor deny to any person within its jurisdiction the equal protection of the laws"; See more in Connally v. General Constr. Co., 269 U.S. 385, 46 S.Ct. 126, 70 L.Ed. 322 (1926); WAYNE R. LAFAVE, CRIMINAL LAW 103–104 (4th ed., 2003).

[65]Almendarez-Torres v. United States, 523 U.S. 224, 118 S.Ct. 1219, 140 L.Ed.2d 350 (1998).

[66]Commonwealth v. Wotan, 422 Mass. 740, 665 N.E.2d 976 (1996); Jones v. United States, 529 U. S. 848, 120 S.Ct. 1904, 146 L.Ed.2d 902 (2000); State v. Colvin, 645 N.W.2d 449 (Minn. 2002).

[67]United States Constitution, art I, §§ 9, 10.

[68]Calder v. Bull, 3 U.S. 386, 1 L.Ed. 648 (1798); Galvan v. Press, 347 U.S. 522, 74 S.Ct. 737, 98 L. Ed. 911 (1954); Rogers v. Tennessee, 532 U.S. 451, 121 S.Ct. 1693, 149 L.Ed.2d 697 (2001).

[69]United States v. Bowman, 260 U.S. 94, 43 S.Ct. 39, 67 L.Ed. 149 (1922); Smith v. United States, 507 U.S. 197, 113 S.Ct. 1178, 122 L.Ed.2d 548 (1993).

Chapter 2
The Legitimate Sources of the Criminal Norm

Contents

The first secondary principle of the principle of legality in criminal law concerns the sources of the criminal norm. Identifying the criminal norm is part of recognizing its legitimacy. For example, the Biblical commandment "Thou shalt not kill"[1] is a moral, not a criminal norm because most legal systems do not identify the Bible as a legitimate source for a criminal norm. In most legal systems, the legitimate source of the prohibition against murder is legislation enacted by parliament, whereas the Bible has not been embraced as a source of criminal norm by any legitimate source of law.[2] Another reason for not recognizing this commandment as a criminal norm is that it does not conform to the structure required of criminal norms.

---

[1]Exodus 20:13.

[2]This is not necessarily a full positivist approach to criminal law. See, e.g., in JOSEPH RAZ, THE AUTHORITY OF LAW 38 (1979); JOHN AUSTIN, THE PROVINCE OF JURISPRUDENCE DETERMINED 9 (1832, 2000); Herbert L. A. Hart, *Legal Positivism and the Separation of Law and Morals*, 71 HARV. L. REV. 593, 601–602 (1958).

G. Hallevy, *A Modern Treatise on the Principle of Legality in Criminal Law*,
DOI 10.1007/978-3-642-13714-3_2, © Springer-Verlag Berlin Heidelberg 2010

2.1 The Structure of the Criminal Norm and Its Identification

Identifying a specific criminal norm within a legitimate legal source is part of the principle of legality in criminal law. Identifying the source of a criminal norm is not necessarily the same as identifying the criminal norm itself. After a source has been identified, it may be possible to derive not only criminal norms from it but also civil and administrative ones. Moreover, to identify the criminal norm, it is not sufficient to identify its source as a legitimate legal source but it is necessary to also verify that its structure matches that of a criminal norm. The structure of the criminal norm may be described as:

A valid conditional clause the result of which is a criminal sanction.

For example, the specific offense of theft may be analyzed as follows[3]:

valid conditional clause — Whoever steals

criminal sanction — shall be punished with imprisonment of not more than three years.

The criminal norm contains two parts: a valid conditional clause and a criminal sanction. Both parts are required to identify the criminal norm. (Another reason why the Biblical commandment "Thou shalt not kill" is not recognized as a criminal norm is that it contains no explicit criminal sanction).

2.1.1 *Valid Conditional Clauses*

Logically there are two types of conditional clauses[4]: valid and invalid. A valid conditional clause refers to a real occurrence; an invalid conditional clause relates to a hypothetical situation that has not, will never, or can never occur. The valid conditional clause can relate to the past, the present, or the future:

[3]See examples for theft offenses, e.g., in Britain article 4(2)(b) of the Theft Act, 1978, c.31 provides: "A person convicted on indictment shall be liable- (a)...(b) for an offence under section 3 of this Act, to imprisonment for a term not exceeding two years"; in Germany subsection 242(1) of the German Penal Code (Strafgesetzbuch) provides: "Wer eine fremde bewegliche Sache einem anderen in der Absicht wegnimmt, die Sache sich oder einem Dritten rechtswidrig zuzueignen, wird mit Freiheitsstrafe bis zu fünf Jahren oder mit Geldstrafe bestraft"; and in France article 311-3 of the French Penal Code (Code Pénal) provides: "Le vol est puni de trois ans d'emprisonnement et de 45,000 euros d'amende".

[4]In fact, there are more than two types of conditional clauses, but all these types may be classified into these two *main* types of conditional clauses.

(1) "If you stole, you would be punished."
(2) "If you steal, you will be punished."
(3) "If you are going to steal, you will be punished."

The invalid conditional clause refers to a counterfactual, unreal, or impossible circumstance.

(4) "Had you stolen, you would have been punished" (but in reality you did not steal and therefore were not punished).

Because criminal law and criminal norms refer to actual occurrences and not to hypothetical ones, only the valid conditional clause is relevant to the identification of the criminal norm, and therefore the structure of the criminal norm contains only valid conditional clauses.

A valid conditional clause that is part of the criminal norm contains the components necessary to impose criminal liability on the offender. Some of these components may be satisfied by the norms of other general criminal laws. For most offenses, the valid conditional clause of the criminal norm includes the components of the factual element (*actus reus*) and the requirements of the mental element (*mens rea*). If all required components of the criminal norm are present, the criminal sanction may be imposed on the offender.

2.1.2 Criminal Sanction

The result of a valid conditional clause is a criminal sanction, which is an integral part of the criminal norm. There is no doubt about the centrality of the sanction within criminal law.[5] Most legal systems refer to this area of law by names that indicate the centrality of the sanction, for example, "**Penal** Law" in English, "**Straf**recht" in German, and "Droit **Pénal**" in French. Some scholars identify the criminal law with the sanction,[6] but the criminal sanction does not stand alone and must necessarily follow from a valid conditional clause.

The criminal sanction is a measure of the distress imposed on the offender. The distress may take various forms, some of which may or may not be considered as such in various societies.[7] But for a penalty to be considered criminal sanction, it must also be considered to cause distress within the given society. Only if the penalty imposed is identified as a criminal sanction can a norm be considered a criminal norm. Although in certain cases any given sanction may cause no distress

---

[5]See, e.g., GEORGE P. FLETCHER, THE GRAMMAR OF CRIMINAL LAW – AMERICAN, COMPARATIVE AND INTERNATIONAL, VOLUME ONE: FOUNDATIONS 69–73 (2007).

[6]JEROME HALL, GENERAL PRINCIPLES OF CRIMINAL LAW 296–321 (2nd ed., 1960, 2005).

[7]E.g., killing a person by the state is considered in most societies as a punishment, while in the Aztec society it was considered as great honor and honorable service to the gods. See FRANCES F. BERDAN, THE AZTECS OF CENTRAL MEXICO: AN IMPERIAL SOCIETY (2nd ed., 2005).

to a specific offender, it may still be considered a criminal sanction if society considers it to be distress.

The general provisions of criminal law can be applied to execute or restrict given criminal norms. The application is applied in the same way that the general provisions of criminal law relating to the mental element, complicity, inchoate offenses, etc. are applied to the valid conditional clause part of the criminal norm. The criminal sanction itself is not enough to identify a criminal norm. To identify a specific norm as criminal, the criminal sanction must be the result of a valid conditional clause. This basic structure of the criminal norm is merely a template that needs to be filled with substance. The template is crucial to identifying criminal norms, but it is not enough. The essence of the criminal norm is its content.

2.1.3 Classification of Offences Based on Content

All criminal offenses can be classified based on their content by two main criteria: according to the social interest of the specific norm and according to its criminal sanction. The first type of classification refers to the valid conditional clause of the criminal norm, the second type relates to the criminal sanction.

2.1.3.1 Classification According to Social Interest

The social interest of the criminal norm is embodied in the valid conditional clause for each individual criminal norm. Its conditional clause contains the specific substantive prohibition and its specific terms. Criminal norms may be classified, for instance, by their mental element requirement, which is crucial in most legal systems for distinguishing between homicide offenses.[8] But in most cases the classification according to social interest has to do with the protected interest of the specific criminal norm.

For example, property offenses are distinguished from national security offenses by the different protected interest embodied in the specific offenses. The protected interests express the general objectives of the legal control society wishes to exercise on individuals in a given context. When the society prohibits stealing, it

[8]In most legal systems murder requires at least premeditation, specific intent or deliberate intent, manslaughter requires at least recklessness, and negligent killing requires at least negligence. In some legal systems there is also a felony murder, which is a strict liability offense. For felony murder see Stuart P. Green, *Six Senses of Strict Liability: A Plea for Formalism*, APPRAISING STRICT LIABILITY 1, 3–4 (A.P. Simester ed., 2005, 2007); Douglas Husak, *Strict Liability, Justice, and Proportionality*, APPRAISING STRICT LIABILITY 81, 84–85 (A.P. Simester ed., 2005, 2007); Antony Robin Duff, *Strict Liability, Legal Presumptions, and the Presumption of Innocence*, APPRAISING STRICT LIABILITY 125, 143–144 (A.P. Simester ed., 2005, 2007). For the common legal definitions of murder See, e.g., in Britain Homicide Act, 1957, 5 & 6 Eliz. II, c.11; in Germany section 211 of the German Penal Code; and in France article 221-1 of the French Penal Code.

controls individual behavior for the purpose of the protection of property. Not all societies relate in the same way to various social interests, which is why not all societies share the same offenses, and why various offenses change their definitions over time.[9]

This type of classification applies mostly to procedures in the criminal process and to evidentiary law. For example, in most legal systems criminal trial on sexual offenses involves different types of procedures governing testimony by the victim, the registration of the offender and to public notification for the protection of the public.[10] These procedures are unique to sexual offenses, and are not applicable in property offenses. In criminal codes worldwide, this type of classification of criminal norms is used to categorize specific offenses.[11]

2.1.3.2 Classification According to Criminal Sanction

The criminal sanction in a specific criminal norm reflects the severity of the offense in the eyes of society. If the maximum penalty for the specific offense of theft is imprisonment for not more than 3 years, whereas for the offense of manslaughter it is imprisonment for not more than 20 years, in this given society manslaughter is considered to be much more severe than theft. The classification is mostly technical, but different legal systems regard it differently.

Until 1967, the **English common law** used to classify offenses into three categories: treason, felony, and misdemeanour. The distinction between treason and felony derived from the feudal law of the middle ages, when it was used to distinguish between offenses committed on the king's soil and on other soil.[12] In 1967, the British Parliament abolished the distinction.[13] The new law regards all offenses as misdemeanors, but it classifies these into arrestable and other offenses. Arrestable offenses are offenses that carry a maximum penalty of 5 years of imprisonment or more.[14]

---

[9]See, e.g., Stuart P. Green, *What's Wrong With Bribery*, DEFINING CRIMES – ESSAYS ON THE SPECIAL PART OF THE CRIMINAL LAW 143, 151–166 (Antony Robin Duff and Stuart P. Green eds., 2005).

[10]See, e.g., in Britain section 80 of the Sexual Offences Act, 2003, c. 42.

[11]The general categorization is into four main types of offenses: Offenses against the National Security, Offenses against the Public Policy and Legal Administration, Offenses against the Human Body and Offenses against Property.

[12]WAYNE R. LAFAVE, CRIMINAL LAW 34 (4th ed., 2003).

[13]Section 1 of the Criminal Law Act, 1967, c. 58 provides: "(1) All distinctions between felony and misdemeanour are hereby abolished. (2) Subject to the provisions of this Act, on all matters on which a distinction has previously been made between felony and misdemeanour, including mode of trial, the law and practice in relation to all offences cognizable under the law of England and Wales (including piracy) shall be the law and practice applicable at the commencement of this Act in relation to misdemeanour".

[14]Section 2 of the Criminal Law Act, 1967, c. 58, as amended by section 24 of the Police and Criminal Evidence Act, 1984, c.60, defines "arrestable offence" as "for which the sentence is fixed

In the **American Law**, the classification distinguishes between felonies and misdemeanors. Felonies carry capital punishment or imprisonment in state prison; misdemeanors are all other offenses, and the borderline between them is a maximum penalty of imprisonment of 1 year: felonies are punishable with 1 year of imprisonment or more, whereas misdemeanors are punishable with less. In some courts this classification is flexible,[15] but all courts in the United States use this classification both in a procedural and a substantive context.[16] **French Law** classifies offenses into three types: crimes, délits, and contraventions.[17]

The **German Law** classifies all offenses into severe (Verbrechen) and light (Vergehen). The borderline between them is a maximum penalty of imprisonment of 1 year or more.[18] Offenses punishable by fines are considered Vergehen. The German penal code of 1871 also contained a type of very light offenses, Übertretungen. This classification was abolished in 1975, and the offenses it covered became the administrative offenses of Ordnungswidrigkeiten.[19] The new classification is used in Germany both in a procedural context and a substantive context.[20]

2.2 The Legal Sources of the Criminal Norm

2.2.1 General Principles

The positivism of the criminal law is partial because it relates only to the identification of the legitimate source of the criminal norm, not to specific sources of the

by law or for which a person (not previously convicted) may be sentenced for a term of five years (or might be so sentenced but for the restrictions imposed by s. 33 of the Magistrates' Courts Act 1980), and to attempts to commit any such offence". See in addition section 3 of the Criminal Law Act, 1977, c.45.

[15]State v. Nagel, 98 Idaho 129, 559 P.2d 308 (1977); Rivett v. State, 578 P.2d 946 (Alaska, 1978); United States v. Schutte, 610 F.2d 698 (10th Cir.1979); Commonwealth v. Rhodes, 920 S.W.2d 531 (Ky.App.1996).

[16]Smith v. Hern, 102 Kan. 373, 170 P. 990 (1918); Pierce v. State, 96 Okl.Cr. 76, 248 P.2d 633 (1952); State v. Merrifield, 180 Kan. 267, 303 P.2d 155 (1956).

[17]Article 111-1 of the French Penal Code provides: "Les infractions pénales sont classées, suivant leur gravité, en crimes, délits et contraventions". The penalties for crimes are in articles 131-1, 131-2, 131-10 and 131-11 of the French Penal Code, the penalties for délits are in articles 131-3–131-11, and the penalties for contraventions are in articles 131-12–131-18.

[18]Section 12 of the German Penal Code provides: "(1) Verbrechen sind rechtswidrige Taten, die im Mindestmaß mit Freiheitsstrafe von einem Jahr oder darüber bedroht sind; (2) Vergehen sind rechtswidrige Taten, die im Mindestmaß mit einer geringeren Freiheitsstrafe oder die mit Geldstrafe bedroht sind; (3) Schärfungen oder Milderungen, die nach den Vorschriften des Allgemeinen Teils oder für besonders schwere oder minder schwere Fälle vorgesehen sind, bleiben für die Einteilung außer Betracht".

[19]Gesetz über Ordnungswidrigkeiten (BGBl. I, S. 602).

[20]Volker Krey, Deutsches Strafrecht Allgemeiner Teil, Teil I: Grundlagen 133–138 (2002).

norms. Theocracies, for example, may embrace religious norms as legitimate criminal norms because from their point of view religious texts are legitimate sources for criminal law.[21] Despite the variety of sources in various legal systems, some general principles relate to the partial positivism of criminal law. These general principles are expressed as social representation, social reflection, and social consensus, in offences of *mala in se* and *mala prohibita*, and in the formal publication of the criminal norm. In order to understand the distinction of *mala in se* offenses and *mala prohibita* offenses and the general principle of the formal publication of the criminal norm under the modern criminal law, they should be compared to the general defense of "mistake of law".

2.2.1.1 Social Representation, Social Reflection, and Social Consensus

The criminal norm is an application of the legal-social control exercised by society on its individuals. Social control reflects the will of society to create legitimate paths of behavior and to encourage individuals to use these paths. The criminal norm must therefore reflect the will of the society because society is the source of all criminal norms. A criminal norm that negates the will of society is considered illegitimate, whatever the content of that norm may be. All societies consist of individuals, therefore social reflection may be expressed as consent among individuals regarding the content of the criminal norm.

The more individuals share a specific consensus, the broader its sway is. Every society has the right to choose the basic rules that the consensus covers and the minimal scope required for it to be considered a consensus. Broad agreement is considered as a social consensus. The social consensus reflects the most legitimate social source of the criminal norm. Unanimous agreement naturally reflects consensus, but a much narrower agreement is sufficient for a consensus.

No government or regime in history was ever based on direct and unanimous consensus.[22] Institutional difficulties made resorting directly to the public in daily decisions inefficient or impossible. Consequently, the forging of consensus became part of the institutional arena. There are various types of social institutions that have the authority to forge consensus, such as parliament, the courts, the government, the constitutional court or council, and others. Different societies use different institutions to formulate social consent or social consensus. These institutions may bear the same name in different countries, but their functions and authorities may be

---

[21]See examples in JOSEPH SCHACHT, AN INTRODUCTION TO ISLAMIC LAW (1964, 1998).

[22]This is correct even as to ancient Athens. Not all topics were raised to vote, and not all inhabitants were allowed to participate in that vote. See, e.g., STEPHEN C. TODD, THE SHAPE OF ATHENIAN LAW 289–298 (1995).

different in different societies.[23] An institution can gain or lose functions and authorities at different times within the same society.[24]

The social representation of certain social institutions is a crucial element in the legitimacy of the norms it creates. Wider representation reflects wider social legitimacy to make decisions. When representatives of parliament are elected by the entire public, parliamentary representation is of all public. But because judges are not elected but appointed or nominated, the social representation of the court is much narrower. As a result, the social legitimacy of legal provisions derived from parliament is much wider than the social legitimacy of court decisions.

In most constitutional legal systems, the superiority of the constitution and of constitutional provisions rests on the reflection of a wide social consensus.[25] If the constitution reflects no social consensus when it is written or with the passage of time, its legal status is undermined. Given that criminal norms reflect society's legal-social control over the individuals, the criminal norm should reflect social consensus, or at least, social consent, even at the institutional level of decision making. Otherwise, the source of the criminal norm is not necessarily considered legitimate.

2.2.1.2 Offences of *mala in se* and *mala prohibita*

In modern criminal law, there is no proper justification for the distinction between offenses of *mala in se* and *mala prohibita*. The first record of this distinction dates back to 1496 in England, when King Henry VII granted an exemption from the duty to obey the criminal norm in some specific areas. Chief Justice Fineux used the distinction and ruled that such authority is given to the king only with regard to *mala prohibita*, not to *mala in se* offenses.[26] The court classified the offenses of

---

[23]See, e.g., the differences of the functions and authorities of the court in different legal systems in NIGEL FOSTER AND SATISH SULE, GERMAN LEGAL SYSTEM AND LAWS 66–78 (3rd ed., 2002, 2007); René Lévy, *Crime, the Judicial System, and Punishment in Modern France*, CRIME HISTORY AND HISTORIES OF CRIME – STUDIES IN THE HISTORIOGRAPHY OF CRIME AND CRIMINAL JUSTICE IN MODERN HISTORY 87–108 (1996).

[24]FRANK PAKENHAM LONGFORD, HISTORY OF THE HOUSE OF LORDS (1999); BARRY FITZPATRICK, THE HOUSE OF LORDS: ITS PARLIAMENTARY AND JUDICIAL ROLES (Brice Dickson and Paul Carmichael eds., 1999); DUNCAN WATTS, TORIES, UNIONISTS AND CONSERVATIVES, 1814–1915 (2nd ed., 2002); Parliament Act, 1911, 1 & 2 Geo. V, c.13.

[25]Thus, for instance, the American constitution emphasizes the public and social elements in its very beginning by stating: "We **the people** of the United States, in order to form a more perfect union, establish justice, insure domestic tranquility, provide for the common defense, promote the general welfare, and secure the blessings of liberty to ourselves and our posterity, do ordain and establish this Constitution for the United States of America" (emphasis not in original).

[26]In Y.B. Mich. 11 Hen. VII, f. 11, pl.35 (1496) Chief Justice Fineux explicitly noted the distinction using the words: "Distinction between malum prohibitum and malum per se". For the analysis of the distinction see Note, *The Distinction between Mala Prohibita and Mala in se in Criminal Law*, 30 COLUM. L. REV. 74 (1930).

murder, adultery, and disruption of the police as *mala in se* offenses, whereas illegal minting of coins and breach of economic embargo were classified as *mala prohibita* offenses.[27]

The distinction between *malum in se* and *malum prohibitum* derives from medieval concepts of morality, religion, and society, as well as from the concept of natural law.[28] When the distinction was transferred to criminal law in the nineteenth and twentieth centuries, it changed according to the domestic social concepts of the countries in which it was applied. For example, in the United States *mala in se* offenses are defined as relating to "natural evil."[29] The belief behind this distinction is that there is a basic core of offenses that are understandable to any rational human being, even if there is no specific provision that explicitly prohibits them. These offenses contain an intrinsic evil and are therefore defined as *mala in se* offenses. All other offenses are *mala prohibita*, that is, if no explicit offenses had been formulated regarding these specific prohibitions, they would not have been considered offenses at all.[30]

Naturally, the debate is about the identity of the offenses, seeking the significant "moral turpitude" that characterizes the *mala in se* offenses.[31] Different legal systems and different societies classify the same prohibitions differently. The criminal sanction of specific offenses became immaterial for the classification, and light offenses were classified as *mala in se* whereas severe offenses were classified as *mala prohibita*. Thus, in the United States offenses of possession of drugs,[32] grand and petit larceny,[33] battery,[34] robbery,[35] injury to property,[36] abortion,[37] and attempted suicide[38] are classified as *mala in se* offenses, whereas

---

[27]Compare Y.B. Hill. 19 Hen. VI, f. 62, pl.1 (1431).

[28]Y.B. Mich. 1 Hen. VII, f. 2, pl.2 (1485); Y.B. Mich. 3 Hen. VII, f. 15, pl.30 (1488); John Fortescue, De Laudibus Legum Angliae c. xv (1470, 1874); St. Augustine, De Vera Religione, c. xxvi (389).

[29]State v. Horton, 139 N.C. 588, 51 S.E. 945 (1905): "An offense malum in se is properly defined as one which is naturally evil as adjudged by the sense of a civilized community, whereas an act malum prohibitum is wrong only because made so by statute"; in Kinney v. State, 927 P.2d 1289 (Alaska App.1996) the *mala in se* offenses were defined as offenses "which reasoning members of society regard a condemnable".

[30]Henry M. Hart Jr., *The Aims of the Criminal Law*, 23 Law & Contemp. Probs. 414, 419 (1958); Stuart P. Green, *Why It's a Crime to Tear the Tag Off a Mattress: Overcriminalization and the Moral Content of Regulatory Offenses*, 46 Emory L.J. 1533 (1997).

[31]*In re* Pearce, 103 Utah 522, 136 P.2d 969 (1943); Compare State v. Anderson, 94 Wash. App. 151, 971 P.2d 585 (1999).

[32]*In re* Gorman, 269 Ind. 236, 379 N.E.2d 970 (1978); Compare State v. Hartzog, 26 Wash. App. 576, 615 P.2d 480 (1980); State v. Hartzog, 96 Wash.2d 383, 635 P.2d 694 (1981).

[33]*In re* Henry, 15 Idaho 755, 99 P. 1054 (1909).

[34]Schlossman v. State, 105 Md.App. 277, 659 A.2d 371 (1995); Gunter v. State, 499 S.W.2d 954 (Tenn.Crim.App. 1973); Creel v. State, 186 Miss. 738, 191 So. 814 (1939).

[35]Bell v. State, 394 So.2d 979 (Fla. 1981); Gregory v. State, 259 Ind. 652, 291 N.E.2d 67 (1973).

[36]People v. Causley, 299 Mich. 340, 300 N.W. 111 (1941).

[37]Peoples v. Commonwealth, 87 Ky. 487, 9 S.W. 509 (1888).

[38]Commonwealth v. Mink, 123 Mass. 422, 25 Am. Rep. 109 (1877).

carrying a concealed weapon,[39] shooting in a public place,[40] tax evasion,[41] passing a toll gate without paying the toll,[42] driving over the speed limit,[43] driving on a suspended or revoked license,[44] leaving the scene of an accident,[45] hunting without permission,[46] selling unregistered securities,[47] false notarization of a document,[48] and defacing the flag[49] are *mala prohibita*.

Moreover, the same offenses were classified both as *mala in se*[50] and *mala prohibita*.[51] For instance, driving under the influence of alcohol was classified both as *mala in se* and *mala prohibita*. The prohibition against intoxication in public was classified as *mala in se*, inspired by the biblical story of Noah,[52] and also as *mala prohibita*.[53] The main reason behind this classification was to counter the "mistake of law" defense, in which the defendant claims ignorance of law. When an offense

---

[39] Potter v. State, 162 Ind. 213, 70 N.E. 129 (1904).

[40] Dixon v. State, 104 Miss. 410, 61 So. 423 (1913); Sparks v. Commonwealth, 66 Ky. 111 (1868).

[41] Blue v. State, 716 So.2d 567 (Miss.1998).

[42] Estell v. State, 51 N.J.L. 182, 17 A. 118 (1889).

[43] Commonwealth v. Adams, 114 Mass. 323, 19 Am.Rep. 362 (1873); Hurt v. State, 184 Tenn. 608, 201 S.W.2d 988 (1947).

[44] Commonwealth v. Guthrie, 420 Pa.Super. 372, 616 A.2d 1019 (1992).

[45] State v. Dyer, 289 A.2d 693 (Me.1972).

[46] State v. Horton, 139 N.C. 588, 51 S.E. 945 (1905).

[47] Hentzner v. State, 613 P.2d 821 (Alaska.1980).

[48] Johnson v. State, 251 Ind. 17, 238 N.E.2d 651 (1968).

[49] State v. Waterman, 190 N.W.2d 809 (Iowa.1971).

[50] Baker v. State, 377 So.2d 17 (Fla.1979); State v. Kellison, 233 Iowa 1274, 11 N.W.2d 371 (1943); State v. Budge, 126 Me. 223, 137 A. 244 (1927); King v. State, 157 Tenn. 635, 11 S.W.2d 904 (1928); State v. Darchuck, 117 Mont. 15, 156 P.2d 173 (1945); Grindstaff v. State, 214 Tenn. 58, 377 S.W.2d 921 (1964); District of Columbia v. Colts, 282 U.S. 63, 51 S.Ct. 52, 75 L.Ed. 177 (1930).

[51] Keller v. State, 155 Tenn. 633, 299 S.W.803 (1927).

[52] People v. Townsend, 214 Mich. 267, 183 N.W. 177 (1921): "Voluntary intoxication is an offense not only *malum prohibitum* but *malum in se,* condemned as wrong in and of itself by every sense of common decency and good morals from the time that Noah in his drunkenness brought shame to his sons so that they backed in to cover his nakedness, and Lot's daughters employed it for incestuous purposes. Drunkenness was declared wrong in and of itself and punishment provided by the Israelites; by the ancient Chinese in an imperial edict about the year 1120 B.C., called 'The announcement about drunkenness'; in ancient India by the ordinances of Manu. In Rome the censors turned drunken members out of the senate and branded them with infamy. In England 300 years ago drunkenness was pilloried as the root and foundation of many sins, such as bloodshed, stabbing, murder, swearing and such like by the statute, 4 Jac. 1, chap. 5, and the ecclesiastical judges and officers were granted power to censure and punish offenders, and Bacon in his Abridgement of the common law lists drunkenness as one of the sins of heresy. In Massachusetts Bay Colony in 1633, 1634, one Robte Coles, for drunkenness, was disfranchised and sentenced to wear a red letter D upon a white background for a year. One of the acts passed at the first session of the general assembly of the Northwest Territory and approved December 2, 1799, provided a penalty for being drunk in a public highway".

[53] Dixon v. State, 104 Miss. 410, 61 So. 423 (1913).

was classified as *mala in se*, the mistake of law defense was automatically rejected.[54] In the modern definition of this defense, however, the classification is entirely irrelevant, as discussed below.[55]

Jeremy Bentham called for the abolition of the classification because it serves no purpose in criminal law.[56] Some Anglo-American courts have also called for the abolition of the classification[57] because it has no relevance to modern criminal law.[58] There are two major difficulties in embracing the classification. First, the classification relies on morality, which has no legal status, especially not in modern criminal law. Many moral behaviors may be considered offenses, and immoral behaviors may be absolutely legal. Adultery is considered immoral behavior in most modern societies, but in most legal systems it is not a criminal offense and therefore not legally prohibited. Moreover, there are various types of moral theories (e.g., teleological vs. deontological morality), and there is no consensus on what is and is not moral.

Second, in modern criminal law, the definition of specific offenses is complicated to such a degree that it is not entirely understandable to a reasonable person. When the offense of murder, traditionally classified as a *mala in se* offense, is defined in complicated terms and combined with all relevant defenses that contain detailed conditions, determining when killing is considered to be murder is not straightforward. In many societies, honor killing is not considered murder or even an offense. Rape of a wife was not considered rape until the end of the twentieth century, and rape was classified as a *mala in se* offense.[59] Furthermore, many former *mala in se* offenses have been abolished.[60]

---

[54]Prince, (1875) L.R. 2 C.C.R. 154, 173.

[55]Hereinafter at Sect. 2.2.1.4.

[56]Jeremy Bentham, A Comment on The Commentaries: A Criticism of William Blackstone's Commentaries on the Laws of England 80 (1776, C.W. Everett ed., 1928): "that acute distinction between *mala in se*, and *mala prohibita*; which being so shrewd and sounding so pretty, and being in Latin, has no sort of an occasion to have any meaning to it; accordingly it has none".

[57]Note, *The Distinction between Mala Prohibita and Mala in se in Criminal Law*, 30 Colum. L. Rev. 74, 86 (1930).

[58]In Bensley v. Bignold, (1822) 5 Barn and Ald 335, 106 E.R. 1214 Justice Best noted: "The distinction between *mala prohibita* and *mala in se* has been long since explored. It was not founded upon any sound principle, for it is equally unfit, that a man should be allowed to take advantage of what the law says he ought not to do, whether the thing be prohibited, because it is against good morals, or weather it be prohibited, because it is against the interest of the State"; See more in Aubert v. Maze, (1801) 2 Bos & Pul 371, 126 E.R. 1333; Jackson v. Harrison, (1978) 138 C.L.R. 438, 455.

[59]Matthew Hale, Historia Placitorum Coronae 629 (1736) [Matthew Hale, History of the Pleas of the Crown (1736)]: "But the husband cannot be guilty of rape committed by himself upon his lawful wife, for by their mutual matrimonial consent and contract the wife hath given herself up this kind unto her husband which she cannot retract"; Clarence, (1888) 22 Q.B.D. 23, [1890] All E. R. 133; Compare R, [1992] 1 A.C. 599, [1991] 4 All E.R. 481, [1991] 3 W.L.R. 767, 94 Cr. App. Rep. 216, 155 J.P. 989, [1992] Crim. L.R. 207, [1992] 1 F.L.R. 217, [1992] Fam. Law 108 and section 1 of the Sexual Offences Act, 2003, c.42.

[60]See, e.g., the Buggery Act, 1533, 25 Hen. VIII, c.6, which was deemed as *mala in se* in Wallis v. Duke of Portland, (1797) 3 Ves. 494 (p.502: "Maintenance is not *malum prohibitum*, but

It may be concluded that in modern criminal law there is no appropriate legal justification for the classification of offenses as *mala in se* and *mala prohibita*.[61] As a result, it is always necessary to identify the source of a specific criminal norm as a legitimate normative source, whether or not the offense involves moral turpitude.

2.2.1.3 Formal Publicity of the Criminal Norm

Without legal justification for classifying specific offenses into *mala in se* and *mala prohibita*, all criminal norms are considered to be *mala prohibita*. As a result, it is always required to identify the source of a specific criminal norm as a legitimate normative source. Based on this understanding, all criminal norms are subject to the general requirement of formal publicity of the criminal norm. Formal publicity requires the publication of the criminal norm, so that it is accessible to the public. Formal publicity has no interest in the contents of the criminal norm, only in its accessibility to the public.

Formal publicity can be contrasted with substantial publicity, which concerns the level of public understanding of the criminal norm,[62] and with substantial publicity, which concerns the clarity and precision of the criminal norm, as required by the fourth secondary principle of the principle of legality in criminal law.[63]

The formal publicity requirement of the criminal norm has two main justifications. First is efficiency and effectiveness in applying the criminal norm. The criminal norm is aimed at guiding the individuals in their behavior, while exercising legal-social control over them. If an individual breaches the norm, a punishment is imposed. An individual who wants to obey the norm must know about it. If a given norm is not publicized, the individual cannot know about it and therefore cannot obey it. An efficient application of criminal norms is carried out by the individuals themselves, without intervention by the sovereign. If a person avoids committing a robbery in light of the criminal norm, there is no need to involve the policing powers of the state. Naturally, individuals can obey only norms that are known to them.

---

malum in se:... parties shall not by their countenance aid the prosecution of suits of any kind; which every person must bring upon his own bottom and at his own expense" by Lord Loughorough), but abolished by subsection 13(1)(a) of the Criminal Law Act, 1967, c.58.

[61]Richard L. Gray, *Eliminating the (Absurd) Distinction between Malum in se and Malum Prohibitum Crimes*, 73 Wash. U. L. Q. 1369 (1995).

[62]Antony Robin Duff, *Rule-Violations and Wrongdoings*, Criminal Law Theory – Doctrines of the General Part 47 (Stephen Shute and A. P. Simester eds., 2005).

[63]The fourth secondary principle of the principle of legality in criminal law relates to the interpretation of the criminal law and shall be discussed hereinafter at Chap. 5.

The second justification is fairness to the individual in the exercise of legal-social control through the criminal norm. Fairness is a complex term.[64] But as it applies to the formal publicity of the criminal norm, it suffices to use a narrow (liberal) meaning of fairness, whereby the individual has the free choice to commit or not to commit the offense. The choice requires a fair notice. Only if the individuals are aware of the criminal norm, they have a *real* opportunity to choose between committing and not committing the offense.

When the criminal norm is not publicized, the opportunity to make the choice is removed, and therefore the formal publicity of the criminal norm is related to the principle of legality and to the rule of law. The justification of fairness is accepted in most legal systems.[65] As a result, when the criminal norm is not publicized, it is considered to be an invalid norm that the individual has no obligation to obey. In legal systems worldwide, there are institutional, formal ways to publicize the criminal norm, usually in a manner that is identical with the formal publicity of other norms within the given legal system.[66]

2.2.1.4 The Mistake of Law Defense in the Modern Criminal Law

The defense of mistake of law, or ignorance of the law, assumes the full existence of both the external elements (factual elements, *actus reus*) and the internal elements (mental elements, *mens rea*) of the specific offense by the specific offender.[67] The defense also assumes that criminal norms exist prohibiting the specific offense and were lawfully promulgated. The mistake of law defense claims that, despite that, the defendant did not know about the specific prohibition (ignorance of the law) or believed the specific action to be legal, due to an incorrect interpretation of the law (mistake of law). Legally, there is no difference between ignorance of the law and mistake of law, and both shall be referred to below as mistake of law, since both of them are legal errors.[68]

---

[64] John Rawls, A Theory of Justice (revised ed., 1971, 1999).

[65] See, e.g., Blackpool Corporation v. Locker, [1948] 1 K.B. 349, 361 [1948] 1 All E.R. 85, 46 L.G. R. 58, 112 J.P. 130, 150 E.G. 477, [1947] E.G.D. 155, [1948] W.N. 27; Lim Chin Aik, [1963] A.C. 160, 171 [1963] 1 All E.R. 223, [1963] 2 W.L.R. 42.

[66] For the legal norms which require formal publicity see, e.g., Lewisham Borough Council v. Roberts, [1949] 2 K.B. 608, [1949] 1 All E.R. 815, 829, 47 L.G.R. 479, 153 E.G. 262, [1949] E.G. D. 187, 65 T.L.R. 423, 113 J.P. 260, 208 L.T. 23, 210 L.T. 322, [1949] W.N. 165, 100 L.Q.R. 588 and Blackpool Corporation v. Locker, *ibid.*

[67] Douglas Husak and Andrew von Hirsch, *Culpability and Mistake of Law*, in Action and Value in Criminal Law 157, 161–167 (Stephen Shute, John Gardner and Jeremy Horder eds., 2003).

[68] Edwin R. Keedy, *Ignorance and Mistake in the Criminal Law*, 22 Harv. L. Rev. 75, 76, 88–96 (1909); Canal Bank v. Bank of Albany, 1 Hill. 287 (1841); Hutton v. Edgerton, 6 S.C. 485 (1876); Athy Poulos-Mobilia, *Ignorance or Mistake of Law – Will the Memory Ever Fade*, 62 St. John's L. Rev. 114 (1988); but compare Jerome Hall, *Ignorance and Mistake in Criminal Law*, 33 Ind. L. J. 1 (1957) and Jerome Hall, General Principles of Criminal Law 405–408 (2nd ed., 1960, 2005).

The social question, which is not necessarily a legal question, is whether a defendant must actually know about the specific law as a precondition for imposing criminal liability. If actual knowledge of a specific law is necessary in order to impose criminal liability upon a defendant, then every slight mistake in the understanding of the law is a legal obstacle to imposing criminal liability. According to this line of reasoning, in order to impose criminal liability, the entire population must become lawyers, who are experts in all aspects of the law. But the entire population cannot become lawyers, and even if they could, lawyers do make mistakes, even in their own spheres of expertise. If actual knowledge of criminal law were an essential precondition to criminal liability, then, in most cases, no enforcement of criminal law could be possible.[69]

Therefore, the state is obliged to promulgate laws, but not necessarily to inculcate them in every person's consciousness.[70] This has been the international consensus since ancient times, that is, until recently. Roman law dictated that ignorance of the law is not an excuse to break the law (*ignorantia juris non excusat*).[71] The reason for that ruling in Roman law was that, while the facts may be complicated to understand, Roman law is simple and logical, and therefore, every person is presumed to know it. That rule also relied on the historical division of offenses into *mala in se* offenses and *mala prohibita* offenses. All offenses in Roman law were considered *mala in se* offenses.[72]

Historically, the division of offenses into *mala in se* and *mala prohibita* was accepted worldwide. *Mala in se* offenses were deemed prohibitions that any person, regardless of culture, origin, gender, religion or age, knows and understands to be forbidden. On the other hand, *mala prohibita* offenses require knowledge of the specific law.[73] One of the main difficulties of this distinction relates to cultural differences. Murder has been considered for ages by western society as a *mala in se* offense, which does not require a specific law prohibiting it because the cultural consensus in western society already accepted that murder is a crime.

However, in countries that recognize murder in the name of family honor, for instance, as an accepted norm, the situation is different.[74] As long as no specific

---

[69]Livingston Hall and Selig J. Seligman, *Mistake of Law and Mens Rea*, 8 U. Chi. L. Rev. 641 (1941); Geoffrey Marston, *Mens Rea and Mistake of Law*, 8 U. W. Austl. L. Rev. 459 (1968); Kumaralingam Amirthalingam, *Mens Rea and Mistake of Law in Criminal Cases: A Lesson from South Africa*, 18 U.N.S.W.L.J. 428 (1995).

[70]Joseph E. Murphy, *The Duty of the Government to Make the Law Known*, 51 Ford. L. Rev. 255 (1982); Brumarescu v. Romania, (2001) 33 E.H.R.R. 35; Kokkinakis v. Greece, (1993) 17 E.H.R.R. 397; C.R. v. United Kingdom, (1995) 21 E.H.R.R. 363.

[71]Digesta, 22.6.9: "juris quidam ignorantiam cuique nocere, facti vero ignorantiam non nocere".

[72]Olivia F. Robinson, The Criminal Law of Ancient Rome 15–22 (1995).

[73]*Note: The Distinction between Mala Prohibita and Mala in se in Criminal Law*, 30 Colum. L. Rev. 74 (1930); Henry M. Hart Jr., *The Aims of the Criminal Law*, 23 Law & Contemp. Probs. 414, 419 (1958); Stuart P. Green, *Why It's a Crime to Tear the Tag Off a Mattress: Overcriminalization and the Moral Content of Regulatory Offenses*, 46 Emory L. J. 1533 (1997).

[74]Richard L. Gray, *Eliminating the (Absurd) Distinction between Malum in se and Malum Prohibitum Crimes*, 73 Wash. U.L.Q. 1369 (1995).

prohibition of murder in the name of family honor exists, then in these societies, an honor killing is not considered murder at all.[75] This is particularly the case in countries where women are considered inferior, as objects, and objects cannot be murdered. This is part of the objectification of women within the context of the commission of specific culture-based crimes. In most legal systems around the world, the past distinction between *mala in se* offenses and *mala prohibita* offenses no longer has any practical significance.[76]

The Roman law's approach towards the mistake of law defense was adopted by all legal systems in the middle ages. The first documented case in English common law of rejecting a mistake of law defense occurred in 1231. A person was convicted of trespassing on his mother's land. He claimed that he had relied on his attorney's advice that the land belongs to him as well, but the attorney was wrong. The court rejected that claim on the grounds of *ignorantia juris non excusat*.[77] This approach was not changed until the beginning of the sixteenth century.

The change occurred during the trial of *Vernon* in 1505, when a man was exonerated of the offense of trespassing for accompanying a married woman to the local church. The defense argument was that the man had accompanied her to the church, where she intended on suing for divorce from her husband. The prosecution claimed that no divorce is allowed in that church. The defense pleaded the mistake of law defense, since the defendant did not know that. The defense was accepted, and the man was exonerated.[78] This exoneration became a precedent, changing the former approach.[79]

However, in most cases during the sixteenth and seventeenth centuries, English common law rejected the mistake of law defense while relying on Roman law.[80] In only a very few cases it was not rejected. The legal literature of that time asserted that English common law accepted that defense if the defendant had no opportunity to seek the advice of an attorney. However, when the defendant was erroneously misled by an attorney, it was not considered a mistake of law defense.[81] The dramatic change occurred during the nineteenth century.

---

[75]See analogously in Gerald Leonard, *Rape, Murder, and Formalism: What Happens if We Define Mistake of Law*, 72 U. Colo. L. Rev. 507 (2001); Gunther Arzt, *The Problem of Mistake of Law*, 1986 BYU L. Rev. 711 (1986).

[76]See e.g. Michael L. Travers, *Mistake of Law in Mala Prohibita Crimes*, 62 U. Chi. L. Rev. 1301 (1995).

[77]The case of *Waggehastr*, as reported in Henry de Bracton, De Legibus et Consuetudinibus Angliae 496 (1260; G. E. Woodbine ed., S.E. Thorne trans., 1968–1977).

[78]Y.B. Trin. 20 Hen. VII, f.2, pl.4 (1505): "Car par cas ils n'avoiet conusance de le Ley on le divorsce seroit sue".

[79]Dialogues II, c.46 (1518): "Ignorance of the law… doth not excuse as to the law but in a few cases; for every man is bound at his peril to take knowledge what the law of the realm is, as well the law made by statute as the common law".

[80]See e.g. Brett v. Rigden, (1568) 1 Plowd. 340, 75 Eng. Rep. 516; R. v. Mildmay, (1584) 1 Co. Rep. 175a, 76 Eng. Rep. 379; R. v. Manser, (1584) 2 Co. Rep. 3, 76 Eng. Rep. 392; R. v. Vaux, (1613) 1 Blustrode 197, 80 Eng. Rep. 885.

[81]Dialogues II, c.46 (1518); Digesta, 22.6.9; Dialogues I, c.26 (1518).

The concept of fault developed tremendously during the nineteenth century in Anglo-American criminal law. Differentiations were made between intent and recklessness, and between recklessness and negligence, which is differentiated by awareness and knowledge. As a result, the mistake of law defense should have been adapted to that new, modern and developed concept of fault.[82] Conceptually, it was thought to change the applicability of the mistake of law defense, so that if the mistake prevented the knowledge from existing in the defendant's mind, and the specific offense required knowledge, no criminal liability should be imposed.[83] It resembles the concept of mistake in good faith (*bona fide* mistake),[84] which was considered relevant in a case of mistake of fact (factual mistake).[85]

When the specific offense requires negligence as its element of fault, the mistake should prevent negligence from existing in the defendant's mind. Such a mistake of law is a mistake that any reasonable person would not have made under the same circumstances.[86] After the development of strict liability offenses during the twentieth century (as developed from the absolute liability offenses of the nineteenth century),[87] a new type of mistake of law was required that would prevent strict liability from existing.[88] Such a mistake is an inevitable mistake, even after all reasonable measures have been taken in order to prevent it.

Of course, it is much more difficult to prove a strict liability mistake than a negligent mistake, and it is much more difficult to prove a negligent mistake than a mistake of awareness. The modern legal systems of the end of the nineteenth century and the beginning of the twentieth century were afraid of a wide expansion

[82]R. v. Bailey, (1818) Russ. & Ry. 341, 168 Eng. Rep. 835; R. v. Esop, (1836) 7 Car. & P. 456, 173 Eng. Rep. 203; R. v. Crawshaw, (1860) Bell. 303, 169 Eng. Rep. 1271; Schuster v. State, 48 Ala. 199 (1872); Grumbine v. State, 60 Md. 355 (1883).

[83]R. v. Hall, (1828) 3 Car. & P. 409, 172 Eng. Rep. 477; State v. Hollyway, 41 Iowa 200 (1875).

[84]Elizabeth Edinger, *Mistake of Law – Bona Fide Diligent Effort to Ascertain and Comply with the Law*, 10 U. Brit. Colum. L. Rev. 320 (1976).

[85]R. v. Forbes, (1835) 7 Car. & P. 224, 173 Eng. Rep. 99; Parish v. R., (1837) 8 Car. & P. 94, 173 Eng. Rep. 413; Allday v. R., (1837) 8 Car. & P. 136, 173 Eng. Rep. 431; Dotson v. State, 6 Cold. 545 (1869); Cutter v. State, 36 N.J.L. 125 (1873); Squire v. State, 46 Ind. 459 (1874).

[86]State v. Goodenow, 65 Me. 30 (1876); State v. Whitoomb, 52 Iowa 85, 2 N.W. 970 (1879).

[87]Dixon v. R., (1814) 3 M. & S. 11, 105 Eng. Rep. 516; Vantandillo v. R., (1815) 4 M. & S. 73, 105 Eng. Rep. 762; R. v. Burnett, (1815) 4 M. & S. 272, 105 Eng. Rep. 835.

[88]See e.g. Sweet v. Parsley, [1970] A.C. 132, [1969] 1 All E.R. 347, [1969] 2 W.L.R. 470, 133 J.P. 188, 53 Cr. App. Rep. 221, 209 E.G. 703, [1969] E.G.D. 123; Jeremy Horder, *Strict Liability, Statutory Construction and the Spirit of Liberty*, 118 Law Q. Rev. 458 (2002); John R. Spencer and Antje Pedain, *Approaches to Strict and Constructive Liability in Continental Criminal Law*, *in* Appraising Strict Liability 237 (A. P. Simester ed., 2005); compare Commonwealth v. Boynton, 84 Mass. 160, 2 Allen 160 (1861); Commonwealth v. Goodman, 97 Mass. 117 (1867); Farmer v. People, 77 Ill. 322 (1875); State v. Sasse, 6 S.D. 212, 60 N.W. 853 (1894); State v. Cain, 9 W. Va. 559 (1874); Redmond v. State, 36 Ark. 58 (1880); State v. Clottu, 33 Ind. 409 (1870); State v. Lawrence, 97 N.C. 492, 2 S.E. 367 (1887).

of the mistake of law defense, due to the new obligations of the state that would derive from such an expansion. These obligations include the duty to make law known, including its current interpretation, to all parts of the population. In addition, modern law is far more complicated than it was during the middle ages or during ancient times. Understanding modern law requires law studies, which are not available to all parts of the population.[89]

As a result, it was accepted in very many legal systems that the only legitimate standard for accepting a mistake of law defense is the standard of a strict liability mistake.[90] This standard significantly reduces the probability that a mistake of law defense shall be accepted. This standard is considered as balancing society's need for public order and a defendant's lack of fault due to a mistake of law. The applicability of the mistake of law defense is identical in specific offenses that require knowledge (with or without intent or recklessness), negligence or strict liability offenses.[91]

Thus, when a defendant did not know what the legal situation was, the mistake of law defense is irrelevant. Even when any reasonable defendant under the same circumstances also would not have known what the legal situation was, the mistake of law defense is still deemed irrelevant. Only if, after taking all reasonable measures to prevent the mistake of law, the mistake was still inevitable, then the mistake of law defense is relevant, regardless of the specific fault element required in the specific offense. The relevant question in this legal situation is: What exactly is an inevitable mistake of law even after all reasonable measures to prevent it have been taken?

This question is examined by courts under an objective standard.[92] All reasonable measures are all of the measures a reasonable person would have taken under

[89]Peter Alldridge, *Making Crimianl Law Known*, *in* CRIMINAL LAW THEORY – DOCTRINES OF THE GENERAL PART 103 (Stephen Shute and A. P. Simester eds., 2005).

[90]E.g. article 17 of the German Penal Code provides: "Fehlt dem Täter bei Begehung der Tat die Einsicht, Unrecht zu tun, so handelt er ohne Schuld, wenn er diesen Irrtum nicht vermeiden konnte. Konnte der Täter den Irrtum vermeiden, so kann die Strafe nach Art. 49 Abs. 1 gemildert werden"; article 122-3 of the French penal code provides: "N'est pas pénalement responsable la personne qui justifie avoir cru, par une erreur sur le droit qu'elle n'était pas en mesure d'éviter, pouvoir légitimement accomplir l'acte"; article 2.04(3)(a) of the American Model Penal Code, THE AMERICAN LAW INSTITUTE, MODEL PENAL CODE – OFFICIAL DRAFT AND EXPLANATORY NOTES 27 (1962, 1985) provides: "A belief that conduct does not legally constitute an offense is a defense to a prosecution for that offense based upon such conduct when: (a) the statute or other enactment defining the offense is not known to the actor and has not been published or otherwise reasonably made available prior to the conduct alleged"; see also the German ruling in explaining the type of mistake in BGH 2, 194; BGH 3, 105; BGH 4, 1; BGH 4, 80; BGH 5, 111; BGH 9, 164; BGH 9, 358; BGH 12, 379; BGH 13, 135; BGH 15, 332; BGH 16, 155; BGH 17, 87; BGH 20, 342; BGH 21, 18; BGH 22, 223; BGH 35, 347; BGH VRS 65, 127; VRS 60, 313.

[91]Gunther Arzt, *Ignorance or Mistake of Law*, 24 AM. J. COMP. L. 646 (1976); Raymond Youngs, *Mistake of Law in Germany – Opening up Pandora's Box*, 64 J. CRIM. L. 339 (2000).

[92]Robert A. Leflar, *Mistake of Law in Arkansas*, 3 LAW SCH. BULL. 28 (1932); George Wilfred Stumberg, *Mistake of Law in Texas Criminal Cases*, 15 TEX. L. REV. 28 (1937); A. T. H. Smith, *Error and Mistake of Law in Anglo-American Criminal Law*, 14 ANGLO-AM. L. REV. 3 (1985).

the specific circumstances in order to prevent the mistake. Sometimes the answer to the question is reached by relying on a legal interpretation of the law. When a person has no reasonable possibility of relying upon a legal interpretation of the law, this is deemed an inevitable mistake. Thus, when the law was not duly promulgated, no person could possibly have known about it. As a result, any mistake of law pertaining to that specific law is inevitable, since no person had a reasonable opportunity to rely on it.[93]

Reliance on court decisions that erroneously interpreted the law may create inevitable mistakes of law. If a competent court has interpreted a law, then it is reasonable to rely on that ruling. If a higher court, or a court of higher instance, overrules the prior decision, but, meanwhile, the defendant acted according to the first decision, then it is deemed an inevitable mistake of law.[94]

Reliance on an erroneous decision of administrative authorities under executive power is deemed reasonable reliance,[95] although the power to interpret is that of the judicial authorities, whether the interpretation is intended for one person or for the entire population.[96] Such a mistake of law is deemed an inevitable mistake.[97] The defendant is considered as having taken all reasonable measures to prevent the mistake from occurring.[98] Similarly, if an administrative authority acted in a manner exceeding its powers (*ultra vires*), a defendant's reliance on that authority is deemed reasonable,

---

[93]Christian v. R., [2006] U.K.P.C. 47, [2007] 2 A.C. 400; Debardelaben v. State, 99 Tenn. 649, 42 S.W. 684 (1897); State v. Click, 2 Ala. 26 (1841); Zakrasek v. State, 197 Ind. 249, 150 N.E. 615 (1926); Jellico Coal-Min. Co. v. Commonwealth, 96 Ky. 373, 29 S.W. 26 (1895); United States v. Casson, 434 F.2d 415 (D.C.Cir.1970).

[94]People v. Fraser, 96 N.Y.2d 318, 728 N.Y.S.2d 115, 752 N.E.2d 244 (2001); People v. Marrero, 69 N.Y.2d 382, 515 N.Y.S.2d 212, 507 N.E.2d 1068 (1987); Livingston Hall and Selig J. Seligman, *Mistake of Law and Mens Rea*, 8 U. Chi. L. Rev. 641 (1941); State v. O'Neil, 147 Iowa 513, 126 N. W. 454 (1910); State v. Longino, 109 Miss. 125, 67 So. 902 (1915); Stinnett v. Commonwealth, 55 F.2d 644 (4th Cir.1932); Lutwin v. State, 97 N.J.L. 67, 117 A. 164 (1922); State v. Whitman, 116 Fla. 196, 156 So. 705 (1934); United States v. Mancuso, 139 F.2d 90 (3rd Cir.1943); State v. Chicago, M. & St.P.R. Co., 130 Minn. 144, 153 N.W. 320 (1915); Coal & C.R. v. Conley, 67 W. Va. 129, 67 S.E. 613 (1910); State v. Striggles, 202 Iowa 1318, 210 N.W. 137 (1926); United States v. Albertini, 830 F.2d 985 (9th Cir.1987).

[95]State v. Patten, 353 N.W.2d 30 (N.D.1984); Edwin C. Walker, *Mistake of Law Defense Based on Reasonable Reliance on Apparent Authority*, 14 Wake Forest L. Rev. 136 (1978); Vernon G. Owen Jr., *Mistake of Law – Reliance upon Advice of Public Official*, 2 W. Res. L. Rev. 91 (1950).

[96]State v. Sheedy, 125 N.H. 108, 480 A.2d 887 (1984); People v. Ferguson, 134 Cal.App. 41, 24 P.2d 965 (1933); compare State v. Foster, 22 R.I. 163, 46 A. 833 (1900).

[97]United States v. Hancock, 231 F.3d 557 (9th Cir.2000); Andrew Ashworth, *Testing Fidelity to Legal Values: Official Involvement and Criminal Justice*, 63 Mod. L. Rev. 663 (2000); Glanville Williams, *The Draft Code and Reliance upon Official Statements*, 9 Legal Stud. 177 (1989).

[98]State v. Davis, 63 Wis.2d 75, 216 N.W.2d 31 (1974); R. v. Arrowsmith, [1975] Q.B. 678, [1975] 1 All E.R. 463, [1975] 2 W.L.R. 484, 60 Cr. App. Rep. 211, 139 J.P. 221; Kingston v. R., [1995] 2 A.C. 355, [1994] 3 All E.R. 353, [1994] 3 W.L.R. 519, [1994] Crim. L.R. 846, 99 Cr. App. Rep. 286, 158 J.P. 717.

and thus, an inevitable mistake of law may be entertained.[99] If the administrative authority deliberately misled the defendant, under American law, it is considered entrapment that may lead to exoneration.[100]

Reliance on the legal advice of a private attorney at law is deemed reasonable reliance if the attorney possesses appropriate legal credentials and the defendant relied on the attorney in good faith (*bona fide* reliance).[101] If not, the mistake is not deemed inevitable and the mistake of law defense is rejected.

2.2.2 Legal Sources

What are the legitimate normative sources of the criminal norm? Although different legal systems use different legal sources, the general principles discussed above are common to all.

2.2.2.1 The Constitution

Can the constitution be considered a legitimate normative source for criminal norms? Generally, the constitution is the basic legal document of a given legal system, embodying its basic principles. The content of constitutions in different regimes may be different, but all constitutions address the same topics, namely the relations between various state authorities and the civil rights of individuals. Thus, the constitution is not the common legal source for criminal norms. Moreover, the

[99] United States v. Barker, 546 F.2d 940 (D.C.Cir.1976); Jones v. State, 32 Tex.Crim. 533, 25 S.W. 124 (1894); State v. Simmons, 143 N.C. 613, 56 S.E. 701 (1907); United States v. Ormsby, 252 F.3d 844 (6th Cir.2001); United States v. Ramirez-Valencia, 202 F.3d 1106 (9th Cir.2000); United States v. Gutierrez-Gonzalez, 184 F.3d 1160 (10th Cir.1999); United States v. Ramos, 179 F.3d 1333 (11th Cir.1999); United States v. West Indies Transport Inc., 127 F.3d 299 (3rd Cir.1997); United States v. Achter, 52 F.3d 753 (8th Cir.1995); Bsharah v. United States, 646 A.2d 993 (D.C. App.1994); State v. DeCastro, 81 Haw. 147, 913 P.2d 558 (App.1996); Miller v. Commonwealth, 25 Va.App. 727, 492 S.E.2d 482 (1997). Compare United States v. Pennsylvania Industrial Chemical Corp., 411 U.S. 655, 93 S.Ct. 1804, 36 L.Ed.2d 567 (1973); United States v. Clegg, 846 F.2d 1221 (9th Cir.1988); United States v. Duggan, 743 F.2d 59 (2nd Cir.1984); United States v. Austin, 915 F.2d 363 (8th Cir.1990); United States v. Tallmadge, 829 F.2d 767 (9th Cir.1987).

[100] Cox v. Louisiana, 379 U.S. 559, 85 S.Ct. 476, 13 L.Ed.2d 487 (1965); United States v. Hancock, 231 F.3d 557 (9th Cir.2000); Commonwealth v. Kratsas, 564 Pa. 36, 764 A.2d 20 (2001); Raley v. Ohio, 360 U.S. 423, 79 S.Ct. 1257, 3 L.Ed.2d 1344 (1959); State v. Guzman, 89 Haw. 27, 968 P.2d 194 (App.1998); People v. Donovan, 53 Misc.2d 687, 279 N.Y.S.2d 404 (Ct. Spec. Sess. 1967).

[101] Rollin M. Perkins, *Ignorance and Mistake in Criminal Law*, 88 U. Pa. L. Rev. 35 (1940); compare People v. McCalla, 63 Cal.App. 783, 220 P. 436 (1923); State v. Bellows, 596 N.W.2d 509 (Iowa 1999); State v. Huff, 89 Me. 521, 36 A. 1000 (1897); State v. Western Union Tel. Co., 12 N.J. 468, 97 A.2d 480 (1953); State v. Brewer, 932 S.W.2d 1 (Tenn.Cr.App.1996); United States v. Poludniak, 657 F.2d 948 (8th Cir.1981); Long v. State, 44 Del. 262, 65 A.2d 489 (1949); State v. Downs, 116 N.C. 1064, 21 S.E. 689 (1895).

legal provisions of the constitution are too abstract to serve as specific criminal norms, and they include general principles rather than concrete legal orders. The level of clarity required for criminal norms is much higher than that of constitutional provisions.[102]

Nevertheless, some constitutions in western countries contain criminal norms. A prominent example is the American Constitution, which defines what is treason and specifies some related criminal procedures.[103] In addition, the 18th Amendment to the Constitution, enacted in 1919, defined the prohibition on the manufacture, sale, transportation, importation, and exportation of intoxicating liquors. The "Prohibition Period" remained in effect until 1933.[104] Specific offenses were enacted on the grounds of this amendment, including specific prohibitions and criminal sanctions. In 1933, the 20th Amendment abolished the prohibition by abolishing the 18th Amendment,[105] and with it all the associated specific offenses.

Formally, these norms do not reference specific offenses because the constitutional provisions contain no criminal sanctions and are not formulated as valid conditional clauses.[106] Therefore, the provisions may be considered to be general directives for the enactment of specific offenses, but they do not define specific offenses in themselves.[107] Analyzing most western constitutions reveals that their tendency to include provisions in a criminal context focuses on criminal procedure, which contains many topics related to human rights.[108] Even then, the constitutional provisions are too abstract, and are used as general directives for the formulation of specific provisions related to criminal procedure or court rulings.

---

[102]See hereinafter at Sect. 5.2.3 in Chap. 5.

[103]The beginning of U.S. Constitution, art. III, § 3 provides: "Treason against the United States, shall consist only in levying war against them, or in adhering to their enemies, giving them aid and comfort. No person shall be convicted of treason unless on the testimony of two witnesses to the same overt act, or on confession in open court".

[104]U.S. Constitution, amend. XVIII, § 1 provides: "After one year from the ratification of this article the manufacture, sale, or transportation of intoxicating liquors within, the importation there of into, or the exportation there of from the United States and all territory subject to the jurisdiction there of for beverage purposes is here by prohibited".

[105]U.S. Constitution, amend. XXI, § 1 provides: "The eighteenth article of amendment to the Constitution of the United States is hereby repealed".

[106]See above at Sect. 2.1.1.

[107]The end of U.S. Constitution, art. III, § 3 provides: "The Congress shall have power to declare the punishment of treason, but no attainder of treason shall work corruption of blood, or forfeiture except during the life of the person attainted ", and U.S. Constitution, amend. XVIII, § 2 provides: "The Congress and the several states shall have concurrent power to enforce this article by appropriate legislation". The American legislator enacted therefore 18 U.S.C.S. § 2381 that provides: "Whoever, owing allegiance to the United States, levies war against them or adheres to their enemies, giving them aid and comfort within the United States or elsewhere, is guilty of treason and shall suffer death, or shall be imprisoned not less than five years and fined under this title but not less than $ 10,000; and shall be incapable of holding any office under the United States".

[108]See, e.g., in Germany, Grundgesetz, Art. 2(2) and in Canada, article 7 of the Canadian Charter of Rights and Freedoms, 1982.

It is therefore unusual to include a specific criminal norm within the constitution. In 1949 the German basic law abolished capital punishment. Although this is a general criminal norm, it has also been considered as a constitutional norm because of its effect on the general outlook of the regime.[109] When provisions of a constitution intervene in specific criminal norms, the courts tend to reject the intervention, as for example, the rulings of the Federal Constitutional Court in Germany.[110]

There is no reason to prevent the inclusion of criminal norms within the constitution as long as these norms are subjected to the general requirements of the principle of legality in criminal law. The constitution is a legal document that represents a social consensus sufficiently wide for the formulation of criminal norms. The institutions that formulate the constitution enjoy a high level of social representation, social reflection, and social consensus, sufficient for the creation of criminal norms.

The constitution is not the most appropriate legal source for the criminal norms, however, because it lacks the flexibility required to respond to social changes. A proper normative source must be able to assimilate social changes into the criminal norm. If not, the criminal norm becomes anachronistic and stops fulfilling its mission of *relevant* legal-social control. When this happens, individuals and the policing powers of the state disregard the criminal norm, which becomes legally dead – a reasonable outcome when the criminal norm lacks the required flexibility to respond to social changes. Therefore, although the constitution can be a legitimate source of criminal norms, the criminal norms captured in the constitution may lack the required flexibility, and become irrelevant and anachronistic.[111]

2.2.2.2 Legislation

In most western legal systems legislation is the dominant legal source of criminal norms.[112] Assimilation of the political ideas of scholars in the age of enlightenment, in the eighteenth century, contributed greatly to this situation. These political ideas urged the separation of the powers of the state and the precedence of the legislator. Generally, the legislator is the parliament, which represents individuals in society. The representatives are elected and subject to public criticism, so that the legislator is subject to public criticism. Representatives who disappoint the public and no longer represent it are not reelected and are replaced.

Because the legislator (parliament) reflects society and the individuals in it at the current time, western legal systems support the idea that the legal-social control should be exercised through the legislator. Institutionally, the legislator reflects the

---

[109]Grundgesetz, Art. 102.

[110]BVerfGE 39, 1, 65; BVerfGE 88, 203, 254–258; BVerfGE 19, 342, 348; BVerfGE 35, 382, 400; BVerfGE 61, 126, 134; HANS-HEINRICH JESCHECK UND THOMAS WEIGEND, LEHRBUCH DES STRAFRECHTS – ALLGEMEINER TEIL 12–13 (5 Auf., 1996); VOLKER KREY, DEUTSCHES STRAFRECHT ALLGEMEINER TEIL, TEIL I: GRUNDLAGEN 24–29 (2002).

[111]See, e.g., in Lawrence v. Texas, 539 U.S. 558, 123 S.Ct. 2472, 156 L.Ed.2d 508 (2003).

[112]WAYNE R. LAFAVE, CRIMINAL LAW 74 (4th ed., 2003).

public under the limitations of representation, so that not all individuals may be represented in the parliament owing to election thresholds.[113] Democratic elections and public criticism of representatives provides society the flexibility required to assimilate social changes within the legal social control expressed by specific criminal norms.

Although legislation does not reflect the same wide consensus as expressed in the constitution, the legislation is sufficiently flexible to assimilate social changes. Legal systems determine the minimal social consensus needed to create, change, or abolish criminal norms. This determination materializes through the definition of the majority required in parliament for the legislative process. For most criminal norms, a standard majority suffices. When the criminal norm requires a wider consensus, a special majority may be required to change the current norm.

The need for fair notice that is public and clear also made legislation the major and dominant legal source of criminal norms.[114] The legislative process embodies the fair notice requirement in relation to most legal norms, including the criminal ones. In some legal systems a legal provision specifies that legislation is the only legitimate or dominant source of criminal norms.[115] In these legal systems, recognition of other legitimate sources for the creation of criminal norms is an exception and it is strictly interpreted.[116]

The European-Continental legal tradition uses the codex as a form of legislation. This tradition goes back to the early Middle Ages, and one of its basic documents is the Justinian Codex enacted in 534 AD.[117] The tradition of codification includes clear formulation of the law, accessible to the public and understandable to the reasonable layman. The codification of criminal law spread from the European-Continental legal systems to the Anglo-American systems since the nineteenth century.[118] In the modern age, codification appears to be the common expression of legislation regarding the criminal law in both European-Continental and Anglo-American legal systems.

The validation of legislation is embodied within the legislative process. Validation includes both formal and substantive requirements. The most common formal requirement of validation is the requirement of formal publicity, as discussed

---

[113] E.g., in 2010 in Germany, New Zealand and Poland the election threshold is 5%, in France 12.5%, in Israel 2%, in Sweden 4% and in Turkey 10%.

[114] George P. Fletcher, The Grammar of Criminal Law – American, Comparative and International, Volume One: Foundations 80–87 (2007).

[115] Section 1 of the German Penal Code provides: "Eine Tat kann nur bestraft werden, wenn die Strafbarkeit gesetzlich bestimmt war, bevor die Tat begangen wurde"; and the beginning of article 111-2 of the French Penal Code provides: "La loi détermine les crimes et délits et fixe les peines applicables à leurs auteurs".

[116] See the end of article 111-2 of the French Penal Code.

[117] Apparently it seems that the Justinian Codex was not the first codex, but Theodosius Codex of 438 AD.

[118] See in Britain, The Law Commission, A Criminal Code for England and Wales (Law Com. No. 177, 1989), and in the United States, The American Law Institute, Model Penal Code – Official Draft and Explanatory Notes (1962, 1985).

above.[119] Substantive requirements of validation originate with the constitution or with common constitutional conventions.[120] Although in most cases validation is done *ex ante*, in some legal systems it is possible to validate or invalidate the criminal norm *ex post*. Validation or invalidation of legal norms *ex post* is done through judicial review. The European-Continental legal systems require special institutions for *ex post* validation,[121] whereas in the Anglo-American legal systems the courts are authorized to do so.[122]

2.2.2.3 Regulations

Occasionally, in order to carry out the legislation provisions, the legislation itself empowers an administrative authority to enact regulations. These regulations may include criminal norms. In some legal systems, the criminal norms captured by regulations are regarded as administrative offenses and not criminal ones.[123] Breach of administrative offenses creates no criminal record, and after the penalty is settled, the offense is forgiven. The common penalty in administrative offenses is a fine of a light or moderate rate.

The justification for using regulations in general is the need for efficiency in carrying out the executive powers of the state. Regulations are much more flexible than the legislation, and are put in effect directly by the executive powers of the state.[124] Nevertheless, the creation of criminal norms within the regulations is not a simple matter. The executive branch is not an elected power of the state, and the social consensus of the government is much narrower than that of parliament. In most legal systems, members of the government are not elected but appointed. They represent only part of the population, and not always a major part. Therefore, questions arise about the legitimacy of regulations to create criminal norms.

There are two main justifications for regulations as a legitimate legal source of criminal norms. First, in most legal systems the formal function of the administrative authorities is to execute the legislation and implement it, as defined by parliament under the rules of the legislator's precedence. Implementation of the legislation may not contradict the legislation itself. In most cases the administrative authority has the professional knowledge and skills to carry out the legislation, and

---

[119] Above at Sect. 2.2.1.3.

[120] See, e.g., in Germany, Grundgesetz, Art. 103 II.

[121] E.g., the Federal Constitutional Court in Germany (Bundesverfassungsgericht) and the Constitutional Council (Conseil Constitutionnel) in France.

[122] E.g., Marbury v. Madison, 5 U.S. 137, 2 L.Ed. 60, 1 Cranch 137 (1803) in the United States, and Bonham, (1610) 8 Co. Rep. 114 in England.

[123] Edmund H. Schwenk, *The Administrative Crime, Its Creation and Punishment by Administrative Agencies*, 42 MICH. L. REV. 51 (1943); Gesetz über Ordnungswidrigkeiten (BGBl. I, S. 602).

[124] United States v. International Minerals & Chemical Corp., 402 U.S. 558, 91 S.Ct. 1697, 29 L. Ed.2d 178 (1971).

the legislation itself requires regulations for various situations to be implemented and applied as a legal-social control.

The second reason has to do with the function of the administrative authority in emergency situations. Parliament cannot respond as efficiently as the administrative authority can in times of emergency, when fast, clear, and efficient action is required. The administrative authority, designed to respond to these situations, functions through regulations. Nevertheless, in order to prevent abuse of the power to enact regulations, full and clear constitutional limits are placed on it in light of the separation of the powers of the state.[125] Excessive power of the government is the path toward dictatorship and the destruction of democracy. Most tyrannies were implemented through regulations that included criminal norms.[126] At the same time, insufficient powers in the hands of the government weaken the state and make it vulnerable.

To balance the powers of the executive branch, criminal norms created by regulations must fulfill four major requirements:

(1) Explicit authorization to enact regulations within the legislation
(2) Substantial match between the regulation and the legislation
(3) Applicability of legislative limitations on the regulations
(4) Sentencing limitations on regulations

Explicit authorization to enact regulations within the legislation is the outcome of the administrative law principle of legality, whereby the administrative authority is subject to the parliament. This concept has its roots in the English Glorious Revolution of the seventeenth century, which created the concept of the "King in Parliament." When the administrative authority is subject to the parliament, only the parliament can authorize it to act in certain ways. Enacting regulations is authorized because the parliament ruled so. Consequently, only when the parliament authorizes the government to enact regulations that include criminal norms, are these regulations legal. The parliament rules through legislation, and therefore the authorization is granted through legislation.

Because of the subordination of regulations to legislation, a substantial match is required between the regulation the legislation authorizing it. Regulations cannot contradict legislation. When regulations do not match the legislation, these regulations are considered to be *ultra vires*, i.e., in other words, lacking in legal authority.

[125]United States v. Grimaud, 220 U.S. 506, 31 S.Ct. 480, 55 L.Ed. 563 (1911); McKinley v. United States, 249 U.S. 397, 39 S.Ct. 324, 63 L.Ed. 668 (1919); Yakus v. United States, 321 U.S. 414, 64 S.Ct. 660, 88 L.Ed. 834 (1944); Mistretta v. United States, 488 U.S. 361, 109 S.Ct. 647, 102 L.Ed.2d 714 (1989); Touby v. United States, 500 U.S. 160, 111 S.Ct. 1752, 114 L.Ed.2d 219 (1991).

[126]See, e.g., RGBL, 1933, Teil I, Nr. 25, S. 141; Martin Broszat, Der Staat Hitlers – Grundlegung und Entwicklung seiner inneren Verfassung 117 (1969).

Ultra vires regulations are invalid and void.[127] In general, the match between regulations and legislation is examined under judicial review.[128]

Applicability of legislative limitations on regulations is necessary because of the derivative nature of regulations. The legislation is not authorized to empower regulations to act in ways the legislation itself is not authorized to use. For example, the legislation has no power to take judiciary actions because of the general concept of separation of the powers of the state. As a result, regulations that empower the administrative authority to take judiciary actions are void.[129] All formal limitations on the legislation are relevant to regulations, including formal publicity,[130] application in time,[131] application in territory,[132] and principles of interpretation.[133]

Sentencing limitations on regulations are part of the differentiation between parliamentary and administrative authority, necessary to maintain the required balance between them. A common type of sentencing limitation on regulations is on in which the legislation itself limits the sentencing to specific types and degrees of punishment.[134] When the legislation does not limit the regulations by determining the punishment for their breach, and the administrative authority is not subject to formal limitations in determining punishment, in most legal systems this constitutes an illegal situation, and the associated regulations are considered void.[135] The same problem can occur when no formal limitation on punishment associated with a regulation is specified by the legislation.[136]

2.2.2.4 Judicial Decisions

The legality of judicial decisions and rulings in creating criminal norms is a basic question in the debate on the concept of separation of powers. Do courts have the power to enact criminal laws? Different legal systems at different times answered this question differently, according to their legal tradition and their interpretation of the concept of separation of powers.

---

[127] State v. Dube, 409 A.2d 1102 (Me.1979); State v. King, 257 N.W.2d 693 (Minn.1977); State v. Smith, 539 P.2d 754 (Okl.Crim.App.1975).

[128] Louis L. Jaffe, Judicial Control of Administrative Action 110 (1965).

[129] Helvering v. Mitchell, 303 U.S. 391, 58 S.Ct. 630, 82 L.Ed.2d 917 (1938).

[130] Above at Sect. 2.2.1.3.

[131] Hereinafter in Chap. 3.

[132] Hereinafter in Chap. 4.

[133] Hereinafter in Chap. 5.

[134] See, e.g., article 111-2 of the French Penal Code.

[135] People v. Grant, 242 App.Div. 310, 275 N.Y.S. 74 (1934); State v. Curtis, 230 N.C. 169, 52 S.E.2d 364 (1949); Gilgert v. Stockton Port Dist., 7 Cal.2d 384, 60 P.2d 847 (1936).

[136] Smallwood v. District of Columbia, 17 F.2d 210 (D.C.Cir.1927); Commonwealth v. Diaz, 326 Mass. 525, 95 N.E.2d 666 (1950); State v. Gallion, 572 P.2d 683 (Utah.1977).

The European-Continental legal systems did not embrace the praxis of the binding precedent (*stare decisis*).[137] The binding precedent praxis empowers the courts to create legal norms by way of judicial decisions. The separation of powers of the state, as accepted in European-Continental legal systems, prefers that parliament enact through legislation rather than the courts through judicial decisions. The main reason for this is that judges are not elected, but appointed, and therefore do not reflect society. The elected representatives of parliament represent society and are subject to public criticism. Thus, in European-Continental legal systems judicial decisions are not authorized to create criminal norms.[138]

A different approach was taken in English common law. Common Law originated in the twelfth century through the creation of new criminal norms by the crown's courts (*curia regis*). Until the middle of the seventeenth century, most criminal offenses were created and defined by judicial decisions using the binding precedent praxis.[139] Although some offenses were enacted through legislation, these were in the minority.[140] Between the years 1660–1860, inspired by the Glorious Revolution, the courts restricted themselves to creating only offenses that are considered to be corrupting of public morals.[141] When the courts did not create such offenses, parliament did so through legislation.[142]

At that time, the House of Commons gained increasing power, which it expressed through excessive legislation. Judicial decisions lost ground to the degree to which parliament gained it.[143] In the middle of the nineteenth century, a new concept was embraced whereby the creation of new offenses was under the ultimate authority of parliament, but the courts were able to interpret the criminal norms (both the offenses and general principles)[144] and rule on the validity and definition of misdemeanors (but not felonies).[145] English criminal law, however, is

---

[137] BERND RÜTHERS, RECHTSTHEORIE 145 (1999).

[138] R. M. Jackson, *Common Law Misdemeanors*, 6 CAMB. L. J. 193 (1936–1938).

[139] JEROME HALL, GENERAL PRINCIPLES OF CRIMINAL LAW 53 (2nd ed., 1960, 2005).

[140] Sedley, [1664] 1 Siderfin 168, 1 Keb. 620.

[141] Scofield, [1784] Cald. 397; Higgins, (1801) 2 East 5, 102 E.R. 269; GLANVILLE WILLIAMS, CRIMINAL LAW: THE GENERAL PART SEC. 189 (2nd ed., 1961).

[142] WAYNE R. LAFAVE, CRIMINAL LAW 75 (4th ed., 2003).

[143] Manley, [1933] 1 K.B. 529; JAMES FITZJAMES STEPHEN, A HISTORY OF THE CRIMINAL LAW OF ENGLAND 359–360 (1883, 1964); William Teulon Swan Stallybrass, *Public Mischief*, 49 L. Q. REV. 183 (1933).

[144] Andrew Ashworth, *Is the Criminal Law a Lost Cause?*, 116 L.Q.R. 225 (2000); Shaw v. Director of Public Prosecutions, [1962] A.C. 220, [1961] 2 All E.R. 446, [1961] 2 W.L.R. 897, 45 Cr. App. Rep. 113, 125 J.P. 437.

[145] P.R. Glazebrook, *How Old Do You Think She Was?*, [2001] C.L.J. 26, 30 (2001): "the materials of our criminal law [are] now so voluminous, chaotic and contradictory, [that] the Law Lords are left free to decide cases as the fancy takes them".

ambiguous on this issue,[146] and as a result there have been attempts to codify it, which would then make it the domain of parliamentary legislation.[147]

In American law, the criminal norm was initially rooted in the English common law, brought to the English colonies by the immigrants. After American independence, English common law and English legislation up to the year 1607 became the formal legal basis of the criminal law in the U.S.A. 1607 was the year of the establishment of the first English colony in north-America, at Jamestown. This legal situation was common to most of the states, but not to all of them. Some other states assimilated English law until 1775, others assimilated English law with no limitations, and others yet assimilated the French law because most of their inhabitants were French or Spanish.[148]

American courts did not consider themselves authorized to create criminal offenses. In *all* cases in which the English common law was assimilated, criminal offenses were created through the constitution or through specific legislation. As a result, the source of the criminal norms derived from English common law was not the English common law itself but specific constitutions or legislations.[149] In the nineteenth century, the use of the English common law in American courts was significantly reduced. Codification abolished Common Law offenses gradually but steadily.[150] The creation of offenses was in the exclusive authority of the legislation,[151] as was the creation of general principles in criminal law.[152] Only in cases of interpretation of legal terms of the codex, which originated in the English common law,[153] was it permitted to use the English common law, and only for the purpose of interpretation.[154]

Thus, there is some uniformity worldwide in that judicial decisions are not a legitimate legal source for creating criminal norms. Not only does legislation reflect a wider consensus, but judicial decisions that create criminal norms are applied, in

---

[146]THE LAW COMMISSION, A CRIMINAL CODE FOR ENGLAND AND WALES (1989); DAVID ORMEROD, SMITH AND HOGAN CRIMINAL LAW 32–33 (12th ed., 2008).

[147]Herbert Pope, *The English Common Law in the United States*, 24 HARV. L. REV. 6 (1911).

[148]WAYNE R. LAFAVE, CRIMINAL LAW 76 (4th ed., 2003).

[149]Robinson v. State, 353 Md. 683, 728 A.2d 698 (1999).

[150]United States v. Hudson, 11 U.S. 32, 3 L.Ed. 259 (1812); United States v. Coolidge, 14 U.S. 415, 4 L.Ed. 124 (1816); Liparota v. United States, 471 U.S. 419, 105 S.Ct. 2084, 85 L.Ed.2d 434 (1985): "The definition of the elements of a criminal offense is entrusted to the legislature, particularly in the case of federal crimes, which are solely creatures of statute"; compare United States v. Davis, 167 F.2d 228 (D.C.Cir.1948); United States v. Sampol, 636 F.2d 621 (D.C. Cir.1980); O'Connor v. United States, 399 A.2d 21 (D.C.Cir.1979).

[151]State v. Tuttle, 730 P.2d 630 (Utah 1986).

[152]Turner v. State, 1 Ohio St. 422 (1853); State v. De Wolfe, 67 Neb. 321, 93 N.W. 746 (1903); State v. Dailey, 191 Ind. 678, 134 N.E. 481 (1922); Sheed v. State, 61 Okl.Cr. 96, 65 P.2d 1245 (1937); State v. Moore, 196 La. 617, 199 So. 661 (1940); State v. Anthony, 179 Or. 282, 169 P.2d 587 (1946); State v. Potts, 75 Ariz. 211, 254 P.2d 1023 (1953).

[153]Moskal v. United States, 498 U.S. 103, 111 S.Ct. 461, 112 L.Ed.2d 449 (1990).

[154]WAYNE R. LAFAVE, CRIMINAL LAW 78–83 (4th ed., 2003).

fact, retroactively.[155] The first time the individual learns about a specific prohibition is on the occasion of the ruling relating to that individual's specific case, as it is being declared for the first time that it is illegal. This damages the requirement of fair notice.[156] Whereas the legislation is generally prospective, judicial decisions are retroactive, as the court deals only with occurrences from the past.

Moreover, judicial decisions are specific because they relate specific cases, whereas legislation is general. To make a judicial decision a general rule, there must be a logical process of induction aimed at identifying the *ratio decidendi* and separating it from the *obiter dictum*. Frequently, this is a matter of perspective rather than a hard a fast rule, and as a result, in most legal systems worldwide, judicial decisions are not a legitimate legal source of criminal norms.

2.2.2.5 International Custom and State Practice, International Covenants, and International Judicial Decisions

International law creates prohibitions with criminal sanctions, and the legal question is whether the normative sources of international law can function as legitimate sources of the criminal norm. The significant development of the human rights agenda after World War II made the norms of international law applicable directly to individuals, even when domestic law contradicted these norms. The establishment of international criminal tribunals accelerated the process.[157] The international law includes three major normative sources: international custom and state practice, international covenants, and international judicial decisions.[158]

The international custom and state practice are considered to be the basic normative source of the international law.[159] International custom is a formulation

[155] In McBoyle v. United States, 283 U.S. 25, 51 S.Ct. 340, 75 L.Ed. 816 (1931) Justice Holmes noted: "Although it is not likely that a criminal will carefully consider the text of the law before he murders or steals, it is reasonable that a fair warning should be given to the world in language that the common world will understand, of what the law intends to do if a certain line is passed. To make the warning fair, so far as possible the line should be clear"; in People v. Brengard, 265 N.Y. 100, 191 N.E. 850 (1934) it was noted that "the abolition of all common-law crimes was accomplished not alone for the advantage of those individuals who might be charged with offenses, but also for the benefit of the people of the State. The bar, the courts, society in general, as well as each private person, were to be specifically informed concerning acts which are criminal and the nature and degrees of particular crimes as defined".

[156] Above at Sect. 2.2.1.3.

[157] International Tribunal for Rwanda, Annex to U.N. Security Council Resolution 955 (1994); International Tribunal for the Prosecution of Persons Responsible for Serious Violations of International Humanitarian Law Committed in the Territory of the Former Yugoslavia, Annex to U.N. Security Council Resolution 808 (1993); Rome Statute of the International Criminal Court, U.N. Doc. PCNICC/1999/INF/3 (1999).

[158] Michael W. Reisman, *The Concepts and Functions of Soft Law in International Politics*, Essays in Honour of Judge Taslim Olawale Elias 135 (Bello and San eds., 1992).

[159] North Sea Continental Shelf Cases, [1969] I.C.J. Rep. 3, 44.

of existing state practices, and as a normative source it does not establish new legal norms. International custom declares what is the existing practice by which states are obligated to abide.[160] Therefore, international custom is examined *ex post*, because it is a declarative and descriptive norm rather than a constitutive one.[161] Some international customs are universal, others are regional.[162] All states are obligated to abide by the universal international customs, even if they expressed no explicit consent to it, as long as an explicit objection has not been expressed by these states.[163]

Most international customs are *jus dispositivum*, i.e., dispositive norms, which means that individual states may reject them. But some of the international customs are *jus cogens*, i.e., peremptory norms that the states have no authority to decide whether or not to accept, and the norms are applied always and unconditionally. Criminal international customs are generally *jus cogens*. For example, genocide, piracy, torture, slave trade, war crimes, and crimes against humanity are criminal norms that are international customs of the *jus cogens* type.[164] No state is allowed to commit genocide, even if domestic legislation does not prohibit it.

Under the Anglo-American legal systems, the international custom is considered to be part of the domestic law of the state.[165] In the European-Continental legal systems, international custom may be considered as part of the domestic law of the state, as long as no specific domestic legislation contradicts it. The significant difficulty in embracing the international custom as a legitimate source of criminal norms is its ambiguity that characterizes generally the content and the sanction in cases of breach. When the international custom is written, it is in the form of an international covenant that declares what the international custom is. The international custom that creates *jus cogens* criminal norms is significant mostly within the principle of legality, because it reflects the applicability in time (retroactive) and in territory (extraterritorial) of the criminal norm.[166]

International covenants are agreements between states. International covenants are legal sources in the international law because of international custom,

---

[160] Raphael M. Walden, *Customary International Law: A Jurisprudential Analysis*, 13 ISR. L. REV. 86, 97 (1978).

[161] Asylum Case, [1950] I.C.J. Rep. 266, 277; Rights of Passage over Indian Territory Case, [1960] I.C.J. Rep. 6.

[162] DANIEL PATRICK O'CONNEL, INTERNATIONAL LAW 15 (2nd ed., 1970).

[163] ROBERT JENNINGS AND ARTHUR WATTS, OPPENHEIM'S INTERNATIONAL LAW 25 (9th ed., 1996).

[164] See, e.g., Convention on the Prevention and Punishment of the Crime of Genocide, January 12, 1951, 78 U.N.T.S. 277.

[165] *In re* Paquete Habana, The Lola 175 U.S. 677, 20 S.Ct 290, 44 L.Ed 320 (1900); West Rand Central Gold Mining Co. Ltd., [1905] 2 K.B. 391.

[166] The applicability in time of the criminal norm shall be discussed hereinafter at Chap. 3, and the applicability in place of the criminal norm shall be discussed hereinafter at Chap. 4.

which the agreements should respect (*pacta sunt servanda*).[167] In general, an international covenant is not applied universally, and it obligates only the states that signed the covenants. Nevertheless, sometimes the covenant itself becomes an international custom after some years in which state practice follows the provisions of the covenant.[168] From that point on, it is considered as an international custom, the details of which are formulated in the covenant.

In order to accept an international covenant within the domestic law of the state, the covenant must be ratified in parliament through legislation. After ratification, the covenant has the status of legislation, and the original source of the legislation is immaterial for purposes of applicability. When the state signs the covenant (through its government) but does not ratify it (through parliament), the covenant is not applicable within the domestic law of the state. Nevertheless, domestic courts regard such covenants as an interpretive source, and the actions of the administrative authority are interpreted in light of these covenants.[169]

Creating a criminal norm based on an international covenant that has been ratified is not different from any other criminal norm created through legislation. But a criminal norm based on an international covenant that has not been ratified has no applicability to individuals in domestic law. State actions may be interpreted according to that norm, but it is not compelling to individuals.

International judicial decisions include all judicial decisions of international tribunals and arbitrations that relate to international affairs.[170] The binding precedent praxis (*stare decisis*)[171] has not been accepted within international law, and therefore judicial decisions cannot become case-laws. Although international tribunals are allowed to follow voluntarily previous judicial decisions, they are not compelled by these judicial decisions.[172] Therefore, international law does not identify international judicial decisions as an independent legal source in the creation of international legal norms. Consequently, international judicial decisions are not considered to be a legitimate normative source for creating criminal norms.

---

[167]Article 26 of the Vienna Convention on the Law of Treaties, May 23, 1969, 1155 U.N.T.S. 331, 342 provides: "Every treaty in force is binding upon the parties to it and must be performed by them in good faith".

[168]See, e.g., *1907 Hague Convention IV Respecting the Laws and Customs of War on Land*, 2 American Journal of International Law Supp. 90–117 (1908).

[169]Salomon v. Commissioner of Customs and Excise, [1967] 2 Q.B. 116, [1966] 3 All E.R. 871, [1966] 3 W.L.R. 1223; Garland v. British Rail Engineering Ltd., [1983] 2 A.C. 751, [1982] 2 All E. R. 402, [1982] 2 W.L.R. 918; Brind v. Secretary of State for the Home Department, [1991] 1 A.C. 696, [1991] 1 All E.R. 720 [1991] 2 W.L.R. 588.

[170]Rome Statute of the International Criminal Court, U.N. Doc. PCNICC/1999/INF/3 (1999); Malcolm N. Shaw, International Law 188–190 (4th ed., 1997).

[171]Above at Sect. 2.2.2.4.

[172]Land and Maritime Boundary between Cameroon and Nigeria, [1998] I.C.J. Rep. 28.

2.2.2.6 Supranational and Federal Sources

Whereas in the international system the sovereign status of the states is preserved, there are supranational systems in which the states give up their sovereignty in specific areas and transfer their authority to the supranational system.[173] This is the major difference between international and supranational systems. Supranational systems are established on a geographic basis for the mutual benefit of the states involved. Some supranational systems are federations (e.g., the United States, Germany, and Australia), and some are not (e.g., the European Union).[174] The relevant question for supranational systems is whether they can establish legitimate legal sources for the creation of criminal norms.

The answer depends on the exact definition of the relations between the domestic state and the supranational organization. If the domestic state surrendered some of its authority to create criminal norms to the supranational organization, the criminal norms created by that organization are legitimate and binding within the domestic state. In this case, the supranational criminal norms apply directly to individuals, as if they were created by the domestic state.

In the United States, according to the constitutional definition, the federal system has the authority to create criminal norms through legislations and regulations.[175] Federal criminal norms in the United States apply directly to individuals, and are considered superior to the criminal norms created by the states.[176] In the European Union, the European Court of Justice ruled that the European Union law applies to individuals as part of a new legal order.[177] Moreover, European Union law is superior to domestic state laws.[178] European Union law governs both domestic legislations[179] and domestic constitutions.[180] In this type of relation between the

[173]Francesco Capotorti, *Supranational Organization*, ENCYCLOPEDIA OF PUBLIC INTERNATIONAL LAW Vol. 5 262 (1983).

[174]Secretary of state for transport, *Ex parte* Factortame Ltd., [1990] 2 A.C. 85.

[175]U.S. Constitution, art. I, § 8 provides: "The Congress shall have Power To make all Laws which shall be necessary and proper for carrying into Execution the foregoing Powers, and all other Powers vested by this Constitution in the Government of the United States, or in any Department or Officer thereof".

[176]United States v. Lopez, 514 U.S. 549, 115 S.Ct. 1624, 131 L.Ed.2d. 626 (1995); United States v. Bell, 70 F.3d 495 (7th Cir.1995); Jones v. United States, 529 U.S. 848, 120 S.Ct. 1904, 146 L. Ed.2d. 902 (2000); George D. Brown, *Constitutionalizing the Federal Criminal Law Debate: Morrison, Jones and the ABA*, 2001 U. ILL. L. REV. 983 (2001).

[177]Case 26/62 Van Gend en Loos v. Netherlands Inland Revenue Administration, [1963] E.C.R. 1, [1963] C.M.L.R. 105.

[178]Case 6/64 Costa v. E.N.E.L., [1964] E.C.R. 585, [1964] 3 C.M.L.R. 425.

[179]Case 106/77 Amministrazione delle Finanze dello Stato v. Simmenthal SpA, [1978] E.C.R. 629, [1978] 3 C.M.L.R. 263.

[180]Case 11/70 Internationale Handelsgesellschaft v. Einfuhr und Varratsstelle füd Futtermittel, [1970] E.C.R. 1125, [1972] C.M.L.R. 255; Wünsche Handelsgesellschaft v. Germany, [1987] 3 C. M.L.R. 225.

domestic states and the supranational organization, the supranational norms are considered to be legitimate sources of criminal norms.

2.2.2.7 Agreements, Organizational Policy, and Disciplinary Norms

In most hierarchic organizations there are internal rules of behavior that are captured in agreements or organizational policies. These rules create norms of behavior within the hierarchic organization, which are enforced by disciplinary laws. Breach of the norms imposes disciplinary sanction on the offender. The disciplinary law resembles the criminal law because the norms are formulated as valid conditional clauses, but there is a difference, as the disciplinary law contains no criminal sanction and has no applicability outside the given hierarchic organization.

The disciplinary law does not exercise the general legal-social control embodied in criminal law, and it is much narrower than criminal law. Even if the disciplinary sanctions resemble the criminal ones (e.g., fines, imprisonment within military organizations, etc.), these sanctions are still not considered criminal sanctions. As a result, disciplinary rules cannot constitute criminal law and cannot be considered as a legitimate source of criminal norms.[181]

2.3 Conflict of Laws Based on Legitimate Sources of the Criminal Norm

It is almost inevitable that the different legitimate sources of the criminal norm would create situations in which laws are in conflict with each other, so that given norms contradict other norms (conflict of laws). In these situations the relevant question is which norm governs and should be followed.[182] The principle of legality in criminal law accommodates four types of situations in which laws conflict, one type for every secondary principle. As far as the legitimate sources of the criminal norm are concerned (the first secondary principle), conflicting laws have to do with norms of different legal sources that contradict one another.

When several criminal norms seem to apply to a given case, each criminal norm has a legitimate source in a specific legal system, but the contents of the various sources are not consistent with one another. Which criminal norm should be applied in this situation, and which one should be rejected, although its source is legitimate? The general rule may be stated in Latin as follows:

---

[181]See more in Gabriel Hallevy, *The Defense Attorney as Mediator in Plea Bargains*, 9 PEPP. DISP. RESOL. L. J. 495 (2009); Gabriel Hallevy, *Is ADR (Alternative Dispute Resolution) Philosophy Relevant to Criminal Justice? – Plea Bargains as Mediation Process between the Accused and the Prosecution*, 5 OR. L. REV. 1 (2009).

[182]LAWRENCE COLLINS, DICEY AND MORRIS THE CONFLICT OF LAWS I 32 (13th ed., 2000).

lex superior derogat inferiori

The Latin maxim means that a superior law derogates an inferior one.[183] The question, of course, is which norm is considered to be superior and which one inferior. Every legal system has rules to determine the superiority and inferiority of legal norms. Given that superiority and inferiority are relative, the criminal norm that governs should be superior to all other criminal norms that appear to be relevant in a given situation.

Suppose, for example, that a person polluted the air, and two criminal norms appear to apply: one is a regulation that creates an air pollution offense that carries a maximum penalty of 6 months of imprisonment; the other is a statute (legislation) which also creates an air pollution offense but it carries a maximum penalty of 1 year of imprisonment. In most legal systems, legislation is superior to regulation and therefore the criminal norm created by legislation governs, and the norm created by regulation is rejected. It is immaterial whether the regulation is newer, more specific, or more lenient in its punishment of the offender. As long as the regulation is inferior to legislation, the regulation is rejected if it comes in conflict with the legislated norm.

[183]See Andrej Malec, *Legal Reasoning and Logic*, 5 Studies in Logic, Grammar and Rhetoric 97 (2002).

Chapter 3
Applicability of the Criminal Norm in Time

Contents

The second secondary principle of the principle of legality in criminal law concerns the applicability of the criminal norm in time, which is an aspect of the legitimacy of the norm as a legal social control. To allow individuals to behave according to the criminal norm, fair notice should be provided. Fair notice means effective and in most cases also early notice. This secondary principle, therefore, addressed the time element of criminal norms.

3.1 Basic Distinctions

Four distinctions are required in order to formulate accurate rules regarding the applicability of the criminal norm in time:

(1) Between procedural and substantive criminal norms
(2) Between relevant points in time

G. Hallevy, *A Modern Treatise on the Principle of Legality in Criminal Law*,
DOI 10.1007/978-3-642-13714-3_3, © Springer-Verlag Berlin Heidelberg 2010

(3) Between continuous, temporary, and fragmented criminal norms
(4) Between mitigating and aggravating criminal norms

These distinctions are discussed below.[1]

3.1.1 Distinction Between Procedural and Substantive Criminal Norms

The distinction between procedural and substantive norms is not within the exclusive domain of criminal law, but it is relevant to all spheres of the law. Different legal systems used different methods of distinction, and the same legal systems used different methods at different times. Nevertheless, the basic distinction is characteristic of all legal systems at all times. It is a theoretical distinction, unaffected by its consequences,[2] relevant not only to the applicability of the norm in time, but in place as well. According to the relevant rules of the conflict of laws, procedural norms are dominated by the law of the domestic jurisdiction (*lex fori*), whereas substantive norms are dominated by the law governing the specific case (*lex causae*).[3]

The traditional approaches to this distinction differentiate between the questions of "what" and of "how." When the specific norm answers the question of "what," it is a substantive norm; when it answers the question of "how," it is a procedural norm. But these traditional approaches are not accurate because the same norm can answer several questions, both "what" and "how," in different resolutions of the law. For example, a criminal norm stating that the suspect has the right to remain silent answers a "what" question (what the suspect is allowed to do) as well as a "how" question (how the arrest procedure should be managed).

An accurate distinction between procedural and substantive criminal norms must be based on the purpose of the specific norms. **The purpose of the substantive criminal norm is to define the criminal liability, whereas the purpose of the procedural criminal norm is to impose the defined criminal liability**. Thus, the major question in the distinction between substantive and procedural norms is about the purpose of the specific norm. In many cases there are interactions between various types of the criminal norms,[4] but the purposes of these norms still remain different.

---

[1]The relevant general rules are discussed hereinafter at Sects. 3.2.1 and 3.3.1.

[2]Compare with Grant v. McAuliffe, 41 Cal.2d 859, 246 P.2d 944 (1953); Kilberg v. Northeast Airlines Inc., 9 N.Y.2d 34, 172 N.E.2d 526 (1961).

[3]Lawrence Collins, Dicey and Morris The Conflict of Laws i 157–158 (13th ed., 2000): "While procedure is governed by the *lex fori*, matters of substance are governed by the law to which the court is directed by its choice of law rule (*lex causae*)"; See also in Huber v. Steiner, (1835) 2 Bing. N.C. 202, 210, [1835] All E.R. 159.

[4]Larry Alexander, *Are Procedural Rights Derivate Substantive Rights?*, 17 Law and Philosophy 19 (1998).

For example, when a criminal norm has to do with the rights of a suspect during arrest, it is a procedural norm and not a substantive one. The purpose of an arrest is to enable imposition of the criminal liability and not to define the criminal liability itself. As a result, criminal norms relating to arrests are not deemed substantive norms but procedural ones. When a criminal norm relates to the offense of theft, it is a substantive norm and not a procedural one. The purpose of specific offenses, including theft, is to define the criminal liability. As a result, criminal offenses are not deemed procedural norms, but substantive ones.

Various types of criminal norms may have similar practical legal consequences, but the distinction still remains based on their purposes. Edifying examples are the different types of obsolescence. Obsolescence can be procedural (after a certain period of time it is illegal to indict or prosecute the individual, although the offense may have been committed) or substantive (after a certain period of time the offense is considered never to have been committed). In both types of obsolescence, no criminal liability is imposed on the individual, but the applicable criminal norms are different because of their different purposes.

The substantive obsolescence defines the criminal liability, whereas the procedural obsolescence is related to its imposition. Practically, their consequences may be different. For example, procedural obsolescence may permit suing an individual in a civil procedure, if not specifically banned by civil procedure norms, but because of substantive obsolescence the event is considered as if it has never occurred, and therefore no civil suit can be brought in relation to that event.[5]

The specific location of the criminal law within a certain statute does not necessarily affect the distinction. Procedural criminal norms can be included in a substantive penal code, and substantive criminal norms in a procedural criminal code (code of criminal procedure).[6] If the purpose of the specific criminal norm is to define criminal liability, it is of no consequence that the norm is included in a procedural criminal code; if its purpose is to impose the defined criminal liability, it is unimportant that it is included in a substantive penal code.

According to legal classification, criminal procedure (criminal justice) and the law of evidence contain procedural criminal norms; general criminal law, including penal law, punishment, sentencing, and the law of specific offenses contain substantive criminal norms. Naturally, each criminal norm must be examined separately regarding its purpose to classify it as a procedural or a substantive norm.

3.1.2 Distinction Between Relevant Points in Time

Four points in time are relevant to the applicability of the criminal norm in time:

(1) The time of the criminal event
(2) The time of the judicial decision

[5]Compare with George P. Fletcher, Basic Concepts of Criminal Law 11 (1998).

[6]See e.g. article 56 of the German penal code.

(3) The time of the enactment of the criminal norm
(4) The time of validation of the criminal norm

The time of the criminal event refers to the point or duration in time when the relevant facts of the event can be considered to be a commission of an offense, so that the criminal norm is relevant to the event.[7] Naturally, it is the relevant criminal norm that defines the event as a criminal event. For example, when the relevant criminal norm is a derivative offense of attempted murder, the criminal event may be considered as such long before it would be considered murder, according to the offense of murder. The exact point in time used for defining the criminal event depends on the relevant definition of the criminal norm. In most cases, the definition of the specific criminal norms is completed by general criminal law norms.[8] Only the criminal norm defines when the event is considered to be a criminal event. As a result, the term "criminal event" is a legal term and not a factual one.

The time of the judicial decision refers to the point in time when the court session reaches a decision about the criminal event. In most cases, the judicial decision occurs after the completion of the criminal event, but it does not have to be so. In some criminal cases, the judicial decision relates to future events that have not yet occurred, to prevent the event from taking place, to protect individuals, etc. For example, a judicial decision that authorizes the police to conduct a search in a suspect's apartment relates to the future event of the search. Nevertheless, judicial decisions about future events do not relate directly to the criminal liability but to certain procedures accompanying the general criminal process.

The criminal process includes several stages, each of which may last for a long period, which raises the question of what should be considered the relevant stage for the judicial decision in this context. The answer varies according to the relevant criminal norm. If the relevant criminal norm refers to a stage during the court session (e.g., admissibility of evidence), the relevant judicial decision falls within the court session (e.g., the judicial decision whether or not the evidence is admissible). As far as the criminal liability and its imposition are concerned, the relevant judicial decision is the verdict, in the first instance or in the appeal instance.[9]

The time of enactment of the criminal norm refers to the point in time when the authorized organ (e.g., parliament) enacts the criminal norm, regardless of its validation. The time of enactment and the time of validation are generally different for two main reasons. First, enacting a criminal norm does not include its publication; therefore until it is published, the norm is not valid. Second, the criminal norm

---

[7]E.g., article 2(2) of the German penal code provides: "Wird die Strafdrohung während der Begehung der Tat geändert, so ist das Gesetz anzuwenden, das bei Beendigung der Tat gilt".

[8]Thus, for instance, article 8 of the German penal code define the beginning point of time of the specific criminal event when the conduct element is completed, stating that "Eine Tat ist zu der Zeit begangen, zu welcher der Täter oder der Teilnehmer gehandelt hat oder im Falle des Unterlassens hätte handeln müssen. Wann der Erfolg eintritt, ist nicht maßgebend".

[9]See e.g. Gabriel Hallevy, *Rethinking the Legitimacy of Anglo-American High Courts' Judicial Review of Determining Factual Findings in Courts of the First Instance in Criminal Cases*, 5 High Ct. Q. Rev. 20 (2009).

may specify that its validation date is a point of time in the future, after its publication, for example 1 year after publication, to enable the individuals and the authorities to prepare for the legal change required by the norm.

The time of validation of the criminal norm refers to a certain point in time when all validation conditions and processes are completed. Generally, the time of validation of the criminal norm is after the time of enactment or simultaneous with it, because enactment is a necessary condition for validation. Often the four relevant points in time are relative one to one other in six possible time relations.[10]

In the **first possible relation** between the four relevant points in time (Fig. 3.1),[11] enactment and validation occur before the criminal event and the judicial decision.

In the **second possible relation** between the relevant points in time (Fig. 3.2),[12] the criminal event takes place between enactment of the criminal norm and the time of its validation, and the judicial decision comes after validation.

In the **third possible relation** between the relevant points in time (Fig. 3.3),[13] the criminal event occurs before the criminal norm is enacted, and validated, and all these occur before the judicial decision.

In the **fourth possible relation** between the relevant points in time (Fig. 3.4),[14] the criminal event takes place first, after which the criminal norm is enacted, the judicial decision is made, and finally the validation of the criminal norm is completed.

In the **fifth possible relation** between the relevant points in time (Fig. 3.5),[15] the criminal norm is enacted before the occurrence of the criminal event, whereas the

---

[10]Figures 3.1, 3.2, 3.3, 3.4, 3.5, 3.6 relate to the position in time of the four relevant points in time on an arrow representing the time from its left side (beginning) to its right side (end). When the specific point is closer to the left side, it is earlier than the point or points positioned on its right side. The periods of time between these points may vary from case to case, but the relativity in time of these points remains constant.

[11]The first possible time relation between the relevant points in time may be demonstrated as follows: On 1.1 in a certain year the criminal norm was enacted, on 1.2 the same year the criminal norm has been completely validated, on 1.3 the same year the criminal event has occurred, and on 1.4 that year the judicial decision has been made.

[12]The second possible time relation between the relevant points in time may be demonstrated as follows: On 1.1 in a certain year the criminal norm was enacted, on 1.2 the same year the criminal event has occurred, on 1.3 the same year the criminal norm has been completely validated, and on 1.4 that year the judicial decision has been made.

[13]The third possible time relation between the relevant points in time may be demonstrated as follows: On 1.1 in a certain year the criminal event has occurred, on 1.2 the same year the criminal norm was enacted, on 1.3 the same year the criminal norm has been completely validated, and on 1.4 that year the judicial decision has been made.

[14]The fourth possible time relation between the relevant points in time may be demonstrated as follows: On 1.1 in a certain year the criminal event has occurred, on 1.2 the same year the criminal norm was enacted, on 1.3 the same year judicial decision has been made, and on 1.4 that year the criminal norm has been completely validated.

[15]The fifth possible time relation between the relevant points in time may be demonstrated as follows: On 1.1 in a certain year the criminal norm was enacted, on 1.2 the same year the criminal event has occurred, on 1.3 the same year judicial decision has been made, and on 1.4 that year the criminal norm has been completely validated.

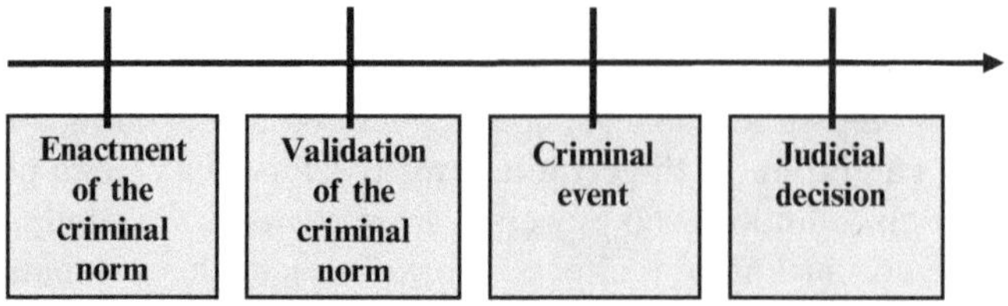

Fig. 3.1 First possible relation between relevant points in time

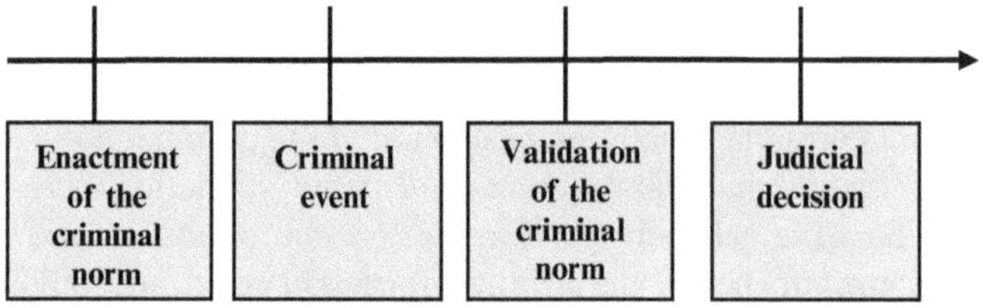

Fig. 3.2 Second possible relation between relevant points in time

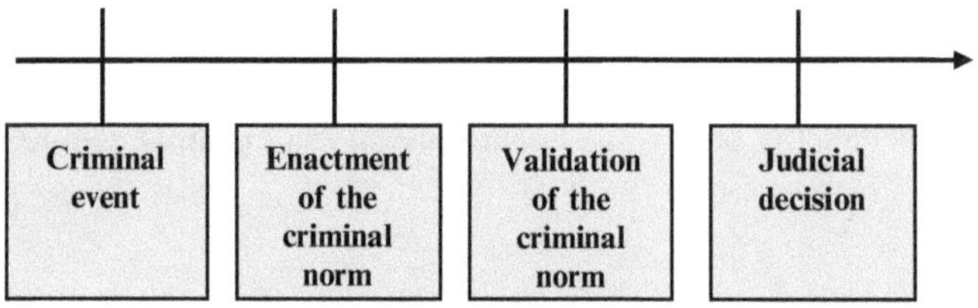

Fig. 3.3 Third possible relation between relevant points in time

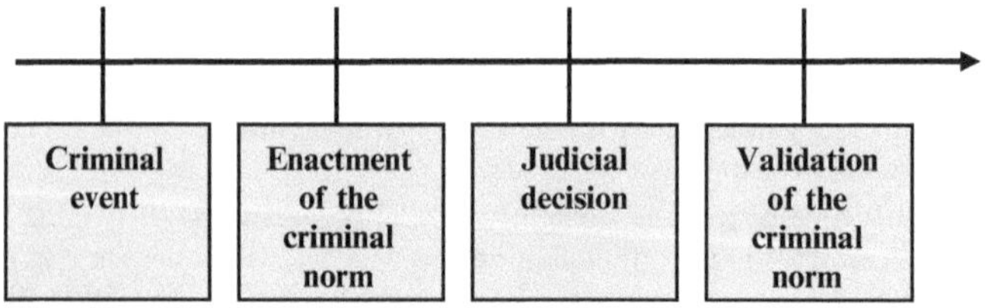

Fig. 3.4 Fourth possible relation between relevant points in time

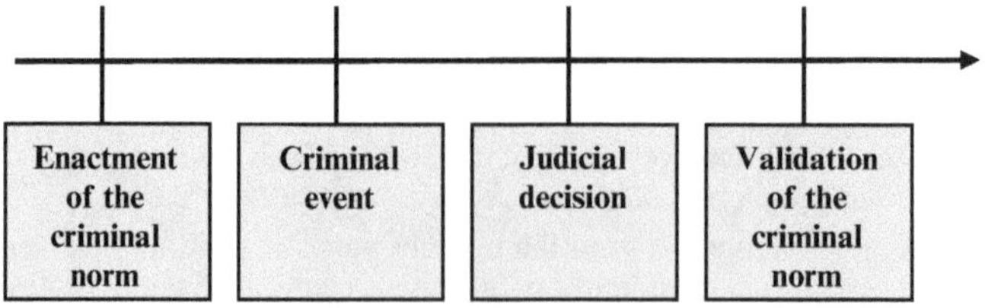

Fig. 3.5 Fifth possible relation between relevant points in time

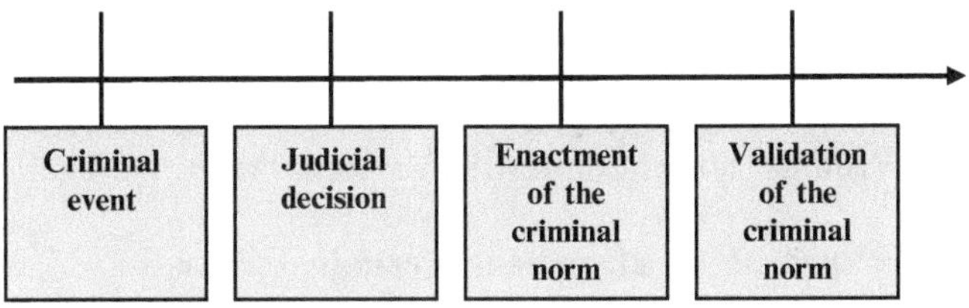

Fig. 3.6 Sixth possible relation between relevant points in time

judicial decision and the validation of the criminal norm take place after the criminal event.

In the **sixth possible relation** between the relevant points in time (Fig. 3.6),[16] criminal event occurs first, after which the judicial decision is made and later the criminal norm is enacted and validated.

The six possible relations between the relevant points in time are the factual ground for the applicability of the criminal norm in time.[17]

3.1.3 Distinction Between Continuous, Temporary, and Fragmented Criminal Norms

From the point of view of continuity, criminal norms can be of three types:

(1) Continuous
(2) Temporary
(3) Fragmentary

This distinction affects the applicability of the criminal norm in time, in other words, its continuity.

A **continuous criminal norm** is applicable constantly and continuously, without internal or external legal provisions that expire, and without limitations on its applicability. Most criminal norms in modern criminal law are continuous. When a new offense is defined, enacted, and validated with no restrictions on its applicability, it applies continuously by default.

In the case of a **temporary criminal norm**, continuity or continuous applicability in time have been restricted. There are two possible ways to restrict the continuity in time of the legal norm: *ex ante* and *ex post*. ***Ex ante***, a criminal norm restricts itself through internal expiry provisions that restrict its applicability

[16]The sixth possible time relation between the relevant points in time may be demonstrated as follows: On 1.1 in a certain year the criminal event has occurred, on 1.2 the same year judicial decision has been made, on 1.3 the same year the criminal norm was enacted, and on 1.4 that year the criminal norm has been completely validated.

[17]See hereinafter in Sects. 3.2.2 and 3.3.2.

for a certain period of time, for example, between specific dates, from a given date onward, or until a given date.[18] ***Ex post***, a criminal norm can be restricted by another provision that has been enacted or validated after the enactment or validation of the said criminal norm. The restrictive norm breaks the continuity of the criminal norm.[19]

The temporary character of a **fragmented criminal norm** is itself temporary. A fragmented criminal norm is a combination of a continuous and a temporary norm. A temporary norm is a norm that has a mechanism of continuous expiration, so that when the temporary norm expires, it is not applicable any more. The applicability in time of a fragmented criminal norm is restricted , but the restriction is itself temporary. Thus, the fragmented norm is a continuous norm whose applicability in time has been restricted by a temporary norm or by a norm whose relevant restrictive provision is not continuous.[20]

3.1.4 Distinction Between Mitigating and Aggravating Criminal Norms

Classification of a legal norm into mitigating and aggravating depends on three main aspects of perspective. First is the identity of the society in which the classification takes place and the type of legal social control being exercised. A norm considered to be aggravating in one society, may be considered as mitigating in another. Second is the identity of the legal area to which the classification relates. Aggravation and mitigation in civil law are not necessarily the same as in criminal or administrative law. Third is the difference in perspective of the individual and of society concerning the norm. A norm that appears to be mitigating from individual's perspective may not be considered as mitigating from society's perspective.

Different societies at different times may classify the same legal provisions as mitigating or aggravating according to their varying social concepts. When trying to classify norms in most societies, the liberal political philosophy appears to be

---

[18]For instance, a specific criminal norm which has been enacted on 1.1 in a certain year, has been validated on 1.2 in the same year, and shall be applicable until 1.3 in the same year due to an internal expiry provision which expires the applicability of this specific norm on that date of 1.3.

[19]For instance, a specific criminal norm which has been enacted on 1.1 in a certain year, has been validated on 1.2 in the same year. Another criminal norm, which has been enacted on 1.3 and validated on 1.4 the same year, provides that the first criminal norm would be expired on 1.5 in the same year. Thus, the first norm becomes a temporary norm, although when it has been enacted it has been considered as a continuous norm.

[20]For instance, a specific criminal norm is enacted and validated on 1.1 in a certain year. This norm is continuous and not restricted by any other norm. Nevertheless, on 1.3 in the same year, a second criminal norm is enacted and validated, and this norm provides that the first norm would be expired from 1.4 to 1.5 this year. The first norm becomes fragmented norm, since its applicability in time is from 1.1 to 1.4 and from 1.5 and on. From 1.5 and on this first criminal norm functions as a continuous norm, but from 1.1 and on it functions as a fragmented norm.

helpful. The liberal perspective of the legal social control and of the socialization process focuses on the tension between society and the individuals.[21] With reference to the three aspects of perspective mentioned above, we can define an **aggravating criminal norm as one that expands the legal possibilities of harming (degrading) the current legal situation of individuals**.

By contrast, we can define a **mitigating criminal norm as one that narrows the legal possibilities of harming the current legal situation of the individuals**. Note that these definitions relate to the legal *possibility* of harming, not to any actual harm. Even if a criminal norm does not harm any individual, it can still be considered as aggravating. For example, in a legal system in which an offense carries a maximum penalty of two-years imprisonment, amending it to three-years imprisonment is considered to be aggravating, because it expands the legal possibilities of the court to impose a harsher penalty (under the initial legal provision, before the amendment, the possibilities were more restricted).[22]

Similarly, when the legislators enact a new defense, it narrows the legal possibilities of the court to impose criminal liability and penalties upon individuals, and therefore the defense is classified as a mitigating criminal norm. The classification applies, naturally, *in abstracto*, to all individuals in all of society, and not *in concreto*, to any specific individual. As a result, if a criminal norm is applied for the benefit of an individual, but it generally expands the possibility to harm others, it is considered to be an aggravating norm.

For example, a legal provision that amends the maximum penalty of an offense from a one-year imprisonment to two years may be helpful to a homeless person who seeks food, shelter, and healthcare, and for whom the detriment to his personal freedom is less important than the daily struggle for physical survival. Nevertheless, such a criminal norm is still classified as aggravating, because it expands the general possibility for harm to other individuals.[23]

The classification *in abstracto* is not affected by the number of individuals who deem the norm to be aggravating or mitigating, or by the balancing of the social (or other) benefit with a social (or other) harm. An aggravating criminal norm can be classified as such even if it bears benefits for a specific individual or individuals, or all of society for that matter. The classification *in abstracto* reflects the analysis of

---

[21]RONALD DWORKIN, A MATTER OF PRINCIPLE 188 (1985): "Liberalism shares the same constitutive principles with many other political theories, including conservatism, but is distinguished from these by attaching different relative importance to different principles. The theory therefore leaves room, on the spectrum it describes, for the radical who cares even more for equality and less for liberty than the liberal, and therefore stands even farther away from the extreme conservative. The liberal becomes the man in the middle, which explains why liberalism is so often now considered wishy-washy, an untenable compromise between two more forthright positions".

[22]Lindsey v. Washington, 301 U.S. 397, 57 S.Ct. 797, 81 L.Ed. 1182 (1937); Flaherty v. Thomas, 94 Mass. 428 (1866); Miller v. Florida, 482 U.S. 423, 107 S.Ct. 2446, 96 L.Ed.2d 351 (1987); Lynce v. Mathis, 519 U.S. 433, 117 S.Ct. 891, 137 L.Ed.2d 63 (1997); United States v. Paskow, 11 F.3d 873 (1993).

[23]See more in Gabriel Hallevy, *The Recidivist Wants to Be Punished – Punishment as an Incentive to Re-offend*, 5 INT'L J. OF PUNISHMENT & SENTENCING 124 (2010).

the criminal norm with respect to the legal possibility of harming individuals, and not to its individual or social benefits. This classification touches on the essence of liberalism, which does not purport to define what is "good" or "evil."[24]

As a result, a substantive criminal norm that creates a new offense, renews an existing one, expands the number of individuals on whom criminal liability may be imposed, imposes harsher maximum penalties or new mandatory penalties, or makes it easier to impose criminal liability is classified as an aggravating criminal norm. By contrast, a criminal norm that abolishes an existing offense, creates a new defense, narrows the number of individuals on whom the criminal liability may be imposed, reduces the maximum penalty, abolishes a mandatory penalty, or makes it more difficult to impose criminal liability is classified as a mitigating criminal norm.

3.2 Applicability of the Procedural Criminal Norm in Time

3.2.1 The General Rule

The general rule of the applicability of the procedural criminal norm in time may be stated as follows:

The procedural criminal norm is applicable to any judicial decision from the time of its validation onward.

The general rule relates only to procedural criminal norms (both mitigating and aggravating), but not to substantive ones. Applicability in time pertains to the judicial decision, not to the criminal event that is the factual ground for the judicial decision. The criminal event has no significance as far as the applicability in time of the procedural criminal norm is concerned. To be applicable, the procedural criminal norm must have completed its validation processes.

In the **European-Continental legal systems** this rule has been fully embraced, and therefore the distinction between procedural and substantive criminal norms is a sharp one. The German legal system has recognized numerous legal amendments in the area of criminal procedure (including with reference to laws that govern criminal evidence) as applicable to judicial decisions that have been decided after the amendments were validated, even if the judicial decisions related to criminal events that occurred before the amendments were validated or even enacted.[25]

[24]Dworkin, *supra* note 21, at p. 191: "...political decisions must be, so far as is possible, independent of any particular conception of the good life, or of what gives value to life".

[25]Volker Krey, Deutsches Strafrecht Allgemeiner Teil, Teil I: Grundlagen 58–65 (2002): "Keine Geltung des Rückwirkungsverbots im Strafprozessrecht".

German courts did not apply in these cases the ban on retroactive criminal legislation that exists in the German basic law[26] because the ban is interpreted as relevant only to substantive criminal norms and not to procedural ones.[27]

German law accepted the time of validation and not of enactment as the relevant time of applicability, whether the procedural norm is aggravating or mitigating.[28] The French legal system also accepted this rule and distinguished the applicability of procedural and substantive criminal norms in time. In the French penal code, the ban on retroactive criminal legislation applies exclusively to substantive criminal norms, not to procedural ones.[29]

The **English common law** also accepted the general rule and duly distinguishes between substantive and procedural criminal norms. As a result, in English common law applying a new procedural criminal norm to a judicial decision relating to a criminal event that occurred before the enactment or validation of the specific procedural criminal norm is not considered as an infringement of the prohibition on retroactive criminal legislation, because this prohibition applies exclusively to substantive criminal norms.[30]

By contrast, the **American law** exercised a more restrictive approach to the applicability of the procedural criminal norm in time. In the eighteenth century, American courts ruled that there was no legal difference between procedural and substantive criminal norms as far as the applicability of the norms in time is concerned.[31] The significant distinction in the American law regarding the applicability of the criminal law in time is the one between an aggravating criminal norm

---

[26]BGH St 2, 300, 305; BVerfG NStZ 1994, 480.

[27]BGH St 4, 379, 385; BGH St 20, 22, 27; BVerfGE 25, 269, 284–287; BVerfGE 39, 155, 166.

[28]BGH St 26, 288, 289: "Dass neue Vorschriften des Verfahrensrechts von ihrem Inkrafttreten an auch für bereits anhängige Verfahren gelten, ist eine Selbstverständlichkeit"; BVerfGE 24, 33, 35; BVerfGE 65, 76, 97.

[29]Article 112-2 of the French penal code provides: "Sont applicables immédiatement à la répression des infractions commises avant leur entrée en vigueur: (1) Les lois de compétence et d'organisation judiciaire, tant qu'un jugement au fond n'a pas été rendu en première instance; (2) Les lois fixant les modalités des poursuites et les formes de la procédure; (3) Les lois relatives au régime d'exécution et d'application des peines; toutefois, ces lois, lorsqu'elles auraient pour résultat de rendre plus sévères les peines prononcées par la décision de condamnation, ne sont applicables qu'aux condamnations prononcées pour des faits commis postérieurement à leur entrée en vigueur; (4) Lorsque les prescriptions ne sont pas acquises, les lois relatives à la prescription de l'action publique et à la prescription des peines".

[30]Joyce v. Director of Public Prosecutions, [1946] A.C. 347, [1946] 1 All E.R. 186, 174 L.T. 206, 62 T.L.R. 208, 31 Cr. App. Rep. 57, [1946] W.N. 31.

[31]Calder v. Bull, 3 U.S. 386, 1 L.Ed. 648 (1798): "I will state what laws I consider ex post facto laws, within the words and the intent of the prohibition. 1st. Every law that makes an action done before the passing of the law, and which was innocent when done, criminal; and punishes such action. 2d. Every law that aggravates a crime, or makes it greater than it was, when committed. 3d. Every law that changes the punishment, and inflicts a greater punishment, than the law annexed to the crime, when committed. 4th. Every law that alters the legal rules of evidence, and receives less, or different, testimony, than the law required at the time of the commission of the offence, in order to convict the offender. All these, and similar laws, are manifestly unjust and oppressive".

and a mitigating one. As a result, the prohibition on retroactive criminal legislation that appears in the United States Constitution[32] is relevant to both substantive and procedural criminal norms if the criminal norm is an aggravating one.

The rationale of the American law for adopting this attitude is that criminal procedure is close to constitutional law, and therefore any infringement of individual rights defined in the American criminal procedure is considered an infringement of constitutional rights.[33] Moreover, according to American criminal procedure, infringement of procedural rights leads to infringement of substantive rights because it expands the legal possibility of imposing criminal liability, and therefore causing harm to individuals.[34] Consequently, in American law the distinction between substantive and procedural criminal norms has no significance with regard to the applicability in time, and only the distinction between aggravating and mitigating criminal norms is consequential.[35]

Three questions arise about the rationale of the general rule of the applicability of the procedural criminal norm in time:

(1) Why is the general rule applied exclusively to procedural criminal norms and not to substantive ones?
(2) Why does the general rule relate to the judicial decision and not to the criminal event?
(3) Why does the general rule relate to the time of validation of the procedural criminal norm and not of its enactment?

These three questions are answered below.

The general rule relates exclusively to the procedural criminal norm because of the general rationale that the individual cannot rightfully rely on procedure. This general rationale is not exclusive to criminal law. Procedure is not regarded as reflecting substantive rights but it is meant to serve the substantive law, and as such has no independent existence. Changes in procedure may derive from changes in technology, the streamlining of processes, etc. These factors do not change the substantive law and the essence of criminal liability. For example, using DNA evidence in court to prove a factual argument does not change the essence of criminal liability.

Society may change procedures for considerations of efficiency, and the individual cannot rightfully rely on the inefficiencies of previous procedures. The individual can rely on substantive rights and on the substantive law, but not on procedure. Thus, it has little or no significance whether a procedural criminal norm

---

[32]United States Constitution, art. I, §9 provides: "...No bill of attainder or ex post facto Law shall be passed".

[33]Breck P. McAllister, *Ex Post Facto Laws in the Supreme Court of the United States*, 15 Cal. L. Rev. 269 (1927); Charles B. Hochman, *The Supreme Court and the Constitutionality of Retroactive Legislation*, 73 Harv. L. Rev. 692 (1960); Wayne A. Logan, *The Ex Post Facto Clause and the Jurisprudence of Punishment*, 35 Am. Crim. L. Rev. 1261 (1998).

[34]People v. Edenburg, 88 Cal.App. 558, 263 P. 857 (1928).

[35]Wayne R. LaFave, Criminal Law 110 (4th ed., 2003).

is aggravating or mitigating, because it does not affect the substantive law. For example, if the legislator changes the maximum period available to appeal from 45 to 30 days, should the change be considered aggravating or mitigating? The defendant has 15 days fewer to appeal (aggravating), but so does the prosecution (mitigating). Neither norm affects the essence of criminal liability.

As long as the individual has no right to rely on procedure, it is not necessary to restrict the applicability of the criminal norm in time. The two points in time that have relevance to the applicability of the criminal norm are that of the criminal event and of the judicial decision. Procedure is relevant to legal processes, therefore the time of the judicial decision is the relevant point to the applicability of the procedural criminal norm in time. The procedural criminal norm determines the way in which the criminal process is managed; therefore it is immaterial for the criminal event itself.

Owing to efficiency considerations of the judicial system, the applicability of the procedural criminal norm in time is dependent on the time of its validity and not necessarily of its enactment. Frequently, to bring about changes in the criminal process, certain systemic, technological, technical, or budgetary changes are required, followed by training and adjustment on the part of the relevant employees. Sometimes the legislator is forced to postpone the applicability of a given norm to make its applicability possible in view of the necessary changes. If the procedural criminal norm had been applicable at the time of its enactment, it may not have been possible to implement it at that point in time.

3.2.2 *Application of the Rule*

The general rule stated above,[36] whereby the procedural criminal norm is applicable to a judicial decision from the time of its validation onward, may be applied in each of the six possible time relations between the four relevant points in time.[37] Because the general rule relates to the applicability in time of the procedural criminal norm, only two points in time are relevant to its application: the time of the judicial decision and of the validation of the (procedural) criminal norm.

As noted, in the **first possible relation** between the relevant points in time, enactment and validation occur before the criminal event and the judicial decision. The relation may be described schematically[38] as shown in Fig. 3.7.[39]

---

[36]Above at Sect. 3.2.1.

[37]Above at Sect. 3.1.2.

[38]Figures 3.7, 3.8, 3.9, 3.10, 3.11, 3.12, as well as Figs. 3.1, 3.2, 3.3, 3.4, 3.5, 3.6, relate to the position in time of the four relevant points in time on an arrow representing the time from its left side (beginning) to its right side (end). When the specific point is closer to the left side, it is earlier than the point or points positioned on its right side. The periods of time between these points may vary from case to case, but the relativity in time of these points remains constant.

[39]The applicability in time of the procedural criminal norm in the first possible time relation between the relevant points in time may be demonstrated as follows: On 1.1 in a certain year the

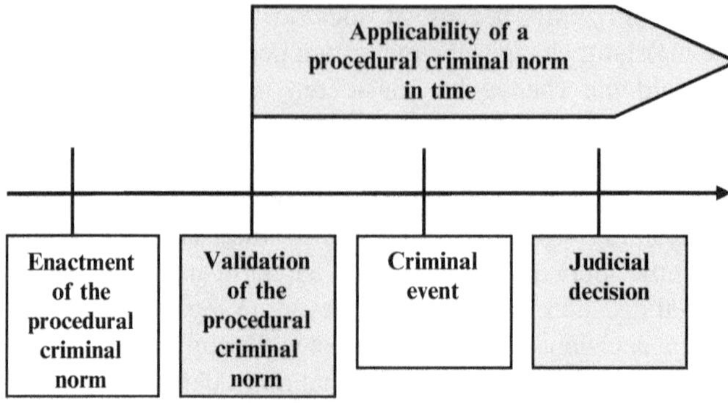

Fig. 3.7 The applicability of the procedural criminal norm in time in the first possible time relation between relevant points in time

In the first possible relation between the relevant points in time, the time of the occurrence of the criminal event is entirely irrelevant to the applicability of the procedural criminal norm in time. The procedural criminal norm relates to the criminal legal process, therefore, it is the time of the judicial decision that is relevant from the point of view of the applicability of the procedural criminal norm in time. As a result, the procedural criminal norm is applicable to any judicial decision that occurs after the validation of the procedural criminal norm, even if the criminal event has occurred after the validation of the procedural criminal norm.

In the **second possible relation** between the relevant points in time, the criminal event takes place between the enactment of the procedural criminal norm and the time of its validation, and the judicial decision occurs after validation. The relation may be described schematically as shown in Fig. 3.8.[40]

In the second possible relation between the relevant points in time, the time of the occurrence of the criminal event is entirely irrelevant to the applicability of the procedural criminal norm in time. The procedural criminal norm relates to the criminal legal process; therefore it is the time of the judicial decision that is relevant from the point of view of the applicability of the procedural criminal norm in time. As a result, the procedural criminal norm is applicable to any judicial decision that occurs after the validation of the procedural criminal norm, whether the criminal event has occurred after the validation of the procedural criminal norm or before it.

In the **third possible relation** between the relevant points in time, the criminal event occurs first, followed by the enactment of the procedural criminal norm and

procedural criminal norm was enacted, on 1.2 the same year the procedural criminal norm has been completely validated, on 1.3 the same year the criminal event has occurred, and on 1.4 that year the judicial decision has been made.

[40]The applicability in time of the procedural criminal norm in the second possible time relation between the relevant points in time may be demonstrated as follows: On 1.1 in a certain year the procedural criminal norm was enacted, on 1.2 the same year the criminal event has occurred, on 1.3 the same year the procedural criminal norm has been completely validated, and on 1.4 that year the judicial decision has been made.

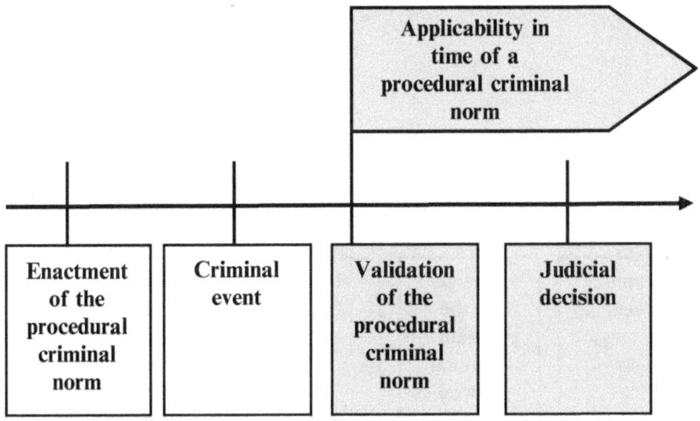

Fig. 3.8 The applicability of the procedural criminal norm in time in the second possible time relation between relevant points in time

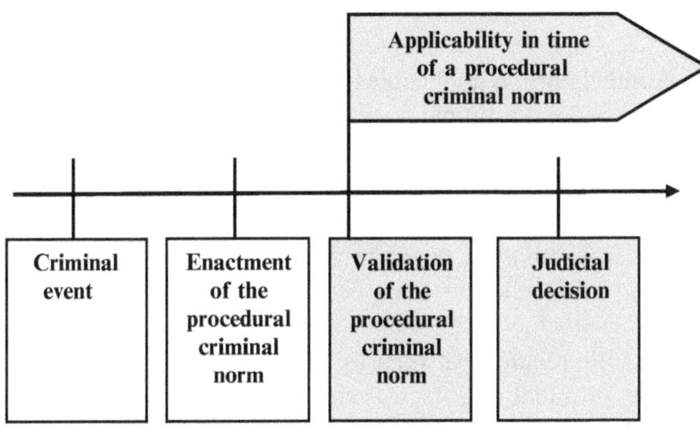

Fig. 3.9 The applicability of the procedural criminal norm in time in the third possible time relation between relevant points in time

by its validation. All these occur before the judicial decision. The relation may be described schematically as shown in Fig. 3.9.[41]

In the third possible relation between the relevant points in time, the time of the occurrence of the criminal event is entirely irrelevant to the applicability of the procedural criminal norm in time. The procedural criminal norm relates to the criminal legal process; therefore, it is the time of the judicial decision that is relevant from the point of view of the applicability of the procedural criminal norm in time. As a result,

[41]The applicability in time of the procedural criminal norm in the third possible time relation between the relevant points in time may be demonstrated as follows: On 1.1 in a certain year the criminal event has occurred, on 1.2 the same year the procedural criminal norm was enacted, on 1.3 the same year the procedural criminal norm has been completely validated, and on 1.4 that year the judicial decision has been made.

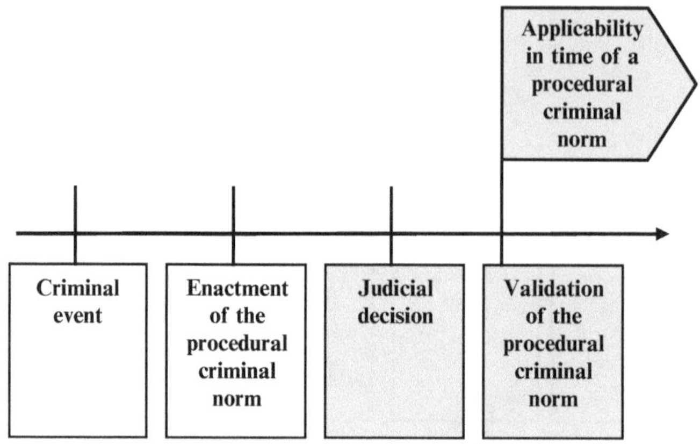

Fig. 3.10 The applicability of the procedural criminal norm in time in the fourth possible time relation between relevant points in time

the procedural criminal norm is applicable to any judicial decision that occurs after the validation of the procedural criminal norm, whether the criminal event has occurred after the validation of the procedural criminal norm or before it.

In the **fourth possible relation** between the relevant points in time, the criminal event occurs first, followed by the enactment of the procedural criminal norm and by the judicial decision. All these occur before validation of the procedural criminal norm is completed. The relation may be described schematically as shown in Fig. 3.10.[42]

In the third possible relation between the relevant points in time, the time of the occurrence of the criminal event is entirely irrelevant to the applicability of the procedural criminal norm in time. The procedural criminal norm relates to the criminal legal process; therefore it is the time of the judicial decision that is relevant from the point of view of the applicability of the procedural criminal norm in time. As a result, the procedural criminal norm is applicable to any judicial decision that occurs after the validation of the procedural criminal norm. Because in this time relation the judicial decision occurs before the procedural criminal norm is fully validated, the procedural criminal norm is not applicable to the judicial decision at hand. But the parties of the criminal process can initiate a relevant criminal process, such as an appeal, re-trial, amnesty request, etc., in which cases the procedural criminal norm is applicable to the judicial decision with regard to the relevant criminal process, e.g., the

[42]The applicability in time of the procedural criminal norm in the fourth possible time relation between the relevant points in time may be demonstrated as follows: On 1.1 in a certain year the criminal event has occurred, on 1.2 the same year the procedural criminal norm was enacted, on 1.3 the same year judicial decision has been made, and on 1.4 that year the procedural criminal norm has been completely validated.

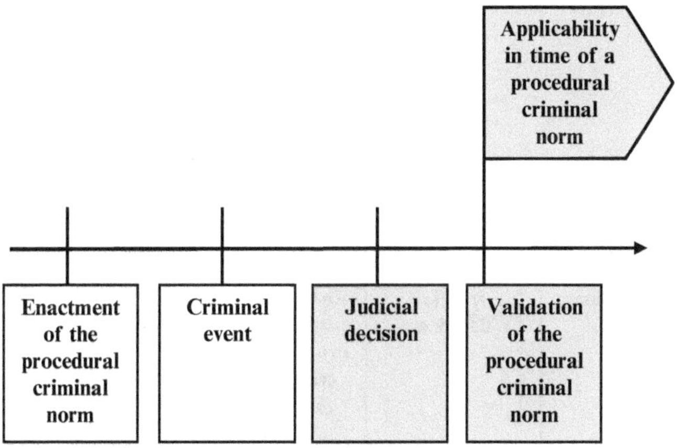

Fig. 3.11 The applicability of the procedural criminal norm in time in the fifth possible time relation between relevant points in time

judicial decision in the appeal, despite the fact that the procedural criminal norm was not applicable to the initial judicial decision.

In the **fifth possible relation** between the relevant points in time, the procedural criminal norm is enacted before the occurrence of the criminal event, followed by the judicial decision and the validation the procedural criminal norm. The relation may be described schematically as shown in Fig. 3.11.[43]

In the fifth possible relation between the relevant points in time, the time of the occurrence of the criminal event is entirely irrelevant to the applicability of the procedural criminal norm in time. The procedural criminal norm relates to the criminal legal process, therefore, it is the time of the judicial decision that is relevant from the point of view of the applicability of the procedural criminal norm in time. As a result, the procedural criminal norm is applicable to any judicial decision that occurs after the validation of the procedural criminal norm, even if the criminal event has occurred after the validation of the procedural criminal norm. Because in this time relation the judicial decision occurs before the procedural criminal norm is fully validated, the procedural criminal norm is not applicable to the judicial decision at hand. But the parties of the criminal process can initiate a relevant criminal process, in which cases the procedural criminal norm is applicable to the judicial decision with regard to the relevant criminal process despite the fact that the procedural criminal norm was not applicable to the initial judicial decision.

[43]The applicability in time of the procedural criminal norm in the fifth possible time relation between the relevant points in time may be demonstrated as follows: On 1.1 in a certain year the procedural criminal norm was enacted, on 1.2 the same year the criminal event has occurred, on 1.3 the same year judicial decision has been made, and on 1.4 that year the procedural criminal norm has been completely validated.

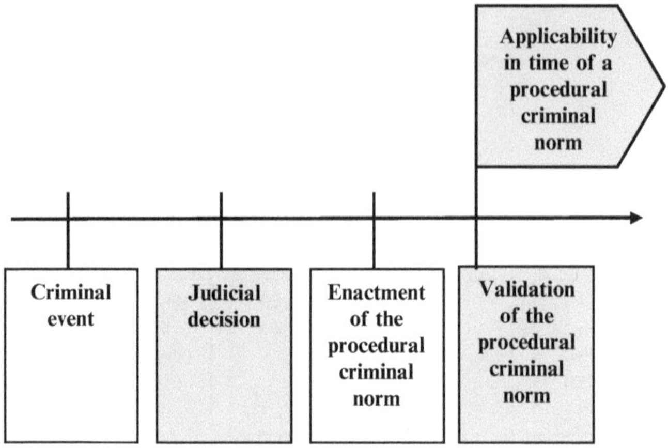

Fig. 3.12 The applicability of the procedural criminal norm in time in the sixth possible time relation between relevant points in time

In the **sixth possible relation** between the relevant points in time, the criminal event takes place first, followed by the judicial decision, the enactment of the procedural criminal norm, and its validation. The relation may be described schematically as shown in Fig. 3.12.[44]

In the sixth possible relation between the relevant points in time, the time of the occurrence of the criminal event is entirely irrelevant to the applicability of the procedural criminal norm in time. The procedural criminal norm relates to the criminal legal process, therefore, it is the time of the judicial decision that is relevant from the point of view of the applicability of the procedural criminal norm in time. As a result, the procedural criminal norm is applicable to any judicial decision that occurs after the validation of the procedural criminal norm, even if the criminal event has occurred after the validation of the procedural criminal norm. Because in this time relation the judicial decision occurs before the procedural criminal norm is fully validated, the procedural criminal norm is not applicable to the judicial decision at hand. But the parties of the criminal process can initiate a relevant criminal process, in which cases the procedural criminal norm is applicable to the judicial decision with regard to the relevant criminal process despite the fact that the procedural criminal norm was not applicable to the initial judicial decision.

[44]The applicability in time of the procedural criminal norm in the sixth possible time relation between the relevant points in time may be demonstrated as follows: On 1.1 in a certain year the criminal event has occurred, on 1.2 the same year judicial decision has been made, on 1.3 the same year the procedural criminal norm was enacted, and on 1.4 that year the procedural criminal norm has been completely validated.

3.3 Applicability in Time of the Substantive Criminal Norm

3.3.1 The General Rule

The general rule of the applicability in time of the substantive criminal norm may be stated as follows:

> **A substantive criminal norm is applicable to any criminal event from the time of its validation onward, but mitigating substantive criminal norms and the substantive criminal law that embraces a cogent international custom (*jus cogens*) are applicable to judicial decisions from the time of their enactment onward.**

The general rule relates only to the substantive criminal norm, not to the procedural criminal norm, as noted above.[45] This general rule has two major parts. The first part relates to aggravating substantive criminal norms. The applicability of aggravating substantive criminal norms in time refers to criminal events that occurred after the validation of the norm, regardless of the time of its enactment or of the judicial decision. The most significant consequence of the first part of the general rule is that the aggravating substantive criminal norm is not applicable retroactively to criminal events that occurred before validation of the norm.

The second part of the general rule relates to two types of substantive criminal norm, mitigating norms, and norms that embrace a cogent international custom (*jus cogens*), whether mitigating or aggravating. The two types of the substantive criminal norm are applicable from the time of their enactment (not of their validation) onward. They are applicable to the judicial decision, not to the criminal event itself. Thus, if the criminal event occurred before the enactment of the norm but the judicial decision has been made after the time of enactment, the norm is applicable to the judicial decision. Although this may appear as retroactive applicability, it is not, because the time of enactment is considered to be the time of declaration about an existing norm and not the time of the norm's constitution, as explained below.

The rationale of the first part of the general rule, namely that the substantive criminal norm is applicable to criminal events from the time of its validation onward, is related to the general liberal concept of the rule of law. The substantive criminal norm is a dominant expression of legal social control, of its application, and implementation. As such, it requires that individuals carefully plan their behavior to prevent any breaches of the norm. The individuals' confidence in the stability and certainty of the social order, unaffected by arbitrary caprice, is assimilated into this general rule. The fair notice required before a behavior

[45]Above at Sect. 3.2.1.

previously permitted becomes prohibited is also necessary for maintaining social stability and certainty.[46]

The individual has the right to be able to rely on the constitutive substantive criminal norm, which lies at the foundation of any regime.[47] Consider, for example, that society decides to prohibit the use of a certain drug. Until such prohibition is validated, the use of the drug is permitted and not considered an offense. With the new norm, a permitted behavior becomes prohibited, and the ensuing social change requires fair notice. This rationale is relevant to all constitutive substantive criminal norms.

The rationale of the second part of the general rule, namely that the mitigating substantive criminal norm and the substantive criminal law that embraces a cogent international custom (*jus cogens*) are applicable to judicial decisions from the time of their enactment onward, is that these types of substantive criminal norms reflect the social recognition of an existing situation. These norms are considered to be declarative norms rather than constitutive ones. Mitigating substantive criminal norms include those that abolish an existing offense, create a new defense, narrow the number of individuals subject to the imposition of criminal liability, impose a more lenient maximum penalty, abolish a mandatory penalty, or make the possibility of imposing criminal liability more difficult. Nevertheless, an *ex ante* temporary substantive criminal norm is not considered to be a mitigating criminal norm when it expires.[48]

The substantive criminal norm that embraces a cogent international custom (*jus cogens*) reflects the social recognition of an existing norm. In this case, society does not constitute a new prohibition but merely recognizes an existing one. The existing prohibition is part of the *delicta juris gentium*, i.e., universal offenses of barbarity, considered to be known and recognized prohibitions by all mankind. These prohibitions form a narrow group. The offender who breaches one of them is considered to be *humani generis hostis*, i.e., hostile to mankind. The norm does not constitute the prohibition, only recognizes it. For example, the prohibition on piracy is known universally to all mankind from the dawn of humanity.[49] An

[46]Phillips v. Eyre, (1870) 6 K.B. 1: "The retrospective Attainder Acts of earlier times, when the principles of law were not so well understood or so closely regarded as in the present day, and which are now looked upon as barbarous and loosely spoken of as ex post facto laws, were of a substantially different character. They did not confirm irregular acts, but voided and punished what had been lawful when done. . . .Here it is impossible that the party could foresee that an action, innocent when it was done, should be afterwards converted to guilt by a subsequent law; he had therefore no cause to abstain from it, and all punishment for not abstaining must of consequence be cruel and unjust".

[47]Thomas Hobbs, Leviathan 226 (1651, 1967).

[48]Article 2(4) of the German penal code provides: "Ein Gesetz, das nur für eine bestimmte Zeit gelten soll, ist auf Taten, die während seiner Geltung begangen sind, auch dann anzuwenden, wenn es außer Kraft getreten ist. Dies gilt nicht, soweit ein Gesetz etwas anderes bestimmt"; BGH St 18, 12, 14.

[49]Philip Gosse, The History of Piracy (1932, 1968).

offence prohibiting piracy does not constitute the offense, only recognizes its existence.[50]

Classifying the mitigating substantive criminal norm and the substantive criminal norm that embraces a cogent universal custom as declarative norms rather than constitutive ones makes it possible to apply these norms to relevant judicial decisions immediately after being enacted, obviating the requirement of fair notice. When the norm embraces a cogent universal custom, the individual cannot argue having been taken by surprise, because the prohibition is universal. Moreover, when the norm is a mitigating one, the individual has no incentive to argue against its applicability to the judicial decision, which is in force even if the criminal event occurred before the enactment of the norm.

The general rule of applicability of the substantive criminal norm in time, including both its parts, has been accepted worldwide, in whole or in part. In **contractual public international law**, the general rule has been accepted as part of Sub-article 11(2) of the Universal Declaration of Human Rights, accepted by the General Assembly of the United Nations on December 10, 1948.[51] As part of the fundamental human rights, the declaration prohibits the retroactive applicability of the substantive criminal norm.

In the **European-Continental legal systems**, the general rule is considered both as a general constitutional rule and as a rule of criminal law under the principle of legality.[52] Article 7 of the European Convention on Human Rights, 1950, is considered to be a fundamental provision for the ban on the retroactivity of the substantive criminal norm.[53] In France, Article 8 of the Declaration of the Rights of Man and of the Citizen, from 1789, became the broad constitutional ground for this general rule.[54] Specifically, the first part of the general rule has been accepted within the beginning and middle parts of Article 112-1 of the French penal code[55]; the second part has been accepted partly in the end of Article 112-1.[56] In Germany

[50]See article 15 of the Convention on the High Seas, 1958, 450 U.N.T.S. 11.

[51]Article 11(2) of the universal declaration of human rights provides: "No one shall be held guilty of any penal offence on account of any act or omission which did not constitute a penal offence, under national or international law, at the time when it was committed. Nor shall a heavier penalty be imposed than the one that was applicable at the time the penal offence was committed".

[52]See e.g. in Germany Grundgesetz, art. 103 (II).

[53]Article 7 of the European convention on human rights from 1950 provides: "No one shall be held guilty of any offence on account of any act or omission which did not constitute a criminal offence under national or international law at the time when it was committed".

[54]Article 8 of the French declaration of rights of the man and the citizen from 1789 provides: "Nul ne peut être puni qu'en vertu d'une loi établie et promulguée anterieurement au délit et légalement appliquée".

[55]The beginning of article 112-1 of the French penal code provides: "Sont seuls punissables les faits constitutifs d'une infraction à la date à laquelle ils ont été commis. Peuvent seules être prononcées les peines légalement applicables à la même date".

[56]The end of article 112-1 of the French penal code provides: "Toutefois, les dispositions nouvelles s'appliquent aux infractions commises **avant** leur entrée en vigueur et n'ayant pas

the general rule is part of the constitutional basic law.[57] Article 2 of the German penal code accepts the general rule explicitly.[58]

The **English common law** accepted the general rule relatively late. Most of the time, English common law applied substantive criminal norms retroactively, even if the offenses were considered severe.[59] Because of acceptance by English law of the binding precedent praxis (*stare decisis*), the courts often decreed new offenses as part of the judicial decision merely because they deemed certain behavior to be immoral. The English courts had no legal difficulty with the retroactivity of the substantive criminal norm.[60] Acceptance of the general rule has been relatively recent, and the courts have refrained since then from decreeing new offenses.[61] Nevertheless, the House of Lords softened the prohibition on retroactivity when amendments of the substantive criminal norm have to do with adjustments.[62] The second part of the general rule has been partly accepted before the first part.[63]

As noted above,[64] the **American law** does not distinguish between the applicability of the substantive and procedural criminal norms in time. Neither criminal norm is applied retroactively, as follows from the United States Constitution.[65] The main rationale is the requirement of fair notice and the need to restrict the police powers of the state from generating arbitrary laws.[66] The ban on retroactivity in the United States applies mostly to legislation rather than to judicial decisions,[67] but the ban includes both the criminal liability and the sentencing aspects of the criminal

---

donné lieu à une condamnation passée en force de chose jugée lorsqu'elles sont moins sévères que les dispositions anciennes" (emphasis not in original).

[57]Grundgesetz, art. 103 (II).

[58]BGH 20, 22, 25; BGH NStZ 1983, 268; BGH NStZ 1992, 535; BVerfG NJW 1990, 1103.

[59]Thurston, (1663) 1 Lev. 91, 83 E.R. 312.

[60]Shaw v. Director of Public Prosecutions, [1962] A.C. 220, [1961] 2 All E.R. 446, [1961] 2 W.L. R. 897, 45 Cr. App. Rep. 113, 125 J.P. 437; A.T.H. Smith, *Judicial Lawmaking in the Criminal Law*, 100 L. Q. REV. 46 (1984).

[61]Knuller (Publishing, Printing and Promotions) Ltd. v. Director of Public Prosecutions, [1973] A. C. 435, [1972] 2 All E.R. 898, [1972] 3 W.L.R. 143, 56 Cr. App. Rep. 633, 136 J.P. 728.

[62]SW and CR v. United Kingdom, (1995) 21 E.H.R.R. 363, 390; Kokkinakis v. Greece, (1993) 17 E.H.R.R. 397.

[63]Mawgan, (1838) 112 E.R. 927; M'Kenzie, (1820) 168 E.R. 881.

[64]Above at Sect. 3.2.1.

[65]Calder v. Bull, *supra* note 31.

[66]Weaver v. Graham, 450 U.S. 24, 101 S.Ct. 960, 67 L.Ed.2d 17 (1981); Warren v. United States, 659 F.2d 183 (1981).

[67]Rogers v. Tennessee, 532 U.S. 451, 121 S.Ct. 1693, 149 L.Ed.2d 697 (2001); Bouie v. Columbia, 378 U.S. 347, 84 S.Ct. 1697, 12 L.Ed.2d 894 (1964); Ross v. Oregon, 227 U.S. 150, 33 S.Ct. 220, 57 L.Ed. 458 (1913).

norm.[68] The second part of the general rule has also been accepted in the United States.[69]

The relevant time for considering the criminal event is the first time when all the factual ingredients that form the criminal offense come together.[70] Abolition of a substantive criminal norm results in the abolition of all criminal procedures accompanying it.[71] Mitigating the maximum penalty for an offense includes all procedures accompanying it as well,[72] regardless of the aspects of the relevant criminal liability.[73] Thus, on many occasions American courts imposed criminal liability on the individual, but pronounced a mitigating penalty.[74] Nevertheless, after the judicial decision becomes final, American courts do not apply the mitigating substantive criminal norm.[75]

3.3.2 Application of the Rule

The general rule[76] whereby the substantive criminal norm is applicable to criminal events from the time of its validation onward, whereas mitigating substantive criminal norms and the substantive criminal law that embraces a cogent international custom (*jus cogens*) are applicable to judicial decisions from the time of their enactment, can be applied in each of the six possible time relations described

---

[68] People v. Stead, 845 P.2d 1156 (1993); Smith v. Doe, 538 U.S. 84, 123 S.Ct. 1140, 155 L.Ed.2d 164 (2003); Seling v. Young, 531 U.S. 250, 121 S.Ct. 727, 148 L.Ed.2d 734 (2001); Kansas v. Hendricks, 521 U.S. 346, 117 S.Ct. 2072, 138 L.Ed.2d 501 (1997); United States v. Crawford, 115 F.3d 1397 (1997).

[69] Lonschein v. Warden, 43 Misc.2d 109, 250 N.Y.S.2d 15 (1964); Commonwealth v. Vaughn, 329 Mass. 333, 108 N.E.2d 559 (1952); McGuire v. State, 76 Miss. 504, 25 So. 495 (1899); Dobbert v. Florida, 432 U.S. 282, 97 S.Ct. 2290, 53 L.Ed.2d 344 (1977); Miller v. Florida, 482 U.S. 423, 107 S.Ct. 2446, 96 L.Ed.2d 351 (1987).

[70] State v. Detter, 298 N.C. 604, 260 S.E.2d 567 (1979); United States v. McKenzie, 922 F.2d 1323 (1991); United States v. Lee, 886 F.2d 998 (1989); United States v. Turpin, 117 F.3d 678 (1997); United States v. Pace, 898 F.2d 1218 (1990); Wright v. Superior Court, 15 Cal.4th 521, 63 Cal. Rptr.2d 322, 936 P.2d 101 (1997).

[71] United States v. Peggy, 5 U.S. 103, 2 L.Ed. 49, 1 Cranch 103 (1801); Bell v. Maryland, 378 U.S. 226, 84 S.Ct. 1814, 12 L.Ed.2d 822 (1964).

[72] Commonwealth v. Kimball, 38 Mass. 373, 21 Pick. 373 (1838); State v. Daley, 29 Conn. 272 (1860).

[73] Note, *Today's Law and Yesterday's Crime: Retroactive Application of Ameliorative Criminal Legislation*, 121 U. PA. L. REV. 120, 127–130 (1972).

[74] *In re* Estrada, 63 Cal.2d 740, 408 P.2d 948, 48 Cal.Rptr. 172 (1965); *In re* Falk, 64 Cal. 2d 684, 414 P.2d 407, 51 Cal.Rptr. 279 (1966); State v. Pardon, 272 N.C. 72, 157 S.E.2d 698 (1967); State v. Tapp, 26 Utah.2d 392, 490 P.2d 334 (1971).

[75] *In re* Manaca, 146 Mich. 697, 110 N.W. 75 (1906); Odekirk v. Ryan, 85 F.2d 313 (1936); People v. Oliver, 1 N.Y.2d 152, 134 N.E.2d 197, 151 N.Y.S.2d 367 (1956); *In re* Moreno, 58 Cal.App.3d 740, 130 Cal.Rptr. 78 (1976).

[76] Above at Sect. 3.3.1.

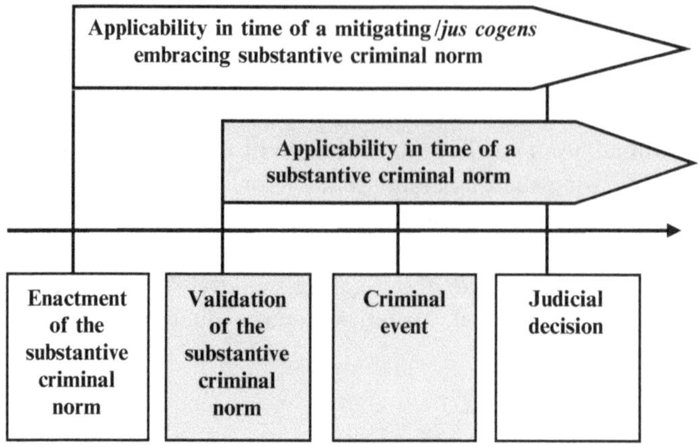

Fig. 3.13 Applicability of the substantive criminal norm in time in the first possible relation between relevant points in time

above[77] between the four relevant points in time. Because the general rule relates to the applicability of the substantive criminal norm in time, all four points in time are relevant to its application.

As noted above, in the **first possible relation** between the relevant points in time enactment and validation occur before the criminal event and the judicial decision. The applicability in time of the substantive criminal norm in the first possible time relation may be described schematically[78] as shown in Fig. 3.13.[79]

In the first possible relation between the relevant points in time, the substantive criminal norm is applicable to the criminal event from the time of its validation onward, as shown by the gray areas of Fig. 3.13. The time of occurrence of the judicial decision and of the enactment of the substantive criminal norm are irrelevant to its applicability in time. Nevertheless, the applicability in time of a mitigating substantive criminal norm and of a substantive criminal norm that embraces a cogent international custom (*jus cogens*) to judicial decisions is from the time of their enactment onward. The time of occurrence of the criminal event and the validation of the norm are irrelevant to its applicability in time. The applicability in time of the

[77]Above at Sect. 3.1.2.

[78]Figures 3.13, 3.14, 3.15, 3.16, 3.17, 3.18, as well as Figs. 3.1, 3.2, 3.3, 3.4, 3.5, 3.6, 3.7, 3.8, 3.9, 3.10, 3.11, 3.12, relate to the position in time of the four relevant points in time on an arrow representing the time from its left side (beginning) to its right side (end). When the specific point is closer to the left side, it is earlier than the point or points positioned on its right side. The periods of time between these points may vary from case to case, but the relativity in time of these points remains constant.

[79]The applicability in time of the substantive criminal norm in the first possible time relation between the relevant points in time may be demonstrated as follows: On 1.1 in a certain year the substantive criminal norm was enacted, on 1.2 the same year the substantive criminal norm has been completely validated, on 1.3 the same year the criminal event has occurred, and on 1.4 that year the judicial decision has been made.

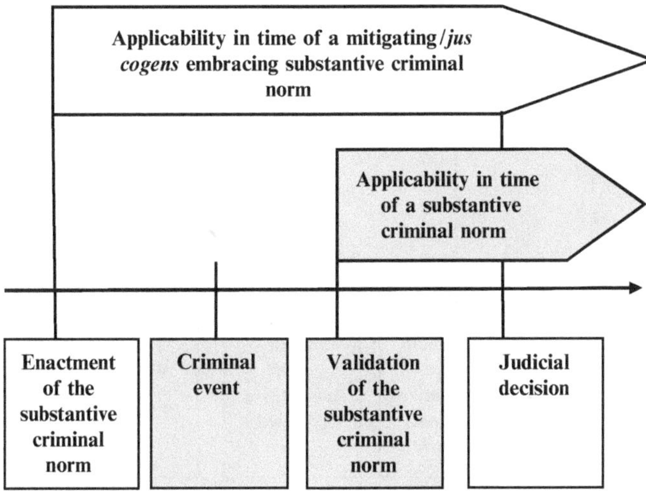

Fig. 3.14 Applicability of the substantive criminal norm in time in the second possible relation between relevant points in time

mitigating substantive criminal norm and of the substantive criminal norm that embraces a cogent international custom (*jus cogens*) are shown in the white areas of Fig. 3.13.

In the **second possible relation** between the relevant points in time the criminal event takes place between the enactment of the procedural criminal norm and the time of its validation, and the judicial decision occurs after validation. The relation may be described schematically as shown in Fig. 3.14.[80]

In the second possible relation between the relevant points in time, the substantive criminal norm is applicable to the criminal event from the time of its validation onward, as shown by the gray areas of Fig. 3.14. The time of occurrence of the judicial decision and of the enactment of the substantive criminal norm are irrelevant to its applicability in time. As a result, in the second possible relation between the relevant points in time, the substantive criminal norm is not applicable to a criminal event that has taken place before its validation has been completed.

Nevertheless, the applicability in time of a mitigating substantive criminal norm and of a substantive criminal norm that embraces a cogent international custom (*jus cogens*) to judicial decisions is from the time of their enactment onward. The time of occurrence of the criminal event and the validation of the norm are irrelevant to its applicability in time. The applicability in time of the mitigating substantive criminal norm and of the substantive criminal norm that embraces a cogent

[80]The applicability in time of the substantive criminal norm in the second possible time relation between the relevant points in time may be demonstrated as follows: On 1.1 in a certain year the substantive criminal norm was enacted, on 1.2 the same year the criminal event has occurred, on 1.3 the same year the substantive criminal norm has been completely validated, and on 1.4 that year the judicial decision has been made.

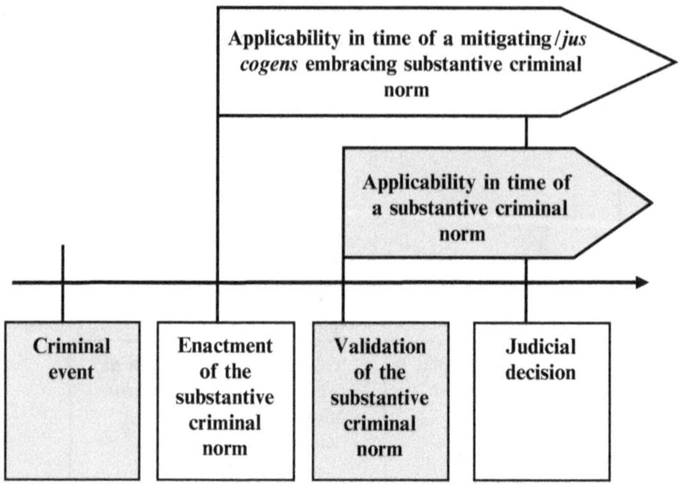

Fig. 3.15 Applicability of the substantive criminal norm in time in the third possible relation between relevant points in time

international custom (*jus cogens*) are shown in the white areas of Fig. 3.14. As a result, in the second possible relation between the relevant points in time, a mitigating substantive criminal norm and a substantive criminal norm that embraces a cogent international custom (*jus cogens*) are applicable to judicial decisions that have been made after their enactment.

In the **third possible relation** between the relevant points in time, the criminal event occurs first, followed by the enactment of the procedural criminal norm and by its validated. All these occur before the judicial decision. The relation may be described schematically as shown in Fig. 3.15.[81]

In the third possible relation between the relevant points in time, the substantive criminal norm is applicable to the criminal event from the time of its validation onward, as shown by the gray areas of Fig. 3.15. The time of occurrence of the judicial decision and of the enactment of the substantive criminal norm are irrelevant to its applicability in time. As a result, in the third possible relation between the relevant points in time, the substantive criminal norm is not applicable to a criminal event that has taken place before its validation has been completed.

Nevertheless, the applicability in time of a mitigating substantive criminal norm and of a substantive criminal norm that embraces a cogent international custom (*jus cogens*) to judicial decisions is from the time of their enactment onward. The time of occurrence of the criminal event and the validation of the norm are irrelevant to

[81]The applicability in time of the substantive criminal norm in the third possible time relation between the relevant points in time may be demonstrated as follows: On 1.1 in a certain year the criminal event has occurred, on 1.2 the same year the substantive criminal norm was enacted, on 1.3 the same year the substantive criminal norm has been completely validated, and on 1.4 that year the judicial decision has been made.

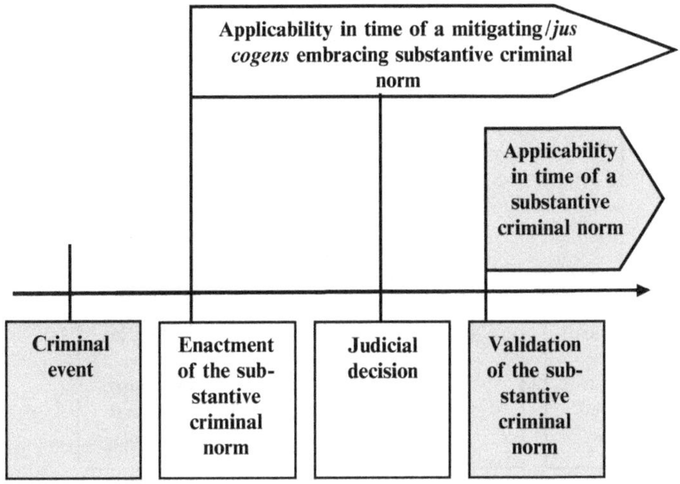

Fig. 3.16 Applicability of the substantive criminal norm in time in the fourth possible relation between relevant points in time

its applicability in time. The applicability in time of the mitigating substantive criminal norm and of the substantive criminal norm that embraces a cogent international custom (*jus cogens*) are shown in the white areas of Fig. 3.15. As a result, in the third possible relation between the relevant points in time, a mitigating substantive criminal norm and a substantive criminal norm that embraces a cogent international custom (*jus cogens*) are applicable to judicial decisions that have been made after their enactment.[82]

In the **fourth possible relation** between the relevant points in time the criminal event occurs first, followed by the enactment of the procedural criminal norm and by the judicial decision. All these occur before validation of the procedural criminal norm is completed. The relation may be described schematically as shown in Fig. 3.16.[83]

[82]A known example for such a time relation is the indictment and conviction of Adolf Eichmann in Israel. Eichmann committed crimes against humanity between 1942 and 1945 and escaped to Argentina. In 1950 the state of Israel enacted the Nazi and their accomplices judgment act, 1950. In 1961–1962 Eichmann was judged in Israel under the Israeli law after being captured and brought into trial by the Israeli Mossad agents. Since this substantive criminal norm embraces a cogent international custom (*jus cogens*), the fact that the criminal events occurred before the enactment and validation of the criminal norm was immaterial. When the judicial decision has been made, the specific criminal norm has already been enacted, and therefore been applicable upon the case. See Cr.App. 336/61 Eichmann v. Attorney General, 16 (3) PD 2032 (1962); See more e.g. in *Transcript of Proceedings of Nuremberg Trials*, 41 American Journal of International Law 1–16 (1947).

[83]The applicability in time of the substantive criminal norm in the fourth possible time relation between the relevant points in time may be demonstrated as follows: On 1.1 in a certain year the criminal event has occurred, on 1.2 the same year the substantive criminal norm was enacted, on

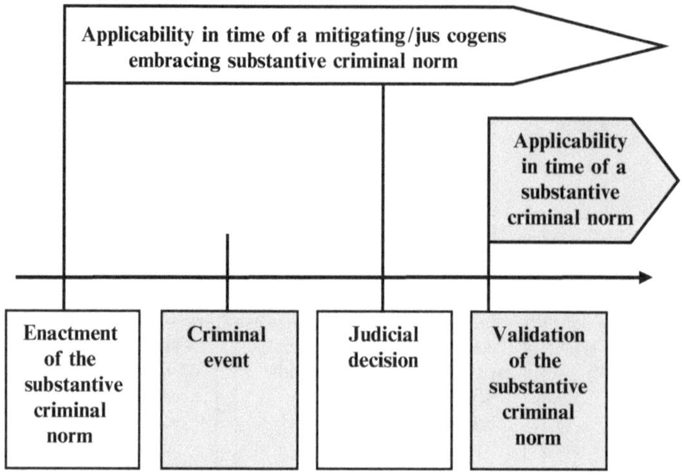

Fig. 3.17 Applicability of the substantive criminal norm in time in the fifth possible relation between relevant points in time

In the fourth possible relation between the relevant points in time, the substantive criminal norm is applicable to the criminal event from the time of its validation onward, as shown by the gray areas of Fig. 3.16. The time of occurrence of the judicial decision and of the enactment of the substantive criminal norm are irrelevant to its applicability in time. As a result, in the fourth possible relation between the relevant points in time, the substantive criminal norm is not applicable to a criminal event that has taken place before its validation has been completed.

Nevertheless, the applicability in time of a mitigating substantive criminal norm and of a substantive criminal norm that embraces a cogent international custom (*jus cogens*) to judicial decisions is from the time of their enactment onward. The time of occurrence of the criminal event and the validation of the norm are irrelevant to its applicability in time. The applicability in time of the mitigating substantive criminal norm and of the substantive criminal norm that embraces a cogent international custom (*jus cogens*) are shown in the white areas of Fig. 3.16. As a result, in the fourth possible relation between the relevant points in time, a mitigating substantive criminal norm and a substantive criminal norm that embraces a cogent international custom (*jus cogens*) are applicable to judicial decisions that have been made after their enactment.

In the **fifth possible relation** between the relevant points in time the procedural criminal norm is enacted before the occurrence of the criminal event, followed by

---

1.3 the same year judicial decision has been made, and on 1.4 that year the substantive criminal norm has been completely validated.

the judicial decision and the validation of the procedural criminal norm. The relation may be described schematically as shown in Fig. 3.17.[84]

In the fifth possible relation between the relevant points in time, the substantive criminal norm is applicable to the criminal event from the time of its validation onward, as shown by the gray areas of Fig. 3.17. The time of occurrence of the judicial decision and of the enactment of the substantive criminal norm are irrelevant to its applicability in time. As a result, in the fifth possible relation between the relevant points in time, the substantive criminal norm is not applicable to a criminal event that has taken place before its validation has been completed.

Nevertheless, the applicability in time of a mitigating substantive criminal norm and of a substantive criminal norm that embraces a cogent international custom (*jus cogens*) to judicial decisions is from the time of their enactment onward. The time of occurrence of the criminal event and the validation of the norm are irrelevant to its applicability in time. The applicability in time of the mitigating substantive criminal norm and of the substantive criminal norm that embraces a cogent international custom (*jus cogens*) are shown in the white areas of Fig. 3.17.As a result, in the fifth possible relation between the relevant points in time, a mitigating substantive criminal norm and a substantive criminal norm that embraces a cogent international custom (*jus cogens*) are applicable to judicial decisions that have been made after their enactment.

In the **sixth possible relation** between the relevant points in time, the criminal event takes place first, followed by the judicial decision, the enactment of the procedural criminal norm, and its validation. The relation may be described schematically as shown in Fig. 3.18.[85]

In the sixth possible relation between the relevant points in time, the substantive criminal norm is applicable to the criminal event from the time of its validation onward, as shown by the gray areas of Fig. 3.18. The time of occurrence of the judicial decision and of the enactment of the substantive criminal norm are irrelevant to its applicability in time. As a result, in the sixth possible relation between the relevant points in time, the substantive criminal norm is not applicable to a criminal event that has taken place before its validation has been completed.

Nevertheless, the applicability in time of a mitigating substantive criminal norm and of a substantive criminal norm that embraces a cogent international custom (*jus cogens*) to judicial decisions is from the time of their enactment onward. The time

[84]The applicability in time of the substantive criminal norm in the fifth possible time relation between the relevant points in time may be demonstrated as follows: On 1.1 in a certain year the substantive criminal norm was enacted, on 1.2 the same year the criminal event has occurred, on 1.3 the same year judicial decision has been made, and on 1.4 that year the substantive criminal norm has been completely validated.

[85]The applicability in time of the substantive criminal norm in the sixth possible time relation between the relevant points in time may be demonstrated as follows: On 1.1 in a certain year the criminal event has occurred, on 1.2 the same year judicial decision has been made, on 1.3 the same year the substantive criminal norm was enacted, and on 1.4 that year the substantive criminal norm has been completely validated.

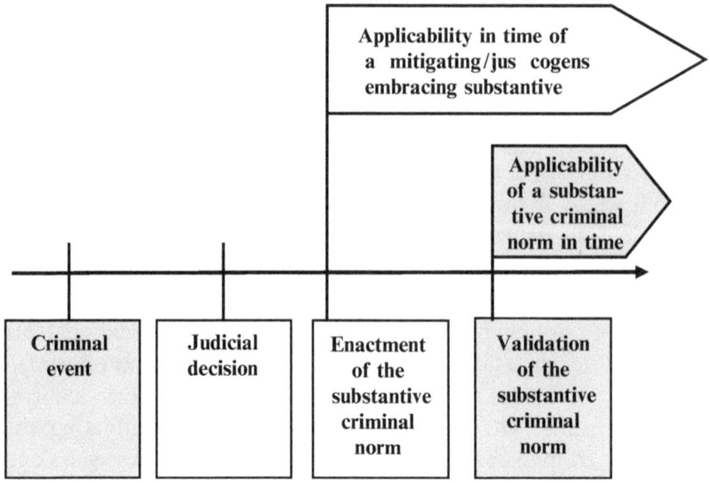

Fig. 3.18 Applicability of the substantive criminal norm in time in the sixth possible relation between relevant points in time

of occurrence of the criminal event and the validation of the norm are irrelevant to its applicability in time. The applicability in time of the mitigating substantive criminal norm and of the substantive criminal norm that embraces a cogent international custom (*jus cogens*) are shown in the white areas of Fig. 3.18. As a result, in the sixth possible relation between the relevant points in time, a mitigating substantive criminal norm and a substantive criminal norm that embraces a cogent international custom (*jus cogens*) are not applicable to judicial decisions that have been made before their enactment.

3.4 Conflict of Laws Based on Applicability of the Criminal Norm in Time

It is almost inevitable that the various options of applicability of the criminal norm in time would create situations in which laws come in conflict with each other, so that given norms contradict others (conflict of laws). The relevant question in these situations is which norm governs and should be followed.[86] The principle of legality in criminal law accommodates four types of situations in which laws conflict, one type for every secondary principle. As far as the applicability of the criminal norm in time is concerned (the second secondary principle), conflicting laws have to do with norms of different applicability in time that contradict one another.

[86] Lawrence Collins, Dicey and Morris The Conflict of Laws I 32 (13th ed., 2000).

In the case of conflicting laws based on applicability of the criminal norm in time, when several criminal norms are applicable to the same event (criminal event or judicial decision), the relevant question is which of the several norms should be applied to the event. The answer is given in two stages. In the first stage we eliminate all the irrelevant criminal norms that do not apply in time to the event. In the second stage we decide which of the remaining criminal norms is the correct one that should be applied to the event.

In the first stage, irrelevant criminal norms are eliminated based on the following three questions about the exact type of the criminal norm:

(1) If the criminal norm is procedural, has it been validated before the judicial decision?
(2) If the criminal norm is substantive, has it been validated before the criminal event?
(3) If the criminal norm is substantive and mitigating, or embracing a cogent international custom (*jus cogens*), has it been enacted before the judicial decision?

If the answer to the relevant question is negative, the criminal norm is irrelevant to the event. If the answer to the relevant question is positive with reference to only one criminal norm, there is no legal problem of conflict of laws because there are no conflicting norms. A legal problem of conflict of laws arises only when the answer to the relevant question is positive with reference to more than one criminal norm. In these cases, it is necessary to proceed to the second stage.

When several criminal norms appear to apply to a given case, each criminal norm is characterized by a certain applicability in time. The rule that determines which criminal norm must be applied in this situation, and which one rejected, can be stated in Latin as follows:

lex posterior derogat priori

In English translation this means that a more recent law prevails over an earlier one.[87] The question, then, becomes which norm is considered to be more recent. The relevant point in time for determining the time of applicability of a criminal norm depends on the type of criminal norm.[88] In the case of a procedural criminal

[87]Henderson v. Sherborne, (1837) 150 E.R. 743; Michell v. Brown, (1858) 120 E.R. 909; Fortescue v. Vestry of St. Mathew Bethnal Green, (1891) 2 Q.B. 170; Smith v. Benabe, (1937) 1 All E.R. 523; Swan v. Moore, 14 La.Ann. 833 (1859); Gouveia v. Vokes, 800 F.Supp. 241 (1992).

[88]Thus, for instance, procedural criminal norm A has been validated on 1.1 in a certain year, and procedural criminal norm B has been validated on 1.2 in the same year. If both procedural criminal norms are applicable on a judicial decision made on 1.3 in the same year, norm B is posterior and norm A is prior, and therefore norm B derogates norm A.

norm, the relevant point in time is that of its validation. As a result, the applicable procedural criminal norm is the one that was validated last. In the case of a substantive criminal norm, the relevant point in time is also that of its validation. As a result, the applicable substantive criminal norm is again the one that was validated last.[89]

Nevertheless, if the criminal norm is a mitigating substantive criminal norm or a substantive criminal norm that embraces a cogent international custom (*jus cogens*), the relevant point in time is the time of its enactment. As a result, the applicable mitigating substantive criminal norm or substantive criminal norm that embraces a cogent international custom (*jus cogens*) is the one that was enacted last.[90]

Naturally, in all three types of conflict of laws, all criminal norms must be applicable to the relevant event (criminal event or judicial decision). Only criminal norms that are applicable to the relevant event (criminal event or judicial decision) can create a situation of conflict of laws. For example, when the later criminal norm is a temporary one that expires before the time of the relevant event, whereas the earlier criminal norm does not expire, the applicable norm is the earlier one because at the relevant time of the event there was no situation of conflict of law, and only one criminal norm was applicable.

---

[89]Thus, for instance, substantive criminal norm A has been validated on 1.1 in a certain year, and substantive criminal norm B has been validated on 1.2 in the same year. If both substantive criminal norms are applicable on a criminal event occurred on 1.3 in the same year, norm B is posterior and norm A is prior, and therefore norm B derogates norm A.

[90]Thus, for instance, mitigating substantive criminal norm or a substantive criminal norm which embraces a cogent international custom (*jus cogens*) A has been enacted on 1.1 in a certain year, and mitigating substantive criminal norm or a substantive criminal norm which embraces a cogent international custom (*jus cogens*) B has been enacted on 1.2 in the same year. If both norms are applicable on a judicial decision made on 1.3 in the same year, norm B is posterior and norm A is prior, and therefore norm B derogates norm A.

Chapter 4
The Applicability of the Criminal Norm in Place

Contents

The third secondary principle of the principle of legality in criminal law concerns the applicability of the criminal norm in place, which is an aspect of the legitimacy of the norm as a legal social control. This secondary principle relates to the place and territory of criminal norms.

4.1 The Basic Distinctions

Five distinctions are required in order to formulate accurate rules regarding the applicability of the criminal norm in place:

(1) Between applicability and jurisdiction in criminal law

G. Hallevy, *A Modern Treatise on the Principle of Legality in Criminal Law*,
DOI 10.1007/978-3-642-13714-3_4, © Springer-Verlag Berlin Heidelberg 2010

(2) Between procedural and substantive criminal norms of different legal systems
(3) Between domestic and foreign criminal norms and criminal events
(4) Between locally restricted and not restricted criminal norms
(5) Between the relevant factors connecting the criminal event with the criminal norm

These distinctions are discussed below.[1]

4.1.1 Distinction Between Applicability and Jurisdiction in Criminal Law

The distinction between applicability and jurisdiction is not within the exclusive domain of criminal law, but it is relevant to all spheres of the law. Applicability of the norm and jurisdiction are different terms relating to different legal aspects. Applicability of a norm means the subordination of a certain event to a relevant legal norm. If the norm is applicable, the event must be judged according to the norm. Jurisdiction is a procedural term describing the authority of a certain court to judge and decide a certain case. Generally, the two terms are distinct. For example, a German court may decide (jurisdiction) in a given case according to French law (applicability). This distinction is highly relevant in the legal domain of private international law and in cases of "conflict of laws."[2]

In the European-Continental legal systems, the distinction is a sharp one, but in Anglo-American legal systems it has become more vague,[3] and at times, the two terms refer to the same idea, so that only in rare cases do Anglo-American courts distinguish between the two terms.[4] The reason for this vagueness is not accidental, and has to do with the effect of the conflict of laws in criminal law.

Criminal law is an instrument of legal social control, necessary to impose the state's sovereignty. Implementation of the criminal law requires solidarity between the organs of society. Courts are organs of society. If there is no solidarity between

---

[1]Hereinafter at Sects. 4.1.1–4.1.5.

[2]LAWRENCE COLLINS, DICEY AND MORRIS THE CONFLICT OF LAWS I 4 (13th ed., 2000).

[3]See e.g. MICHAEL HIRST, JURISDICTION AND THE AMBIT OF THE CRIMINAL LAW 9–12 (2003) who claims as to the British Parliament that "Parliament's chronic inconsistency in its use of the term 'jurisdiction' is, however, a major problem in this context. Sometimes that term is used in order to extend the ambit of criminal offences, and sometimes it is used, as in . . ., in relation only to the power of a court to try an offence, assuming that the substantive law already applies to the conduct that is alleged to amount to that offence"; Geoff Gilbert, *Crimes sans Frontiers: Jurisdictional Problems in English Law*, 63 BRITISH YEARBOOK OF INTERNATIONAL LAW 415, 416 (1992).

[4]Treacy v. Director of Public Prosecutions, [1971] A.C. 537, 559, [1971] 1 All E.R. 110, [1971] 2 W.L.R. 112, 55 Cr. App. Rep. 113, 135 J.P. 112: "the question in this appeal is not whether the Central Criminal Court had jurisdiction to try the appellant on that charge, but whether the facts alleged and proved against him amounted to a criminal offence under the English Act of Parliament".

the courts and the basic values of society, the courts can fail in their attempt to achieve legal social control through criminal law. To avoid such failure, the courts can resort to the doctrine of public policy, according to which a foreign law is rejected in favor of a domestic one.[5] For example, when a person is indicted for bigamy in a country in which it is prohibited for having committed it in a country where it is permitted, the court would normally convict him. But, if the court shows no solidarity with the prohibition against bigamy, it may subordinate its decision to the foreign law, and exonerate the person.

The global rule in criminal law is that a domestic court would not apply a foreign law but only the domestic one. In other spheres of the law, foreign laws can be applied in domestic courts.[6] Thus, German criminal courts decide only according to German criminal law, and American criminal courts according to American criminal law, etc. Moreover, the jurisdiction of the domestic criminal law extends only to domestic courts.[7] In other spheres of law, however, domestic courts can decide according to foreign law.

In light of the rule of applicability in criminal law, the vagueness of the distinction between applicability and jurisdiction becomes immaterial. Jurisdiction follows the applicability of the criminal law, in other words, if the law relevant to the event is applicable on a certain territory, the courts in that territory have automatic jurisdiction over the case.

4.1.2 Distinction Between Procedural and Substantive Criminal Norms in Different Legal Systems

The distinction between procedural and substantive norms is not within the exclusive domain of criminal law, but it is relevant to all spheres of the law. Different legal systems used different methods of distinction, and the same legal systems

---

[5] MAURO-RUBINO SAMMARTANO AND C. G. J. MORSE, PUBLIC POLICY IN TRANSNATIONAL RELATIONSHIPS (1992).

[6] BGH 10, 63; Ogden v. Folliot, (1790) 3 T.R. 726; Lynch v. Paraguay Provisional Government, [1861–1873] All E.R. 934, [1861–73] All E.R. 934; Huntington v. Attrill, [1893] A.C. 150; Attorney General for Canada v. Schulze, (1901) 9 S.L.T. 4; Raulin v. Fischer, [1911] 2 K.B. 93; Banco De Vizcaya v. Don Alfonso De Borbon Y Austria, [1934] All E.R. 555, [1935] 1 K.B. 140; 104 L.J.K.B. 46;151 L.T. 499; 50 T.L.R. 284; 78 Sol.Jo. 224; Frankfurter v. W. L. Exner Ltd., [1947] Ch. 629; Novello v. Hinrischen Edition Ltd., [1951] Ch. 595; Schemmer v. Property Resources Ltd., [1975] Ch. 273; Attorney General of New Zealand v. Ortiz, [1984] 1 A.C. 1, [1983] 2 W.L.R. 809, [1983] 2 All E.R. 93; United States of America v. Inkley, [1989] Q.B. 255, [1988] 3 W.L.R. 304, [1988] 3 All E.R. 144; Larkins v. N.U.M., [1985] I.R. 671; Bank of Ireland v. Meeneghan, [1994] 3 I.R. 111.

[7] *In re* The Antelope, (1825) 10 Wheat. 66: "The common law considers crimes as altogether local, and cognisable and punishable exclusively in the country where they are committed... The courts of no country execute the penal laws of another"; State v. Pelican Insurance Co., 127 U.S. 265, 8 S. Ct. 1370, 32 L.Ed. 239 (1888); SA Consortium General Textiles v. Sun & Sand Agencies Ltd., [1978] Q.B. 279, [1978] 2 All E.R. 339, [1978] 2 W.L.R. 1.

used different methods at different times. Nevertheless, the basic distinction is characteristic of all legal systems at all times. It is a theoretical distinction, unaffected by its consequences,[8] relevant not only to the applicability of the norm in time, but in place as well. According to the relevant rules of the conflict of laws, procedural norms are dominated by the law of the domestic jurisdiction (*lex fori*), whereas substantive norms are dominated by the law governing the specific case (*lex causae*).[9]

The traditional approaches to this distinction differentiate between the questions of "what" and of "how." When the specific norm answers the question of "what," it is a substantive norm; when it answers the question of "how," it is a procedural norm. But these traditional approaches are not accurate because the same norm can answer several questions, both "what" and "how," in different resolutions of the law. For example, a criminal norm stating that the suspect has the right to remain silent answers a "what" question (what the suspect is allowed to do) as well as a "how" question (how the arrest procedure should be managed).

An accurate distinction between procedural and substantive criminal norms must be based on the purpose of the specific norms. **The purpose of the substantive criminal norm is to define the criminal liability, whereas the purpose of the procedural criminal norm is to impose the defined criminal liability**. Thus, the major question in the distinction between substantive and procedural norms is about the purpose of the specific norm. In many cases there are interactions between various types of the criminal norms,[10] but the purposes of these norms still remain different.

For example, when a criminal norm has to do with the rights of a suspect during arrest, it is a procedural norm and not a substantive one. The purpose of an arrest is to enable imposition of the criminal liability and not to define the criminal liability itself. As a result, criminal norms relating to arrests are not deemed substantive norms but procedural ones. When a criminal norm relates to the offense of theft, it is a substantive norm and not a procedural one. The purpose of specific offenses, including theft, is to define the criminal liability. As a result, criminal offenses are not deemed procedural norms, but substantive ones.

Various types of criminal norms may have similar practical legal consequences, but the distinction still remains based on their purposes. Edifying examples are the different types of obsolescence. Obsolescence can be procedural (after a certain period of time it is illegal to indict or prosecute the individual, although the offense may have been committed) or substantive (after a certain period of time the offense

---

[8]Compare with Grant v. McAuliffe, 41 Cal.2d 859, 246 P.2d 944 (1953); Kilberg v. Northeast Airlines Inc., 9 N.Y.2d 34, 172 N.E.2d 526 (1961).

[9]LAWRENCE COLLINS, DICEY AND MORRIS THE CONFLICT OF LAWS I 157–158 (13th ed., 2000): "While procedure is governed by the *lex fori*, matters of substance are governed by the law to which the court is directed by its choice of law rule (*lex causae*)"; See also in Huber v. Steiner, (1835) 2 Bing.N.C. 202, 210, [1835] All E.R. 159.

[10]Larry Alexander, *Are Procedural Rights Derivate Substantive Rights?*, 17 LAW AND PHILOSOPHY 19 (1998).

is considered never to have been committed). In both types of obsolescence, no criminal liability is imposed on the individual, but the applicable criminal norms are different because of their different purposes.

The substantive obsolescence defines the criminal liability, whereas the procedural obsolescence is related to its imposition. Practically, their consequences may be different. For example, procedural obsolescence may permit suing an individual in a civil procedure, if not specifically banned by civil procedure norms, but because of substantive obsolescence the event is considered as if it has never occurred, and therefore no civil suit can be brought in relation to that event.[11]

The specific location of the criminal law within a certain statute does not necessarily affect the distinction. Procedural criminal norms can be included in a substantive penal code, and substantive criminal norms in a procedural criminal code (code of criminal procedure).[12] If the purpose of the specific criminal norm is to define criminal liability, it is of no consequence that the norm is included in a procedural criminal code; if its purpose is to impose the defined criminal liability, it is unimportant that it is included in a substantive penal code.

According to legal classification, criminal procedure (criminal justice) and the law of evidence contain procedural criminal norms; general criminal law, including penal law, punishment, sentencing, and the law of specific offenses contain substantive criminal norms. Naturally, each criminal norm must be examined separately regarding its purpose to classify it as a procedural or a substantive norm.

Nevertheless, a legal problem may arise if one legal system classifies a norm as procedural, whereas the other classifies it as substantive. The problem that ensues is part of a wider legal problem having to do with private international law and known as the problem of classification (formulated by Kahn and Bartin).[13] In private international law, the legal problem is wider, because in addition to the distinction between procedure and substance, it also involves different spheres of law, for example, when one legal system classifies a case as belonging to contract law and another legal system classifies it as belonging to tort law.[14]

In the context of criminal law, there are two problematic classifications:

(1) Classifying a case as criminal in one legal system and as non-criminal in another
(2) Classifying a norm as procedural in one legal system and as substantive in another

The accepted solution to this problem worldwide is that **the classification of the norm follows the general legal concept of the domestic law in the domestic**

---

[11]Compare with GEORGE P. FLETCHER, BASIC CONCEPTS OF CRIMINAL LAW 11 (1998).

[12]See e.g. article 56 of the German penal code.

[13]EDOUARD BARTIN, PRINCIPES DE DROIT INTERNATIONAL PRIVÉ I (1930); Franz Kahn, *Gesetzeskollisionen: Ein Beitrag zur Lehre des internationalen Privatrechts*, 30 JHERING'S JAHRBüCHER FüR DIE DOGMATIK DES HEUTIGEN RöMISCHEN PRIVATRECHTS 1 (1891, 1928); Ernest G. Lorenzen, *The Qualification, Classification, or Characterization Problem in The Conflict of Laws*, 50 YALE L. J. 743 (1940).

[14]Collins, *supra* note 2, at pp. 33–45.

court. This means that the court would classify the case according to the *lex fori* concept embodied in the domestic law.[15] Thus, the domestic court (*forum*) should use domestic conceptions when classifying the norm as criminal or non-criminal, procedural or substantive. This is the most efficient method of classification when several legal systems are involved. The court is under no obligation to embrace foreign conceptions and decide whether domestic or foreign conceptions apply.

4.1.3 Distinction Between Domestic and Foreign Criminal Norms and Criminal Events

The dominant interest in the legal applicability of a legal norm is its applicability to a factual event. With respect to the applicability of the criminal norm in place, there are two distinctions that must be clarified:

(1) Between domestic and foreign criminal norms
(2) Between domestic and foreign criminal events

Both distinctions are discussed below.

In criminal norms, there is a distinction between domestic or internal norms and foreign or external ones. **A domestic legal norm is one that has been embraced by the sovereign as a binding norm, and its origin is immaterial to the classification**. The domestic sovereign applies legal social control through its various relevant organs. The origin of a norm may be local or foreign (as when an international covenant is adopted), but if domestic society regards it as a binding norm within the domestic legal system the norm is classified as domestic, whatever its origin. Naturally, the norm must derive from a legitimate source of law, as required by the first secondary principle of the principle of legality.[16]

A foreign legal norm is one that has not been embraced by the domestic sovereign as a binding norm. For a norm to be considered domestic, the sovereign must embrace it and its form. Even if domestic law includes the same legal norm, the foreign norm is still considered foreign if it has not been explicitly embraced by the domestic sovereign. For example, the criminal norms prohibiting theft in Japan and South Korea are similar, reflecting the same values toward property. Nevertheless, the Japanese prohibition against theft is not considered a domestic norm in

---

[15] De Nicols v. Curlier, [1900] A.C. 21, 69 L.J.Ch. 109, 81 L.T. 733, 16 T.L.R. 101, 48 W.R. 269; Ogden v. Ogden, [1908] P. 46, 77 L.J.P. 34, 97 L.T. 827, 24 T.L.R. 94; *In re* The Colorado, [1923] All E.R. 531, [1923] P. 102, 92 L.J.P. 100, 128 L.T. 759, 16 Asp. M.L.C. 145.

[16] The first secondary principle of the principle of legality in criminal law is discussed above at Chap. 2.

South Korea, and vice versa. Even if one legal system has been inspired by the other, it does not follow that a foreign norm has been embraced domestically.[17]

A similar distinction exists between domestic or internal criminal events and foreign or external ones. **A domestic factual event is one that occurs within a territory that the domestic sovereign perceives as its own.** The general rule in international law is that domestic sovereignty exists within the domestic territory. Without territory there can be no sovereignty. When a factual event occurs within a domestic territory, it is considered to be a domestic event. This would be a straightforward matter if there was global consent regarding the borders of all territories in the world.

Unfortunately, there is no such consent, and at times, when a factual event occurs on a given territory, more than one state claims that the event is a domestic one. Many territorial wars were fought in response to such controversies.[18] Therefore, when a factual event occurs on a territory that is contested by two sovereigns, both consider it to be a domestic event. Because generally there is no territorial agreement between sovereigns, an event should be considered domestic if it occurred on territory that the domestic sovereign considers to be domestic.[19]

A solution of this type can create another problem. If two states claim that a factual event is a domestic one in their perspective, what is the right law that applies to that event? Although this appears to be a legal problem, in reality it is an issue that needs to be settled between the states involved. In this context of criminal law, a problem exists when no domestic law can be applied to a factual event, and the individual escapes judgment. When more than one legal system is relevant to a criminal event, the individual does not escape judgment. Naturally, the states must agree on the appropriate jurisdiction and use such legal means as extradition, or agree to judge the individual on the current the territory where he was captured.

From the definition of the domestic event we can derive that of a foreign event, which is **a factual event that occurs outside the territory that the domestic sovereign perceives as its own.** Recognition of a factual event as foreign depends on the recognition of the domestic sovereign that the territory on which the event occurred on is located outside its sovereignty. In this sense, the definition of a foreign event is complementary to the definition of a domestic event. All factual events are therefore either domestic or foreign. There can be no factual event that is neither domestic nor foreign, and no factual event that can be both.

---

[17]See e.g. in Norman Bentwich, *The Criminal Code of Palestine*, 83 L.J. 390 (1937); Norman Abrams, *Interpreting the Criminal Code Ordinance, 1936 – The Untapped Well*, 7 ISR. L. R. 25 (1972).

[18]E.g. the first gulf war (1991) on the identity of Kuwait as a sovereign territory or as part of Iraq; the struggle on Tibet as a sovereign territory or as part of China; the war on the Falkland Islands between Britain and Argentina (1982) as part of Britain or as part of Argentina.

[19]Yehuda Z. Blum, *The Missing Reversioner: Reflections on the Status of Judea and Samaria*, 3 ISR. L. REV. 279 (1968).

Table 4.1 Applicability in place of domestic and foreign norms to domestic and foreign events

The event		The norm	
		Criminal norm	
		Domestic	Foreign
Factual event	Domestic	**(1)**	**(3)**
	Foreign	**(2)**	**(4)**

The combination of distinctions between domestic and foreign criminal norms and events produces four possible situations for the applicability of the criminal norm to the criminal event, as shown in Table 4.1.

Situation (1) refers to the applicability of domestic norms to domestic events. From the point of view of the domestic sovereign, this situation involves the standard application of legal social control to factual events that occur within its territorial sovereignty. This is the territorial applicability of the criminal norm.[20]

Situation (2) refers to the applicability of domestic norms to foreign events. From the point of view of the domestic sovereign, the factual event occurred outside its territorial sovereignty, therefore both the foreign and domestic criminal norms may be applicable to event. For the domestic sovereign, this situation expresses the extraterritorial applicability of the criminal norm.[21]

Situation (3) refers to the applicability of foreign norms to domestic events. Most legal systems accept the concept that domestic courts do not apply foreign criminal norms to a criminal event, and that the jurisdiction of the domestic court is the only legitimate jurisdiction applicable to a domestic criminal event.[22] In certain cases, however, the domestic court may take into account foreign norms among other considerations, if the domestic norm requires that it do so.[23]

Situation (4) refers to the applicability of foreign norms to foreign events. From the point of view of the relevant foreign sovereign, this situation parallels situation (1), and from the point of view of the domestic sovereign, this situation is irrelevant. Occasionally, however, within situation (2), when the factual event is foreign, the domestic norm requires consideration of a foreign norm in a certain manner, matching a situation (4), in which a domestic court applies foreign norms to a foreign event.[24]

[20]For instance, a factual criminal event occurs in France, and the French court applies a French criminal norm on it.

[21]For instance, a factual criminal event occurs in Germany, and the French court applies a French criminal norm on it.

[22]See above at Sect. 4.1.1.

[23]For instance, a factual criminal event occurs in France, and the French court considers the German criminal norm as to the punishment, if the French criminal norm requires such considerations.

[24]For instance, a factual criminal event occurs in Germany, and the French court considers the German criminal norm as to the punishment, if the French criminal norm requires such considerations.

All four situations may be relevant and exist simultaneously in the eyes of different territorial sovereignties. But the relevant point of view for the applicability in place of the criminal norm is always the point of view of the domestic sovereign.

4.1.4 Distinction Between Locally Restricted and Not Restricted Criminal Norms

The same way a criminal norm may be restricted in its applicability in time, it may be restricted in its applicability in place. A locally restricted criminal norm is applicable within a certain territory and cannot be applied directly outside it. The restriction may be *ex ante,* through provisions of the criminal norm that restrict its applicability in place, or *ex post*, if later provisions or criminal norms restrict an earlier one. The restriction may cover the entire sovereign territory or parts of it.[25]

Not all criminal norms are locally restricted, however, to the territory of the sovereign or to a specific area within that territory. The most common examples are the criminal norms that embrace a cogent international custom (*jus cogens*),[26] which may be applicable outside a sovereign territory. The location where an event took place is immaterial as to the applicability of these norms.

In some cases, the criminal norm is not applicable in a certain territory that is nominally part of the sovereign territory of the state. This is the legal situation in Indian Country in the United States, which is under American sovereignty but enjoys legal autonomy. In these territories the tribal criminal law and not the general American law is applicable.[27] The autonomy is not absolute, however, and in certain cases it is subordinate to federal[28] or state[29] jurisdiction.

In legal systems in which the concept of sovereignty is absolutely territorial, a criminal norm is locally restricted *ex ante* because the sovereign is not authorized to

[25] E.g. municipal criminal norms are generally restricted to the relevant municipal territory, and outside it they are not applicable.

[26] For the term "*jus cogens*" see above at Sect. 2.2.2.5.

[27] WILLIAM C. CANBY, AMERICAN INDIAN LAW IN A NUTSHELL 23–113 (3rd ed., 1998); *Ex parte* Crow Dog, 109 U.S. 556, 3 S.Ct. 396, 27 L.Ed. 1030 (1883).

[28] WAYNE R. LAFAVE, CRIMINAL LAW 224 (4th ed., 2003); United States v. Blue, 722 F.2d 383 (8th Cir.1983); United States v. Yannott, 42 F.3d 999 (6th Cir.1994); United States v. Burns, 529 F.2d 114 (9th Cir.1975); United States v. Young, 936 F.2d 1050 (9th Cir.1991); Stone v. United States, 506 F.2d 561 (8th Cir.1974); Draper v. United States, 164 U.S. 240, 17 S.Ct. 107, 41 L.Ed. 419 (1896); United States v. McBratney, 104 U.S. 621, 26 L.Ed. 869 (1881); Donnelly v. United States, 228 U.S. 243, 33 S.Ct. 449, 57 L.Ed. 820 (1913); Henry v. United States, 432 F.2d 114 (9th Cir.1970); Keeble v. United States, 412 U.S. 205, 93 S.Ct. 1993, 36 L.Ed.2d 844 (1973); United States v. Antelope, 430 U.S. 641, 97 S.Ct. 1395, 51 L.Ed.2d 701 (1977).

[29] Hagen v. Utah, 510 U.S. 399, 114 S.Ct. 958, 127 L.Ed.2d 252 (1994); Williams v. United States, 327 U.S. 711, 66 S.Ct. 778, 90 L.Ed. 962 (1946); Rice v. Rehner, 463 U.S. 713, 103 S.Ct. 3291, 77 L.Ed.2d 961 (1983); Fort Belknap Indian Community v. Mazurek, 43 F.3d 428 (9th Cir.1994).

enact laws outside its territory.[30] The criminal norm is an expression of legal social control, and must therefore overlap with social control exercised by the sovereign in time and place. Some legal systems, however, are not restricted in place, and their criminal norms are applicable universally, and even beyond the confines of Planet Earth. Monotheistic religions, for example, are not restricted in place, and their criminal prohibitions apply everywhere.

4.1.5 Distinction Between the Relevant Factors Connecting the Criminal Event with the Criminal Norm

The term "connecting factor," taken from private international law, refers to specific aspects of a factual event that connect it with the relevant legal norm and applicable law.[31] Although connecting factors originate with private international law, they are not exclusive to it. Any factual event, criminal or not, can match the connecting factors. For example, if a murder is committed in France and the appropriate connecting factor within the relevant legal system is *lex loci delicti* (the law of the place where the criminal offense took place), the applicable law is the French law.

Although the criminal event may include many additional factual aspects, the connecting factors focus on one or on some of these aspects. The other factual aspects are immaterial for the applicability of the relevant criminal norm. The resolution of the connecting factors is at the national level. Thus, applicable criminal norms can be German, French, Australian, etc. It makes no sense to use a higher resolution for the criminal norm because the criminal law is applied at least at national level and in some cases at the federal or international level.

The use of connecting factors requires the classification of an event as a criminal event. Every legal sphere has its relevant connecting factors. To apply the correct connecting factors, the factual event must be classified correctly. For example, in most legal systems the appropriate connecting factor in procedural matters is *lex fori*, i.e., the law of the domestic courts. In most cases of substantive criminal law the connecting factor is *lex loci delicti*, i.e., the law of the place where the criminal offense was committed.

When a question arises in a French court concerning an arrest for an offense committed in Germany, the correct classification is crucial. If the case is classified as procedural, the correct connecting factor is *lex fori*, and French law is applicable. If the case is classified as substantive, the correct connecting factor is *lex loci*

---

[30]See in Attorney General v. Nikolaiovitch, [1940] A.L.R. 3, (1940) 7 P.L.R. 1; Macleod v. Attorney General for New South Wales, [1891] A.C. 455, 459; United States v. Davis, 25 F.Cas. 786 (C.C.D.Mass.1837); Articles 5-7 of the German penal code; Articles 113-6–113-12 of the French penal code.

[31]JOHN D. FALCONBRIDGE, SELECTED ESSAYS ON THE CONFLICT OF LAWS 129–133 (2nd ed., 1954).

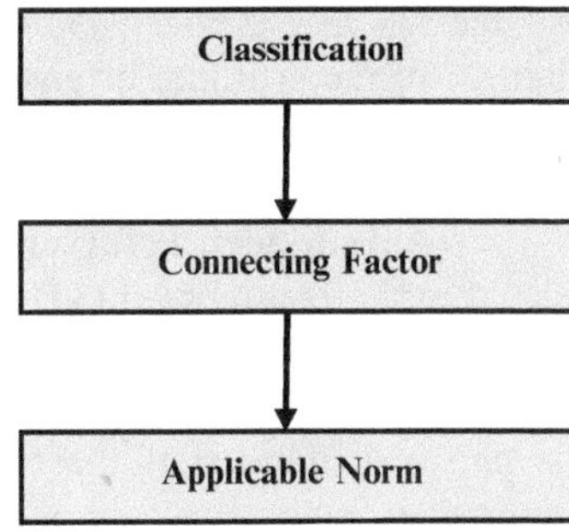

Fig. 4.1 The legal process of matching the applicable norm

delicti, and German law is applicable. In this instance, arrests are part of criminal procedure law, and therefore the correct connecting factor is *lex fori*, which makes the French law applicable in this case. The legal process involves three stages, as shown in Fig. 4.1.

Not all connecting factors are relevant in criminal law.[32] The relevant connecting factors of criminal law can be divided into three major groups as follows:

(1) Procedural connecting factors
(2) Territorial connecting factors
(3) Personal connecting factors

Procedural connecting factors in criminal law refer to the *lex fori*, i.e., the law of the domestic court.[33] Within this connecting factor, the only relevant factual aspect is the national identity of the court that exercises its jurisdiction over the case. If the court is French, the *lex fori* is the French law, if the court is German, the *lex fori* is the German law, etc. The place where the criminal event occurred and the national identity of the parties are immaterial when using this connecting factor. Thus, when a French citizen commits an offense in Germany and is brought before the Australian court, the applicable *lex fori* is the Australian law.

Territorial connecting factors in criminal law refer to the territorial aspects of the factual events. This group contains two main connecting factors in criminal law: the *lex loci delicti*, i.e., the law of the place where the criminal offense took place,

---

[32]The popular connecting factors of the private international law are *lex fori* – the law of the domestic court; *lex domicilii* – the law of the relevant domicile of the party; *lex patriae* – the national law of the relevant party; *lex loci contractus* – the law of the place where the contract has been done (not necessarily where it was signed); *lex loci solutionis* – the law of the place where the contract should have been executed; *lex loci delicti* – the law of the place where the criminal offense has taken place (in criminal law) or the law of the place where the tort has taken place (in tort law); *lex situs* – the law of the place where the object is situated; *lex loci celebrationis* – the law of the place of marriage; *lex monetae* – the law of the monetary means; and *lex loci disgraziae* – the law of the place where the obligation has been violated.

[33]Chevron International Oil Co. Ltd. v. A/S Sea Team, [1983] Lloyd's Rep. 356; ERNEST G. LORENZEN, SELECTED ARTICLES ON THE CONFLICT OF LAWS 97–100, 123–127 (1947).

and the *lex loci delicti commissi*, i.e., the law of the place where the conduct element of the criminal offense manifested itself. The first is general, the second is specific to the element of conduct. These connecting factors also affect the question of jurisdiction.[34]

Personal connecting factors in criminal law refer to aspects of personal identity related to the factual event. This group contains two main connecting factors: the *lex patriae*, i.e., the national law of the relevant party, and the *lex domicilii*, i.e., the law of the place where the relevant party resides. These connecting factors focus on the personal identity of the relevant parties, regardless of the place where the criminal event occurred or the court that has jurisdiction over the case. These connecting factors also affect the question of jurisdiction.[35]

4.2 Applicability of the Procedural Criminal Norm in Place

4.2.1 The General Rule

The general rule of the applicability of the procedural criminal norm in place may be stated as follows:

> **The procedural criminal norm is applicable to any judicial decision where it is considered domestic.**

This general rule refers to both mitigating and aggravating procedural criminal norms, but not to substantive one. The applicability in place extends to all judicial decisions, not the criminal event that is the factual ground for the judicial decision. The criminal event has no significance for the applicability in place of the procedural criminal norm. The applicability of the procedural criminal norm in place

[34]See above at Sect. 4.1.1; Ogden v. Folliot, (1790) 3 T.R. 726; Lynch v. Paraguay Provisional Government, [1861–1873] All E.R. 934, [1861–73] All E.R. 934; Huntington v. Attrill, [1893] A. C. 150; Attorney General for Canada v. Schulze, (1901) 9 S.L.T. 4; Raulin v. Fischer, [1911] 2 K. B. 93; Banco De Vizcaya v. Don Alfonso De Borbon Y Austria, [1934] All E.R. 555, [1935] 1 K.B. 140; 104 L.J.K.B. 46;151 L.T. 499; 50 T.L.R. 284; 78 Sol.Jo. 224; State v. Pelican Insurance Co., 127 U.S. 265, 8 S.Ct. 1370, 32 L.Ed. 239 (1888).

[35]See above at Sect. 4.1.1; Frankfurter v. W. L. Exner Ltd., [1947] Ch. 629; Novello v. Hinrischen Edition Ltd., [1951] Ch. 595; Schemmer v. Property Resources Ltd., [1975] Ch. 273; Attorney General of New Zealand v. Ortiz, [1984] 1 A.C. 1, [1983] 2 W.L.R. 809, [1983] 2 All E.R. 93; United States of America v. Inkley, [1989] Q.B. 255, [1988] 3 W.L.R. 304, [1988] 3 All E.R. 144; Larkins v. N.U.M., [1985] I.R. 671; Bank of Ireland v. Meeneghan, [1994] 3 I.R. 111; SA Consortium General Textiles v. Sun & Sand Agencies Ltd., [1978] Q.B. 279, [1978] 2 All E.R. 339, [1978] 2 W.L.R. 1.

extends to all judicial decisions in which the criminal procedural norm is considered to be domestic. Therefore, to be applicable, the procedural criminal norm must be classified as domestic and function as the *lex fori*.

This general rule has been accepted worldwide following its enactment in French law in 1265. In the original case, the defendant did not appear before the legal instance in Paris and argued that the procedure in Normandy, the place of his domicile, was different and did not obligate him to appear at all court sessions. The legal instance in Paris rejected the defendant's argument and decreed that this was a procedural matter (*de processu causae*), and was therefore governed by the *lex fori*, which was the Parisian law in this case.[36]

The English common law embraced this general rule in the fifteenth century, after it had been accepted in the European continental law.[37] Modern criminal law accepts this general rule as an axiom, so that in procedural issues, the foreign criminal norm is not applicable in domestic courts.[38] Only domestic procedural criminal norm is applicable in domestic courts, so that French courts rule according to the French procedural criminal norm in procedural issues, the German court according to the German procedural criminal norm, and so on.[39]

When the same criminal norm is classified in one legal system as procedural and in other as substantive, it is the legal concept of the domestic court that counts, as embodied in the general concept behind the *lex fori*.[40] The rationale for the classification itself is considered to be a procedural action, and therefore it should also be carried out according to the *lex fori*. Furthermore, it would not be efficient to force the domestic court to embrace foreign legal concepts in its daily judicial activities. Nevertheless, the domestic court may apply the *lex fori* in classification matters as a general concept, and not necessarily in individual details.

The general rule of the applicability of the procedural criminal norm in place raises three questions about its rationale:

(1) Why is the general rule applicable exclusively to the procedural criminal norm and not to the substantive criminal norm?
(2) Why does the general rule relate to the judicial decision and not to the criminal event?
(3) Why does the general rule relate to the domestic norms and not to foreign norms?

These questions are answered below.

---

[36] Edgar H. Ailes, *Substance and Procedure in the Conflict of Laws*, 39 MICH. L. REV. 392, 397 (1941).

[37] Y.B. I Edw. IV, Mich. pl. 13 (1460); Dupleix v. De Roven, (1705) 2 Vern. 540, (1705) 23 E.R. 950.

[38] Ailes, *supra* note 36, at p. 398.

[39] Hansen v. Dixon, (1906) 96 L.T. 32, (1906) 23 T.L.R. 56.

[40] Huber v. Steiner, (1835) 2 Bing.N.C. 202, 210, [1835] All E.R. 159; Société Anonyme Metellurgique de Prayon v. Koppel, (1933) 77 S.J. 800; Grant v. McAuliffe, 41 Cal.2d 859, 246 P.2d 944 (1953); Kilberg v. Northeast Airlines Inc., 9 N.Y.2d 34, 172 N.E.2d 526, 211 N.Y.S.2d 133 (1961).

The general rule relates exclusively to the procedural criminal norm because of the general rationale that the individual cannot rightfully rely on procedure.[41] This general rationale is not exclusive to criminal law. Procedure is not regarded as reflecting substantive rights but it is meant to serve the substantive law, and as such has no independent existence. Changes in procedure may derive from changes in technology, the streamlining of processes, etc. These factors do not change the substantive law and the essence of criminal liability. For example, using DNA evidence in court to prove a factual argument does not change the essence of criminal liability.

Society may change procedures for considerations of efficiency, and the individual cannot rightfully rely on the inefficiencies of previous procedures. The individual can rely on substantive rights and on the substantive law, but not on procedure. Thus, it has little or no significance whether a procedural criminal norm is aggravating or mitigating, because it does not affect the substantive law. For example, if the legislator changes the maximum period available to appeal from 45 to 30 days, should the change be considered aggravating or mitigating? The defendant has 15 days fewer to appeal (aggravating), but so does the prosecution (mitigating). Neither norm affects the essence of criminal liability.

When the individual has no right to rely on procedure, it is not necessary to restrict the applicability of the criminal norm in place. There are two points in place that may be relevant to the applicability in place of the criminal norm. The first is the place of the criminal event and the second is the place of the judicial decision (the place of the domestic court). Procedure is relevant to legal processes; therefore the place of the judicial decision is the relevant point in place which is relevant to the applicability in place of the procedural criminal norm. The procedural criminal norm dominates the way the criminal process is managed; therefore it is immaterial to the criminal event itself.

The general rule relates to domestic norm and not to foreign norms, so that the relevant connecting factor in these matters is always the *lex fori*. All legal systems have accepted this rule for two major reasons: efficiency considerations and the convenience of the judicial system. Using foreign procedure and foreign evidentiary rules in a domestic court requires a drastic change in the judicial system throughout the legal process followed in court. For example, accepting a foreign procedure that uses a jury to make the judicial decision in a domestic court of a legal system that does not ordinarily employ juries requires a drastic change of the judicial system.[42] Applying the foreign law in substantive matters does not require such a change in the judicial system.

To identify the domestic norm, it is necessary to identify the relevant court as a domestic court. When the court is situated within the domestic territory of a given country and activated by domestic sovereign organs, it is considered to be a

---

[41]See above at Sect. 3.2.1.

[42]See e.g. in Nancy Jean King, *The American Criminal Jury*, WORLD JURY SYSTEMS 93 (Neil Vidmar ed., 2000, 2003).

domestic court. But a domestic sovereign can establish courts outside its territory, in which case the question arises whether these courts can be considered domestic even when located outside the domestic territory. The courts established in Nuremberg and Tokyo after World War II are examples of such courts.[43] According to international law, when a territory is occupied, the occupying army must establish courts in the occupied territory in order to keep the public order.[44]

As long as a court is activated by a domestic sovereign, it is considered to be a domestic court even if the individual court is located outside the domestic territory. When the court is subordinated directly to the domestic sovereign it is considered to be a domestic court, and the *lex fori* in this court is the domestic law of the sovereign. Even when the domestic law imports foreign provisions in its procedure, it is still considered to be domestic law, unless the domestic law is no longer applicable to the domestic procedure. If the domestic law points to a foreign law, it is no longer considered to be a domestic law but foreign law, because the domestic law is no longer applicable.

4.2.2 Application of the Rule

The general rule of the applicability of the procedural criminal norm in place[45] is applicable to the factual events in all four possible situations listed above.[46] The combination of the two distinctions, between domestic and foreign, and between procedural criminal norms and factual events,[47] produces four possible situations of the applicability of procedural criminal norm to the criminal event, as shown in Table 4.2.

Table 4.2 Applicability in place of domestic and foreign procedural criminal norms to the domestic and foreign events

The event		The norm	
		The procedural criminal norm	
		Domestic	Foreign
The factual event	Domestic	**(1)**	**(3)**
	Foreign	**(2)**	**(4)**

[43]See more in International Tribunal for Rwanda, Annex to U.N. Security Council Resolution 955 (1994); International Tribunal for the Prosecution of Persons Responsible for Serious Violations of International Humanitarian Law Committed in the Territory of the Former Yugoslavia, Annex to U.N. Security Council Resolution 808 (1993); *Transcript of Proceedings of Nuremberg Trials*, 41 AMERICAN JOURNAL OF INTERNATIONAL LAW 1–16 (1947).

[44]See e.g. Convention (IV) relative to the Protection of Civilian Persons in Time of War, Geneva, 12 August 1949.

[45]Above at Sect. 4.2.1.

[46]See above at Table 4.1.

[47]See above at Sect. 4.1.3.

Situation (1) refers to the applicability of domestic procedural criminal norms to domestic events. In this situation, the domestic court applies the domestic procedural criminal norm as its *lex fori*, not because the event is domestic, but only because the relevant court is a domestic one and must apply the *lex fori* in procedural matters. The fact that the factual event has occurred within the domestic territory is immaterial.[48]

Situation (2) refers to the applicability of domestic procedural criminal norms to foreign events. Naturally, it is assumed that the domestic court has jurisdiction over the case (owing to extraterritorial protective applicability, passive personality applicability, active personality applicability, or universal applicability, as discussed below[49]). But because the relevant norm is a procedural criminal norm, the place where the factual event occurred is immaterial. In this situation, the domestic court applies the domestic procedural criminal norm as its *lex fori* only because the relevant court is a domestic court and must apply the *lex fori* in procedural matters.[50]

Situation (3) refers to the applicability of foreign procedural criminal norms to domestic events. This situation arises only when the relevant court is not a domestic court but a foreign one. No domestic court can apply a foreign law, which is not its *lex fori* in procedural matters. From the point of view of the foreign court, this situation parallels situation (2).[51]

Situation (4) refers to the applicability of foreign procedural criminal norms to the foreign events. This situation arises only when the relevant court is not a domestic court but a foreign one. No domestic court can apply a foreign law, which is not its *lex fori,* in procedural matters. From the point of view of the foreign court, this situation parallels situation (1). Nevertheless, the relevant point of view for the applicability of the procedural criminal norm in place is always that of the domestic sovereign.[52]

---

[48]For instance, a factual criminal event occurs in France, and the French court applies a French criminal norm on it.

[49]The extraterritorial protective applicability of the criminal norm is discussed hereinafter at Sect. 4.3.3.2; the extraterritorial passive personality applicability of the criminal norm is discussed hereinafter at Sect. 4.3.3.3; the extraterritorial active personality applicability of the criminal norm is discussed hereinafter at Sect. 4.3.3.4; the extraterritorial universal applicability of the criminal norm is discussed hereinafter at Sect. 4.3.3.5.

[50]For instance, a factual criminal event occurs in Germany, and the French court applies a French criminal norm on it.

[51]For instance, a factual criminal event occurs in France, and the French court considers the German criminal norm as to the punishment, if the French criminal norm requires such considerations.

[52]For instance, a factual criminal event occurs in Germany, and the French court considers the German criminal norm as to the punishment, if the French criminal norm requires such considerations.

4.3 Applicability of the Substantive Criminal Norm in Place

4.3.1 The General Rule

The general rule of the applicability of the procedural criminal norm in place may be stated as follows:

> **The domestic substantive criminal norm is applicable to domestic factual events decided domestically. In addition, the domestic substantive criminal norm is applicable according to domestic interests to foreign factual events that are decided domestically under legitimate extraterritorial applicability (protective, passive personality, active personality, or universal).**

This general rule refers only to mitigating or aggravating substantive criminal norms but not to procedural criminal norms. The applicability in place is to factual events, not to the judicial decision. The general rule contains two major parts: the applicability in place of domestic substantive criminal norms to domestic factual events and to foreign factual events. This first part of the general rule includes the following three elements:

(1) Substantive criminal norm[53]
(2) Domestic factual event[54]
(3) Domestic judicial decision

These three elements function as conditions. When they are met, the domestic substantive criminal norm is applied to the domestic factual event in the domestic judicial decision. This is the legal duty of the domestic court whether the substantive criminal norm is a specific offense or part of the general provisions of the criminal law. The discretion of the domestic courts with regard to the first part of the general rule is limited to the fulfillment of these three conditions (elements); if all three conditions are met, the courts must apply the domestic substantive criminal norm.

The second part of the general rule, which refers to the applicability in place of domestic substantive criminal norms to foreign events, contains the following four elements:

---

[53]For the distinction between procedural and substantive criminal norms between different legal systems see above at Sect. 4.1.2.

[54]For the distinction between domestic and foreign criminal norms and criminal events see above at Sect. 4.1.3.

(1) Substantive criminal norm[55]
(2) Foreign factual event[56]
(3) Domestic judicial decision
(4) Domestic interests relevant to legitimate extraterritorial applicability

These four elements function as conditions. When they are met, the domestic substantive criminal norm is applied to the foreign factual event in the domestic judicial decision. The domestic interests in the fourth condition are embodied in the legitimate extraterritorial applicability, which can be of four types: protective, passive personality, active personality, and universal. These types are discussed below.[57]

The rationale of the general rule has to do with international political reality since the rise of the nation state. If the human society had been organized as one global or universal society, governed by one universal law, there would have been no need for such a general rule. Under a universal organization of human society, any criminal norm would have been applicable to any criminal event in any judicial decision. This type of applicability exists in all monotheistic religions, which are universal. A Christian is bound to Christianity worldwide, regardless of any specific location. But the organization of the human society is territorial, and therefore the general rule of the applicability of the substantive criminal norm in place is a necessity.

Because the substantive criminal norm is considered to be an act of sovereignty, and because sovereignty is territorial, the substantive criminal norm is territorial. A territorial substantive criminal law is not necessarily restricted within domestic territorial boundaries, but it is applied on a territorial basis. Applying the domestic substantive criminal norm outside the domestic territory is regarded as legitimate only if there is no option available for applying the domestic norms of the relevant territory. This is the principal ground of the territorial state in the international law, although some modern processes after World War II have weakened this concept through the international concepts of human rights.

The modern roots of the territorial basis of the applicability of the criminal norm are found in the English common law of the Middle Ages. By contrast, the European-Continental legal systems continued to apply the *jus commune* (which advocated a common legal system throughout Western Europe) through the end of

[55]For the distinction between procedural and substantive criminal norms between different legal systems see above at Sect. 4.1.2.

[56]For the distinction between domestic and foreign criminal norms and criminal events see above at Sect. 4.1.3.

[57]The extraterritorial protective applicability of the criminal norm is discussed hereinafter at Sect. 4.3.3.2; the extraterritorial passive personality applicability of the criminal norm is discussed hereinafter at Sect. 4.3.3.3; the extraterritorial active personality applicability of the criminal norm is discussed hereinafter at Sect. 4.3.3.4; the extraterritorial universal applicability of the criminal norm is discussed hereinafter at Sect. 4.3.3.5.

the eighteenth century.[58] In England, jury praxis has been exercised since the twelfth century, restricted to local events in a given county, where only local inhabitants could participate in the jury. This praxis was in force for both civil and criminal cases, and members of the jury were usually witnesses to the said event.[59] In 1705 this praxis was abolished in civil cases and was retained only in criminal ones.

If there were difficulties in drafting members for a jury, English law permitted drafting other than local inhabitants who resided in the relevant county in England.[60] The jurisdiction of the relevant court depended on the identity of the jury members;[61] only later became members of the jury distinct from the witnesses.[62] To provide English courts the relevant jurisdiction, English law used certain legal presumptions that allow the courts to consider foreign events as domestic. For example, if a person entered England with goods stolen outside the country, the theft has been considered as if it had occurred in England itself, and therefore English courts had jurisdiction over the case.[63]

These legal presumptions weakened the territorial approach of the courts' jurisdiction and the applicability of the criminal norm in place. In 1883 there were already 18 exceptions to the territorial approach in England,[64] but the English common law preferred not to weaken the territorial approach as a formal policy.[65]

---

[58]Harold J. Berman and Charles J. Reid Jr., *Roman Law in Europe and the Jus Commune: A Historical Overview with Emphasis on the New Legal Science of the Sixteenth Century*, 20 SYRACUSE J. INT'L L. & COM. 1 (1994); HAROLD J. BERMAN, LAW AND REVOLUTION: THE FORMATION OF THE WESTERN LEGAL TRADITION 3 (1983); CHARLES RADDING, THE ORIGINS OF MEDIEVAL JURISPRUDENCE: PAVIA AND BOLOGNA, 850–1150 (1988); KENNETH PENNINGTON, THE PRINCE AND THE LAW, 1200–1600: SOVEREIGNTY AND RIGHTS IN THE WESTERN LEGAL TRADITION (1993); HAROLD J. BERMAN, FAITH AND ORDER: THE RECONCILIATION OF LAW AND RELIGION 187 (1993); RICHARD H. HELMHOLZ, ROMAN CANON LAW IN REFORMATION ENGLAND (1990); Gino Gorla and Luigi Moccia, *A "Revisiting" of the Comparison Between "Continental Law" and "English Law" (16th to 19th Centuries)*, 2 J. OF L. HIST. 143 (1981); PETER STEIN, ROMAN LAW AND ENGLISH JURISPRUDENCE: YESTERDAY AND TODAY (1969); HELMUT COING, EUROPäISCES PRIVATRECHT, BAND II: 19 JAHRHUNDERT: ÜBERBLICK ÜBER DIE ENTWICKLUNG DES PRIVATRECHTS IN DEN EHEMALS GEMEINRECHTLICHEN LäNDERN 2 (1989); FRIEDRICH KARL VON SAVIGNY, SYSTEM DES HEUTIGEN RöMISCHEN RECHTS 1–8 (1840–1849).

[59]THOMAS ANDREW GREEN, VERDICT ACCORDING TO CONSCIENCE 15 (1985).

[60]Act for the Trial of Murders and Felonies in Several Counties, 1548, 2 & 3 Edw. VI, c. 24.

[61]Lacy's Case, (1582) 1 Leon. 270.

[62]Bennet v. Hundred of Hartford, (1650) Style 233, 82 E.R. 671.

[63]2 Geo. II, c. 21 (1728); MATTHEW HALE, HISTORIA PLACITORUM CORONAE vol. II 273 (1736) [MATTHEW HALE, HISTORY OF THE PLEAS OF THE CROWN (1736)].

[64]JAMES FITZJAMES STEPHEN, HISTORY OF THE CRIMINAL LAW OF ENGLAND vol. I 277 (1883).

[65]Thus, for instance, the English court had ruled in Page, [1954] 1 Q.B. 170, 175, [1953] 2 All E.R. 1355, [1953] 3 W.L.R. 895, 37 Cr. App. Rep. 189: "It is, no doubt, true that the general rule of English law is that offences committed by British subjects out of England are not punishable by the criminal law of this country. We need not explore the origin of this doctrine. Suffice it to say that it depends partly on the law of nations which would regard an offence committed on the soil of one nation as, at least primarily, the concern of the sovereign of that country, but one can also see the procedural difficulty which would have occurred to a medieval lawyer who would be unable to

Only in 1925 did British legislators state formally that the English court is not closed to foreign events.[66] From that point on, British legislation widened the applicability of the domestic law over foreign events.[67] This approach has been accepted worldwide, and territorial applicability is considered only a primary basis of applicability, which may be widened in certain circumstances.[68]

In the modern criminal law, in both European-Continental and Anglo-American legal systems, the basic structure of the applicability of the substantive criminal law in place includes a primary territorial applicability and several expansions governed by the protective extraterritorial applicability, the passive personality extraterritorial applicability, the active personality extraterritorial applicability, or the universal extraterritorial applicability.

4.3.2 The Territorial Application of the General Rule

4.3.2.1 The Senior Status of Territoriality

Although domestic law may be applied to both domestic and foreign factual events, the applicability in place that is based on territoriality has a senior status among all other types of applicability. The senior status of territoriality has been accepted worldwide[69] because of the territorial approach of modern sovereignty, as discussed above.[70] The senior status of territoriality in the applicability of the substantive criminal norm in place is necessary as long as modern sovereignty is based on territory and not on persons or other legal entities.

The senior status of territoriality is consistent with the legal overlap between the legal social control and the sovereignty of a given sovereign. Because application of the substantive criminal norm is part of sovereignty, it is restricted to the territorial borders of that sovereignty. The major significance of the senior status of

understand how the jury presentment consisting of persons taken from the vicinage could have knowledge of crimes committed abroad sufficient to present them to the sovereign's courts. It is enough to say that, certainly from the reign of Henry VIII, this rule has been subject to statutory exceptions"; See more in Casement, [1917] 1 K.B. 98.

[66]Criminal Justice Act, 1925, c.86.

[67]See e.g. in article 46(2) of the Courts Act, 1971, c.23; Supreme Court Act, 1981 [Senior Courts Act, 1981], c.54 that states: "The jurisdiction of the Crown Court with respect to proceedings on indictment shall include jurisdiction in proceedings on indictment for offences wherever committed, and in particular proceedings on indictment for offences within the jurisdiction of the Admiralty of England".

[68]See e.g. in American Banana Co. v. United Fruit Co., 213 U.S. 347, 29 S.Ct. 511, 53 L.Ed. 826 (1909).

[69]Ibid: "The general and almost universal rule is that the character of an act as lawful or unlawful must be determined wholly by the law of the country where the act is done".

[70]Above at Sect. 4.3.1.

territoriality is that domestic courts are not bound to consider any criminal norm other than the substantive domestic criminal norms. In this type of case, there is no significance to any foreign circumstances of the factual event (e.g., the identity of the parties, which may be of foreign nationality). Territorial applicability is a direct applicability of the relevant substantive criminal norm, and foreign laws or foreign sovereignties are immaterial for this applicability.

The senior status of the territoriality is also significant internally, and domestic courts are affected by it. Because domestic courts function as organs of the domestic sovereign, they are bound to prefer the domestic substantive criminal norm on a territorial basis. Thus, when a foreign citizen causes harm to a domestic citizen on domestic territory, although the domestic court may apply the domestic substantive criminal law through the domestic passive personality, its preference should be to apply the domestic substantive criminal law through the domestic territorial characteristics of the factual event. When applying the domestic substantive criminal norm not based on territoriality, it generally requires considering the foreign norm, but foreign norms are immaterial when application of the norm is based on territoriality.

The senior status of territoriality is also significant in cases of conflicts of laws between different legal systems. When the domestic substantive criminal norms of two or more legal systems may apply, the legal system to be preferred is the one that can apply its domestic substantive criminal norm through territoriality, in which the *lex fori* and the *lex loci delicti* are identical in reference to the specific case.

For example, if a Dutch citizen causes harm to a German citizen in France, both French and German courts have jurisdiction over the case. The French court has jurisdiction through territoriality, whereas the German court has jurisdiction through passive personality extraterritorial applicability. But in this case, the French court and the French law are preferable because the domestic French law is applicable through territoriality and not through extraterritoriality, whereas the German law is applicable through extraterritoriality.

4.3.2.2 Subjective and Objective Territoriality

To characterize a domestic event as such, the Anglo-American legal systems have distinguished between two types of territoriality: subjective and objective. **Subjective territoriality** refers to cases in which the factual element occurred physically within the territorial boundaries of the domestic sovereignty.[71] **Objective territoriality** refers to cases in which the factual element did not occur within the

[71]Frank Tuerkheimer, *Globalization of U.S. Law Enforcement: Does The Constitution Come Along?*, 39 HOUSTON L. REV. 307, 315 (2002); Bruce Zagaris and Julia Padierna Peralta, *Mexico-United States Extradition and Alternatives: From Fugitive Slaves to Drug Traffickers – 150 Years and beyond the Rio Grande's Winding Courses*, 12 AM. U. J. INT'L L. & POL'Y 519, 553 (1997).

territorial boundaries of the domestic sovereignty, but the factual event has some consequences within these territorial boundaries.[72] Objective territoriality examines the effect of the factual event on the domestic sovereignty, whereas subjective territoriality examines the location of its physical occurrence. For this reason, objective territoriality is also referred to as "the effects principle" or "the effects doctrine."[73]

For example, if a person commits a theft in Italy, the Italian substantive criminal norms are applicable to that case because it is an Italian domestic event under subjective territoriality. But when two persons conspire in England to commit a theft in Italy, the conspiracy cannot be considered an Italian domestic event based on subjective territoriality because the conspiracy has not been committed in Italy. Nevertheless, because conspiracy has an effect in Italy, Italian substantive criminal norms are applicable through objective territoriality.

The Anglo-American distinction between subjective and objective territoriality may cause some difficulties in classification. Objective territoriality is too vague, because the effects of an offense committed on one territory upon another territory vary from case to case, and therefore objective territoriality is not entirely accurate. A more effective distinction regarding the territorial applicability of the substantive criminal norm is between constructive and *de facto* territoriality.

4.3.2.3 Constructive and *De facto* Territoriality

The distinction between constructive and *de facto* territoriality was recognized in order to accurately characterize a domestic event as such. **Territoriality *de facto*** refers to the physical occurrence of the factual event within the boundaries of a specific sovereignty. This territoriality is direct. **Constructive territoriality** refers to situations in which the factual event occurred physically outside a given sovereignty, but the physical event was just part of a process that continued within the boundaries of the given sovereignty, although it has begun outside it.

If the process continued within the boundaries of a given sovereignty, the domestic substantive criminal norm is applicable through *de facto* territoriality. If the process ended prematurely outside the given sovereignty but it was intended to be continued inside it, the domestic substantive criminal law is applicable through constructive territoriality. In both cases, the event is considered to be a domestic event. Foreign events are factual events that cannot be considered domestic through either *de facto* or constructive territoriality.

---

[72]Strassheim v. Daily, 221 U.S. 280, 31 S.Ct. 558, 55 L.Ed. 735 (1911); Ellen S. Podgor, *International Computer Fraud: A Paradigm for Limiting National Jurisdiction*, 35 U.C. DAVIS L. REV. 267, 289 (2002); Michael Akehurst, *Jurisdiction in International Law*, 46 BRITISH YEARBOOK OF INTERNATIONAL LAW 145, 154 (1972).

[73]Lowell H. Brown, *Extraterritorial Jurisdiction Under the 1998 Amendments to the Foreign Corrupt Practices Act: Does the Government's Reach Exceed Its Grasp?*, 26 N.C. J. INT'L L. & COM. REG. 239, 328 (2001).

When considering *de facto* territoriality for the applicability of the domestic substantive criminal norm, only ingredients of the factual element of the offense (*actus reus*) are relevant.[74] Other ingredients, including the mental element (*mens rea*), are not considerable because of the simplicity of the examination of these ingredients and their objectiveness. The factual element requirement is manifest mainly in acts or omissions (conduct).[75] At times, other factual elements are required in addition to conduct, such as specific results of the conduct and particular circumstances underlying it.[76]

As a result, to define a factual event as domestic through *de facto* territoriality, the factual element requirement of the offense is analyzed, and if even only one of its ingredients occurred within the boundaries of the given sovereignty, the entire factual event is considered to be domestic. It is not necessary for all the ingredients of the factual element requirement to have taken place within the boundaries of the domestic sovereignty;[77] a single insignificant ingredient is sufficient to consider the entire factual event as a domestic one.

For example, if an offender gives a victim a poisonous drink in Sicily, a few moments before the victim boards a plane to Brazil, and the poison takes effect after the victim's arrival in Brazil, the offender's conduct took place in Sicily, but the result occurred in Brazil. This is sufficient to consider the entire factual event as domestic both from a Sicilian point of view (because the conduct ingredient of the offense occurred in Sicily) and from a Brazilian point of view (because the result ingredient of the offense occurred in Brazil). Even if only one sub-ingredient occurred domestically (e.g., part of the conduct), it is still considered to be a domestic factual event in domestic eyes.

In legal systems that recognize the chain-offense doctrine (*delictum continuatum*), *de facto* territoriality applies to the entire chain. Thus, when the factual event consists of chain of offenses (e.g., burglary of 30 safes at the same time and in the same place), it is sufficient for one sub-ingredient of one of the offenses to have occurred domestically in order to consider the entire chain of offenses as a domestic factual event.

---

[74]Article 402(1)(a) of the American third Restatement states: "has jurisdiction to prescribe law with respect to... **conduct** that, wholly or in substantial part, takes place within its territory" (emphasis not in original); HANS-HEINRICH JESCHECK UND THOMAS WEIGEND, LEHRBUCH DES STRAFRECHTS – ALLGEMEINER TEIL 131 (5 Auf., 1996).

[75]Walter Harrison Hitchler, *The Physical Element of Crime*, 39 DICK. L. REV. 95 (1934); MICHAEL MOORE, ACT AND CRIME: THE PHILOSOPHY OF ACTION AND ITS IMPLICATIONS FOR CRIMINAL LAW (1993).

[76]JOHN WILLIAM SALMOND, ON JURISPRUDENCE 505 (Glanville Williams ed., 11th ed., 1957); GLANVILLE WILLIAMS, CRIMINAL LAW: THE GENERAL PART §11 (2nd ed., 1961); OLIVER W. HOLMES, THE COMMON LAW 54 (1881, 1923); Walter Wheeler Cook, *Act, Intention, and Motive in Criminal Law*, 26 YALE L. J. 645 (1917).

[77]United States v. Guiteau, 12 D.C. 498 (1882); United States v. Parker, 622 F.2d 298 (8th Cir.1980); United States v. Flores, 289 U.S. 137, 53 S.Ct. 580, 77 L.Ed. 1086 (1993).

Constructive territoriality is necessary only if the offense is **an inchoate offense** committed outside the boundaries of the domestic sovereignty, but with the intention of completing the offense within the domestic sovereignty.

The modern development of inchoate offenses in criminal law began as a social response to the "terrorism" of the sixteenth century, which had been expressed mainly by offenses committed against national security, such as high treason. When these offenses were fully perpetrated, there was no legal problem, but the need for a new legal doctrine began when police became more efficient, and succeeded in arresting the offenders before they fully perpetrated the offense. Then, because no offense had been committed, the defendant could argue: On what charge? At the end of the fifteenth century, the English crown established a new court – the Star Chamber Court (*camera stellata*).[78]

By the sixteenth century, the efficiency of the police in England had increased and a doctrinal legal change was required. The Star Chamber Court developed the maxim of *voluntas reputabitur pro facto*[79] (the desire will be regarded as the act) and formulated a doctrine that criminalized inchoate offenses. Under that doctrine, a specific strong desire to harm society may fulfill the *actus reus* requirement for the imposition of criminal liability – the desire will be regarded as the act. This was the legal birth of the modern offenses of attempt, conspiracy and solicitation that were called "inchoate offenses."

Incriminating inchoate offenses differ from other specific offenses. Usually, an offense is defined as such, due to the social harm caused by its commission. The more severe the social harm, the more severe the offense. In most modern societies, murder is more severe crime than theft, since the social harm caused by murder is more severe than that caused by theft. Nevertheless, an inchoate offender causes no physical harm to anyone. A person who attempted to murder someone, but did not succeed in committing the murder, while the victim, or the potential victim, did not even know about the attempt, causes no social harm. If that is the case, then, under the old doctrine, such a person cannot be indicted for any offense relating to murder, since no murder has been committed.

Under the modern doctrine of inchoate offenses, the social harm is immaterial, while the significant factor for criminalizing inchoate offenses is the danger to society that they pose. The attempt to commit murder causes no harm to society, since no one was actually murdered, but it endangers society. The person who attempted to commit murder and did not succeed in perpetrating the specific offense of murder is not less dangerous to society than the murderer. Once a murderer has murdered the victim, in most cases, no other danger is expected, since the murder was completed. But a person who attempted, but failed to murder, will attempt over

---

[78]Thomas G. Barnes, *Due Process and Slow Process in the Late Elizibethan-Early Stuart Star Chamber*, 6 AM. J. LEGAL. HIST. 221 (1962); Thomas G. Barnes, *Star Chamber Mythology*, 5 AM. J. LEGAL. HIST. 1 (1961).

[79]HENRY DE BRACTON, DE LEGIBUS ET CONSUETUDINIBUS ANGLIAE 337, f. 128, 13 (1260; G. E. Woodbine ed., S. E. Thorne trans., 1968–1977); JAMES FITZJAMES STEPHEN, A HISTORY OF THE CRIMINAL LAW OF ENGLAND 222 (1883, 1964).

and over again to complete the murder. Thus, an inchoate offender is not less dangerous to society than the offender who succeeded in committing the specific offense.

Thus, the need for a response to the social endangerment caused by a criminal who committed an incomplete offense led to the modern doctrine of inchoate offenses. Most legal systems around the world recognize three main inchoate offenses: attempt, conspiracy and solicitation. In some legal systems, the list of inchoate offenses became longer.[80] All three original inchoate offenses became part of modern criminal law under the same rationale, that social endangerment should be criminalized, as well as social harm. The lack of harm in these offenses is counteracted by the strong and focused desire of the offender.

As to an attempted offense – after the abolition of the Star Chamber Court in 1640, the case law created by it was transferred to the ordinary criminal courts. These courts accepted the maxim *voluntas reputabitur pro facto*, and "attempt" was accepted as a general legal structure that may be applied to all serious specific offenses, and not only to national security offenses.[81] That was accepted in the

---

[80]E.g. in Britain, in addition to the attempt, conspiracy and solicitation, the accessory and abettor are also considered inchoate offenders since 2008 due to art. 44 of the Serious Crimes Act, 2007, c.27.

[81]JAMES FITZJAMES STEPHEN, A HISTORY OF THE CRIMINAL LAW OF ENGLAND 223–224 (1883, 1964); SIR EDWARD COKE, INSTITUTIONS OF THE LAWS OF ENGLAND – THIRD PART 5, 69, 161 (6th ed., 1681, 1817, 2001); William Hudson, *Treatise of the Court of Star Chamber*, 2 HARGRAVE COLLECTANEA JURIDICA 8 (1882): argues "Attempts to coin money, to commit burglary, or poison or murder, are in ordinary example; of which the attempt by *Frizier* against *Baptista Basiman*, in 5. *Eliz.* is famous; and that attempt of the two brothers who were whipped and gazed in Fleet-street in 44. *Eliz.* is yet fresh in memory", and concludes (pp. 12–13): "Infinite more are the causes usually punished in this court, for which, for which the law provideth no remedy in any sort or ordinary course, whereby the necessary use of this court to the state appeareth; and the subjects may as safely repose themselves in the bosoms of those honourable lords, reverend prelates, grave judges, and worthy chancellors, as in the heady current of burgesses and meaner men, who run too often in a stream of passion after their own or some private man's affections, the equality of whose justice let them speak of who have made trial of it, being no subject fit for me to discourse of". See more e.g. in Sidley, (1664) 1 Sid. 168, 1 Keble 620, 82 E.R. 1036; Bacon, (1664) 1 Lev. 146, 1 Sid. 230, 1 Keble 809, 83 E.R. 341; Johnson, (1678) 2 Shaw. K.B. 1, 89 E.R. 753; Cowper, (1696) 5 Mod. 206, 87 E.R. 611; Langley, (1703) 2 Salk. 697, 91 E.R. 590; Pigot, (1707) Holt 758, 90 E.R. 1317; Sutton, (1736) Cas. T. Hard. 370, 95 E.R. 240; Vaughan, (1769) 4 Burr. 2494, 98 E.R. 308; Scofield, (1784) Cald. Mag. Rep. 397, 400; Higgins, (1801) 2 East 5, 102 E.R. 269: "All offences of a public nature, that is, all such acts or attempts as tend to the prejudice of the community, are indictable..."; Butler, (1834) 6 Car. & P. 368, 172 E.R. 1280: "an attempt to commit a misdemeanour created by statute is a misdemeanour itself"; Roderick, (1837) 7 Car. & P. 795, 173 E.R. 347: "an attempt to commit a misdemeanour is a misdemeanour, whether the offense is created by statute, or was an offense at common law"; State v. Redmon, 121 S.C. 139, 113 S.E. 467 (1922); Whitesides v. State, 79 Tenn. 474 (1883); Criminal Attempts Act, 1981, c.47, art. 1(1) provides: "If, with intent to commit an offence to which this section applies, a person does an act which is more than merely preparatory to the commission of the offence, he is guilty of attempting to commit the offence"; and thus interpreted, e.g. in Walker, (1989) 90 Cr. App. Rep. 226, [1990] Crim. L.R. 44; Tosti, [1997] Crim. L.R. 746; MH, [2004] W.L. 137 2419.

European-Continental legal systems as well.[82] Solicitation was also accepted pursuant to that maxim, as a special form of attempt.[83] In time, it became a separate inchoate offense, which is based on the criminal attempt concept. Solicitation was accepted as a general inchoate offense that may be applied to any severe offense both in the Anglo-American legal systems[84] and in the European-Continental systems.[85]

Although the roots of conspiracy lie in the thirteenth and fourteenth century,[86] the modern concept of the criminal conspiracy was formulated in the Star Chamber Court. In 1611, the Court ruled that an offense does not have to have been completed in order to impose criminal liability on conspirators.[87] The very agreement between the parties creates the social endangerment, and therefore, it is sufficient to impose criminal liability. If the conspirators completed the commission of the specific offense, criminal liability for the specific offense shall be imposed on them. If they were caught before that, or even before they began their attempt, it suffices for conspiracy, as long as they banded together by an agreement to commit

---

[82]See e.g. art. 22-24, 26, 30-31 of the German Penal Code and art. 121-5, 121-6, 121-7 of the French Penal Code.

[83]John W. Curran, *Solicitation: A Substantive Crime*, 17 MINN. L. REV. 499 (1933); James B. Blackburn, *Solicitation to Crimes*, 40 W.VA. L. REV. 135 (1934); Walter Harrison Hitchler, *Solicitations*, 41 DICK. L. REV. 225 (1937); Herbert Wechsler, William Kenneth Jones and Harold L. Korn, *The Treatment of Inchoate Crimes in the Model Penal Code of the American Law Institute: Attempt, Solicitation, and Conspiracy*, 61 COLUM. L. REV. 571 (1961); Daniell, (1704) 6 Mod. 99, 87 E.R. 856; Collingwood, (1704) 6 Mod. 288, 87 E.R. 1029; Vaughan, (1769) 4 Burr. 2494, 98 E. R. 308; Higgins, (1801) 2 East 5, 102 E.R. 269.

[84]State v. Lampe, 131 Minn. 65, 154 N.W. 737 (1915); Gregory, (1867) 1 Crim. C.R. 77; United States v. Lyles, 4 Cranch C.C. 469, Fed.Cas.No. 15,646 (1834); Cox v. People, 82 Ill. 191 (1876); Allen v. State, 91 Md.App. 705, 605 A.2d 960 (1992); Commonwealth v. Barsell, 424 Mass. 737, 678 N.E.2d 143 (1997); Commonwealth v. Flagg, 135 Mass. 545 (1883); State v. Beckwith, 135 Me. 423, 198 A. 739 (1938); State v. Hampton, 210 N.C. 283, 186 S.E. 251 (1936); State v. Avery, 7 Conn. 266 (1828); State v. Foster, 379 A.2d 1219 (Me.1977); State v. Blechman, 135 N.J.L. 99, 50 A.2d 152 (1946); Smith v. Commonwealth, 54 Pa. 209 (1867); State v. Sullivan, 110 Mo.App. 75, 84 S.W. 105 (1904); Director of Public Prosecutions v. Armstrong, (1999) 143 S.J. L.B. 279, [2000] Crim. L.R. 379; Goldman, [2001] Crim. L.R. 894; Jessica Holroyd, *Incitement – A Tale of Three Agents*, 65 J. CRIM. L. 515 (2001).

[85]E.g. art. 26 of the German Penal Code provides: "Als Anstifter wird gleich einem Täter bestraft, wer vorsätzlich einen anderen zu dessen vorsätzlich begangener rechtswidriger Tat bestimmt hat"; art. 121-7 of the French Penal Code provides: "Est également complice la personne qui par don, promesse, menace, ordre, abus d'autorité ou de pouvoir aura provoqué à une infraction ou donné des instructions pour la commettre"; See more e.g. in the German court decisions in RG 36, 402; RG 53, 189; BGH 6, 359; BGH 7, 234; BGH 8, 137; BGH 34, 63.

[86]Francis B. Sayre, *Criminal Conspiracy*, 35 HARV. L. REV. 393, 394–409 (1922); JOHN HAGAN, VICTIMS BEFORE THE LAW – THE ORGANIZATIONAL DOMINATION OF CRIMINAL LAW 8 (1983); 13 Edw. I, c.12 (1285); 33 Edw. I, c.10 (1307); 4 Edw. III, c.11 (1330); Y.B., 24 Edw. III, f.75, pl.99 (1351).

[87]Poulterers' Case, (1611) 9 Coke Rep. 55b, 77 E.R. 813.

the offense.[88] The agreement endangers society, even though the agreement is not much more than a preparatory action.[89] Conspiracy was accepted as a general inchoate offense that may be applied to any severe offense, as were the offenses of attempt and solicitation.

The acceptance of inchoate offenses as instruments of criminal law empowers the police powers of the night-watchman state[90] to fulfill their destiny of protecting society from danger before the danger transpires. A police officer does not have to wait until the potential offender shoots the bullet into the potential victim's heart; the police officer is authorized to arrest the potential offender before the offense is completed and thus, prevent the crime. As a result, criminal liability would be imposed on the potential offender, not just as a potential offender, but as an offender who completed the perpetration of the offense.[91]

In the competition between social harm and social endangerment, social endangerment won.[92] Now, it is not only the murderer who is convicted, but also the person who attempted to murder using a gun, but the shot missed the intended victim by two inches. This sounds fair, but what about a person who attempts to murder using a voodoo doll or a toy gun? If a person attempts to murder someone using a toy gun, and he really believes it will kill the intended victim, then he is certainly criminally liable for attempted murder. Although his conduct can never cause anyone to die, the desire to kill will be regarded as being tantamount to killing (*voluntas reputabitur pro facto*).[93]

---

[88]Timberley, (1663) 1 Sid. 68, 1 Keble 203, 82 E.R. 974, 83 E.R. 900; Starling, (1664) 1 Sid. 174, 82 E.R. 1039; Sidley, (1664) 1 Sid. 168, 1 Keble 620, 82 E.R. 1036; Daniell, (1704) 6 Mod. 99, 87 E.R. 856; Jones v. Randall, (1774) Lofft 383, 98 E.R. 706.

[89]Jones, (1832) 4 B. & Ad. 345, 110 E.R. 485; State v. Burnham, 15 N.H. 396 (1844); Pettibone v. United States, 148 U.S. 197, 13 S.Ct. 542, 37 L.Ed. 419 (1893); Commonwealth v. Hunt, 4 Metc. 111 (Mass.1842); Kamara v. Director of Public Prosecutions, [1974] A.C. 104, [1973] 2 All E.R. 1242, [1973] 3 W.L.R. 198, 57 Cr. App. Rep. 880, 137 J.P. 714; Criminal Law Act, 1977, c.45 art. 1(1), (2) as amended due to art. 5 of the Criminal Attempts Act, 1981, c.47.

[90]ROBERT NOZICK, ANARCHY, STATE, AND UTOPIA (1974); JONATHAN WOLFF, ROBERT NOZICK: PROPERTY, JUSTICE AND MINIMAL STATE (1981).

[91]David Lewis, *The Punishment that Leaves Something to Chance*, 18 PHILOSOPHY AND PUBLIC AFFAIRS 53 (1989); Sanford H. Kadish, *The Criminal Law and the Luck of the Draw*, 84 J. CRIM. L. &. CRIMINOLOGY 679 (1994); Leo Kats, *Why the Successful Assassin is More Wicked than the Unsuccessful One*, 88 CAL. L. REV. 791 (2000); Paul H. Robinson, *Some Doubts About Argument by Hypothetical*, 88 CAL. L. REV. 813 (2000).

[92]See e.g. Robin Antony Duff, *Criminalizing Endangerment*, DEFINING CRIMES – ESSAYS ON THE SPECIAL PART OF THE CRIMINAL LAW 43 (Robin Antony Duff and Stuart P. Green eds., 2005); Markus Dirk Dubber, *The Possession Paradigm: The Special Part and the Police Power Model of the Criminal Process*, DEFINING CRIMES – ESSAYS ON THE SPECIAL PART OF THE CRIMINAL LAW 91 (Robin Antony Duff and Stuart P. Green eds., 2005).

[93]Jerome B. Elkind, *Impossibility in Criminal Attempts: A Theorist's Headache*, 54 VA. L. REV. 20, 33–34 (1968); John J. Yeager, *Effect of Impossibility on Criminal Attempts*, 31 KY. L. J. 270 (1943); Arnold N. Enker, *Impossibility in Criminal Attempts – Legality and Legal Process*, 53 MINN. L. REV. 665 (1969); David D. Friedman, *Impossibility, Subjective Probability, and Punishment for Attempts*, 20 J. LEGAL STUD. 179 (1991); Peter Westen, *Impossibility Attempts: A Speculative Thesis*,

The question is, whether it is fair. The answer embraces the concept of the moral luck.[94] When a shooter misses his intended victim by two inches, he will probably try again. In fact, he will probably try again and again until he succeeds. Although he missed the victim the first time, he is still dangerous to society. If we consider his desire: since he desires to shoot and not miss, therefore, he is dangerous. If the shooter missed the intended victim and the police immediately arrested him, it was just a matter of luck that the intended victim was not eventually shot. Luck is not legitimate grounds for criminal liability; therefore the shooter is criminally liable, whether the victim was actually shot (on the charge of murder), or was not injured at all (on the charge of attempted murder).

Such is the legal situation with the shooter who uses a toy gun or a voodoo doll. Initially, the shooter really thinks that a toy gun will cause death. After a few attempts, the shooter understands that such a device is incapable of causing death, but he still desires the victim's death. Consequently, it is highly likely that he will exchange the toy gun for a lethal device. When he uses a lethal device, the social endangerment very quickly progresses to social harm. As long as the desire to murder still exists, the road from a voodoo doll, that does not do the deed, to a lethal device that gets the deed done, is not a very long road. This justifies deeming offenses that pose a danger to society as more serious than those that cause harm to society.

When an inchoate offense has been committed within the boundaries of a domestic sovereignty, it is considered to be a domestic factual event regardless of its aim, that is, even if the complete offense was aimed at a target outside the domestic territorial sovereignty. It is considered a domestic factual event based on *de facto* territoriality, because the ingredients of the factual element occurred within the boundaries of the domestic sovereignty. But when an inchoate offense is committed outside the domestic sovereignty, but aimed to be completed within the domestic sovereignty, it is necessary to use constructive territoriality to consider the inchoate offense as a domestic factual event because the inchoate offense functions as a preliminary stage in the conduct of the complete offense.

The general course of conduct of a specific offense contains three consecutive stages. The first is the stage of preparation, which is not punishable in most legal systems. The second is the criminal attempt. The third and final stage is the complete perpetration of the offense. The second and third stages are deemed punishable in most legal systems. The crucial question is: Where exactly do the legal borders lie between these three stages? Although some tests have been proposed, all failed to formulate an accurate distinction that satisfied the response

5 OHIO ST. J. CRIM. L. 523 (2008); Kunkle v. State, 32 Ind. 220 (1869); People v. Elmore, 128 Ill. App.2d 312, 261 N.E.2d 736 (1970); State v. Smith, 262 N.J.Super. 487, 621 A.2d 493 (1993).

[94]Nils Jareborg, *Criminal Attempts and Moral Luck*, 27 ISR. L. REV. 213 (1993); Benjamin C. Zipursky, *Two Dimensions of Responsibility in Crime, Tort, and Moral Luck*, 9 THEORETICAL INQ. L. 97 (2008); Russell Christopher, *Does Attempted Murder Deserve Greater Punishment than Murder – Moral Luck and the Duty to Prevent Harm*, 18 NOTRE DAME J.L. ETHICS & PUB. POL'Y 419 (2004).

to social endangerment sought by society. Such tests included the proximity test,[95] the last act test[96] and the unequivocality test.[97]

The first stage in the course of conduct of the specific offense is preparation. Preparation is the stage when the preliminary planning of the offense is performed. The criminal scheme or criminal plan (*iter criminis*) is constituted. This is the stage when the criminal idea is formulated into a plan. The plan may or may not be operative, may or may not be well planned, may or may not be detailed, but there should be a plan, any plan, to commit the specific offense. Formulating the criminal plan is nothing more than thoughts; therefore, it should not be punishable. When only one person is involved in the formulation of the criminal plan, the social endangerment at this stage is very low, if any.

The preparatory stage ends at a very particular point – when the planner makes the decision to carry out his criminal plan and commit the specific offense. The decision is mental and does not necessarily receive immediate expression by particular actual activities. As a result, the decision itself is part of the preparation, but it is the final stage of the preparation. The making of the decision is not punishable in and of itself, as it is still only preparation. However, from that point on, that person becomes a danger to society, since he intends to carry out his criminal plan and commit the offense. The specific point in time when the personal decision is made to execute the criminal plan is the moment when he becomes a danger to society.

Many people fantasize from time to time about killing their partners, about robbing a bank or stealing something. This is part of human nature and does not necessarily pose a threat to society. It becomes a threat to society only when a

---

[95]See e.g. in the United States People v. Bracey, 41 N.Y.2d 296, 392 N.Y.S.2d 412, 360 N.E.2d 1094 (1977); Sizemore v. Commonwealth, 218 Va. 980, 243 S.E.2d 212 (1978); People v. Mahboubian, 74 N.Y.2d 174, 544 N.Y.S.2d 769, 543 N.E.2d 34 (1989); People v. Acosta, 80 N.Y.2d 665, 593 N.Y.S.2d 978, 609 N.E.2d 518 (1993); People v. Warren, 66 N.Y.2d 831, 498 N.Y.S.2d 353, 489 N.E.2d 240 (1985); Hyde v. United States, 225 U.S. 347, 32 S.Ct. 793, 56 L.Ed. 114 (1912); and in the English Common Law Eagleton, [1855] 6 Cox C.C. 559; Button, [1900] All E.R. 1648, [1900] 2 Q.B. 597, 69 L.J.Q.B. 901, 83 L.T. 288, 64 J.P. 600, 48 W.R. 703, 16 T.L.R. 525, 44 Sol. Jo. 659, 19 Cox. C.C. 568; Robinson, [1915] 2 K.B. 342; Compare United States v. Desena, 287 F.3d 170 (2nd Cir.2002); Henderson, [1948] 91 C.C.C. 97.

[96]United States v. Colpon, 185 F.2d 629 (1950); Commonwealth v. Peaslee, 177 Mass. 267, 59 N.E. 55 (1901); Compare ANTONY ROBIN DUFF, CRIMINAL ATTEMPTS 37–42 (1996).

[97]J. W. Cecil Turner, *Attempts to Commit Crimes*, 5 CAMBRIDGE L. J. 230 (1933); LEON RADZINOWICZ AND J. W. CECIL TURNER, THE MODERN APPROACH TO CRIMINAL LAW 279–280 (1948); Barker, [1924] N.Z.L.R. 865, 874–875; State v. Stewart, 143 Wis.2d 28, 420 N.W.2d 44 (1988); Campbell and Bradley v. Ward, [1955] N.Z.L.R. 471; Compare United States v. Cruz-Jiminez, 977 F.2d 95 (3rd Cir. 1992); United States v. McDowell, 714 F.2d 106 (11th Cir. 1983); United States v. Everett, 700 F.2d 900 (3rd Cir. 1983); Lemke v. United States, 14 Alaska 587, 211 F.2d 73 (9th Cir. 1954); State v. Mandel, 78 Ariz. 226, 278 P.2d 413 (1954); People v. Buffum, 40 Cal.2d 709, 256 P.2d 317 (1953); Larsen v. State, 86 Nev. 451, 470 P.2d 417 (1970); People v. Downer, 57 Cal.2d 800, 22 Cal. Rptr. 347, 372 P.2d 107 (1962); Wylie, [1976] 2 N.Z.L.R. 167.

specific decision is made to fulfill that fantasy and commit that specific offense.[98] Dreaming or fantasizing is legal and not punishable, but making the dream or fantasy come true poses a danger to society when it involves an offense. The exact borderline between legitimate thoughts, dreams or fantasies, which pose no threat to society, and fulfilling those fantasies, which might pose a danger to society, lies in the decision-making: whether or not to act upon those fantasies and fulfill them.

From the moment the decision has been made to carry out a criminal plan, any activity performed pursuant to that criminal plan poses a danger to society, and therefore, is no longer attributed to the preparatory stage. Any activity performed pursuant to a criminal plan already constitutes part of the attempt to commit the specific offense. The attempt to commit an offense is not a fixed point on the time axis, but rather, is a range of conduct that may vary from case to case. An attempt, *per se*, is formed once the decision has been made to execute a criminal plan. Any conduct performed pursuant to a criminal plan is considered an attempt and is no longer deemed part of the preparatory stage. This borderline between the preparatory stage and the criminal attempt reflects the borders of social endangerment.

From the moment the decision has been made to commit an offense, any subsequent conduct is deemed within the wide range of criminal attempt, which is punishable. Criminal attempt continues as long as the specific offense has not yet been completely perpetrated. An offense is deemed completely perpetrated when all elements of the specific offense exist. When only one element is still missing, it is deemed an attempt. It is immaterial what precise element is missing, in order to deem the event an attempt. The missing element might be the conduct element, the circumstantial element or the consequential element.[99]

Thus, when a person desires to rape a woman, but discovers that he is temporarily impotent, the conduct element of the specific offense of rape is missing, and it is deemed attempted rape. When a person desires to kill his partner by shooting him at night when he is asleep, and he shoots the figure that seems to be asleep in bed, but it turns out to be a dog and not his partner, the circumstantial element of the specific offense of murder is missing, and it is deemed attempted murder. When a person desires to kill his partner by shooting him in the street, but the bullet misses him, the consequential element of the specific offense of murder is missing, and it is deemed attempted murder.

Whether an element is missing or not depends entirely on the precise definition of the specific offense. The inchoation of a criminal attempt relates to the complete perpetration of the specific offense. An attempt to commit murder is always relative to the specific offense of murder. When an offense is completely perpetrated, it is no longer an attempt to commit the specific offense, but rather is the offense itself. In

---

[98]See e.g. People v. Hawkins, 311 Ill.App.3d 418, 243 Ill.Dec. 621, 723 N.E.2d 1222 (2000); United States v. Doyon, 194 F.3d 207 (1st Cir.1999).

[99]Donald Stuart, *The Actus Reus in Attempts*, [1970] CRIM. L.R. 505 (1970); Mark Thornton, *Attempting the Impossible (Again)*, 25 CRIM. L. Q. 294 (1983).

legal systems where criminal attempt and the specific offense are punishable identically, there is no significant relevance to the classification of an activity as either an attempt or a specific offense. Under such legal systems, it is sufficient to prove that the offender made the decision to commit the offense and acted accordingly.

This is the general course of conduct of specific offenses, but when more than one offender is involved, another inchoate offense is relevant – criminal conspiracy. In fact, criminal conspiracy is the preparatory stage of joint-perpetration or co-perpetration, in the sense that it constitutes an agreement between the conspirators. The general course of conduct of specific offenses is applied when it involves one offender or more. The only difference is that when more than one person is involved, criminal conspiracy may also be deemed part of the preparatory stage.

The specific inchoate offense of conspiracy does not replace preparatory action entirely, and, of course, it does not replace the criminal attempt. Criminal conspiracy incriminates part of the preparatory stage when committed by more than one person. Criminal conspiracy is constituted when an agreement between conspirators is made that relates to the commission of an offense.[100] Thus, when two persons are chatting in a café about their fantasy to rob a bank, it is not deemed a conspiracy. If these two agree to fulfill their fantasy by committing the specific offense of robbery, they become a danger to society, and are culpable for criminal conspiracy. If the commission of the criminal plan has been initiated, but not completed, it is a joint-attempt or a co-attempt. When completed, it is the full joint-perpetration or co-perpetration.

A person who makes an agreement with himself to commit an offense, in fact, is making a decision to commit an offense. Conspiracy does not change the general course of conduct of inchoate offenses, but adapts it to situations when more than one person is involved. The change is minor. While the decision itself is not punishable when made by one person, since it is still deemed a preparatory stage, agreement made by two or more persons is punishable as a criminal conspiracy. In both cases, whatever preceded the decision or agreement is not punishable, since it is still deemed a preparatory stage. In both cases, whatever comes after the decision or agreement is punishable, since it is deemed a criminal attempt. The only difference is in the decision or agreement: when made by one person, it is not punishable (preparatory), but, when made by two or more persons, it is punishable (conspiracy).

The reason for this differentiation lies in the joint commitment in the agreement between the conspirators to commit the specific offense. That joint commitment, *per se*, poses a danger to society, even if, in the final analysis, the conspiracy to commit the offense was not carried out. This is the difference between a joint fantasy and an operative criminal plan, and reflects a basis for a criminal organization between the offenders. This reason is at the core of incriminating complicity

---

[100]Theodore W. Cousens, *Agreement as an Element in Conspiracy*, 23 VA. L. REV. 898 (1937); Paul Marcus, *Conspiracy: The Criminal Agreement in Theory and in Practice*, 65 GEO. L. J. 925 (1977).

and explains why sentencing of conspirators is harsher than for a sole offender who committed an offense. The very gathering for criminal objectives embodies a greater potential for actually committing the offense.[101]

According to the relativity of inchoation concept, an attempt to commit conspiracy is inevitable.[102] If conspiracy is deemed a specific offense in most Anglo-American legal systems, then when two or more parties attempt to agree about committing a specific offense, it is deemed attempted conspiracy. One example of attempted conspiracy: two people meet at the apartment of one of them in order to agree about committing a joint-robbery, but just before they agree, the police enter the apartment and arrest them both. They attempted to conspire, but the conspiracy was not accomplished, due to their arrest.

The danger to society that derives from attempted conspiracy is not of a lesser degree than the conspiracy itself. If the parties did not succeed to come to an agreement between them to commit a specific offense for reasons not under their control, it is highly likely that they will attempt to do that over and over again until an agreement is made. The attempt to conspire poses no less a danger to society than the conspiracy itself. Of course, the social harm might be different, but the social harm is immaterial in relation to inchoate offenses. The danger to society is the same and justifies incrimination as an inchoate offense, and such is the case with attempted conspiracy. The factual element requirement (*actus reus*) of attempted conspiracy shall be discussed hereunder.

Solicitation is an activity whereby the perpetrator persuades another person to commit a specific offense. The persuasion may contain various methods for persuading the potential perpetrator, such as requests, threats, intimidation, encouragement, entreaties, etc. The general course of conduct of solicitation is identical to that of a specific offense. Thus, it has three consecutive stages: preparatory, attempt and complete perpetration. A person is culpable for attempted solicitation if he made a decision to solicit, but the solicitation was not completed. For instance, when the potential target is not convinced and does not intend to commit any specific offense, or when the attempting solicitor is trying to say something, but words do not come out because of his excitement. If the potential target is solicited and intends to commit the specific offense, the solicitation is deemed completed.

The danger to society that derives from solicitation is not of a lesser degree than the specific offense itself. The solicitor himself does not actually commit the specific offense, but the solicitor planted the criminal idea in the target's mind. The solicitation is the very cause of the perpetration, and the solicitor is deemed the intellectual perpetrator (*auteur intellectuel*) of the specific offense. The intellectual perpetrator is not less dangerous to society than the actual perpetrator. Moreover,

---

[101] For the different association theory behind that concept See EDWIN H. SUTHERLAND AND DONALD R. CRESSEY, CRIMINOLOGY 173 (4th ed., 1970).

[102] Note, *Criminal Conspiracy*, 72 HARV. L. REV. 920 (1958–1959); Nick Zimmerman, *Attempted Stalking: An Attempt-to-Almost-Attempt-to-Act*, 20 N. ILL. U. L. REV. 219 (2000); Charles H. Rose III, *Criminal Conspiracy and the Military Commissions Act: Two Minds That May Never Meet*, 13 ILSA J. INT'L & COMP. L. 321 (2007).

the solicitor could plant his criminal idea in more than one person's mind, and thus, pose far greater danger to society than the actual perpetrator. Of course, the social harm might be different between the solicitor and the perpetrator, but the social harm is immaterial in relation to inchoate offenses. The danger to society justifies incrimination as an inchoate offense, and such is the case with solicitation and attempted solicitation.[103] The factual element requirement (*actus reus*) of solicitation and attempted solicitation shall be discussed hereunder.

Obviously, solicitation to commit an attempted offense is inherent in the solicitation itself. Obviously, a solicitor does not solicit a person to commit attempted murder, but to murder the victim. If the perpetrator attempted to murder, but the specific offense of murder was not completed, it does not change the culpability of the solicitation itself. If a person solicits someone to intimidate a victim by shooting near him, the victim would think that this is an attempt to murder him. This is not really solicitation of attempted murder, but it is solicitation to intimidate. If the potential perpetrator does not succeed in committing the offense, this has no impact on the offense of solicitation. Therefore, solicitation to attempt an offense is already inherent in the solicitation itself.

When the inchoate offense functions as a preliminary stage in the conduct of a complete offense, and the offense is intended to be completed within domestic territorial sovereignty, the inchoate offense endangers domestic sovereignty not less than it endangers the foreign sovereignty where it has been committed. But because the inchoate offense has not been committed inside the domestic sovereignty, its domestic territoriality is constructive rather than *de facto*. It is entirely immaterial for constructive territoriality whether the inchoate offense has actually been completed, because in the case of inchoate offenses it is not the social harm but the social endangerment that is examined.[104] In some legal systems it is required to prove the effect of an inchoate offense on domestic sovereignty in order to apply the constructive territoriality, but the essence of the inchoate offense incorporates such an effect.[105]

4.3.2.4 Boundaries of Territoriality in Land, Sea, Airspace, Outer Space, and Transport Crafts

To identify a factual event as domestic it is necessary to identify the domestic territory as such, whether the domestic substantive criminal norm is applicable through *de facto* or constructive territoriality. Identification should parallel the identification of the territorial boundaries of the sovereignty, but the context of

---

[103]See e.g. Anthony LaCroix, *Attempted Online Child Enticement: Not Impossible, but Not That Simple*, 5 DARTMOUTH L.J. 97 (2007); Sam E. Fowler, *Criminal Attempt Conspiracy and Solicitation under the Criminal Code Reform Bill of 1978*, 47 GEO. WASH. L. REV. 550 (1979).

[104]United States v. Postal, 589 F.2d 862 (5th Cir.1979); United States v. Ricardo, 619 F.2d 1124 (5th Cir.1980); United States v. Wright-Barker, 784 F.2d 161 (3rd Cir.1986).

[105]United States v. Plummer, 221 F.3d 1298 (11th Cir.2000).

the applicability of the substantive criminal norm, territoriality should cover issues other than the territorial borders of the domestic sovereignty: for example, the applicability of the substantive criminal norm on the high seas (e.g., a robbery aboard a ship cruising the Pacific), in the outer space (e.g., aboard a space ship approaching Mars), etc.

Generally, domestic territorial borders may be derived from international law as well as from the domestic laws of individual sovereignties (states). According to international law, the borders of the domestic territory should match the territory of the sovereignty agreed in international covenants or accepted by virtue of the applicability of the domestic sovereignty on no-man's-land (*terra nullius*).[106] According to domestic law, however, the territorial borders of the state are within the territorial boundaries where its domestic law is applicable through legislation, administrative actions, or judicial decisions. These territorial boundaries are not necessarily the same as the borders accepted in international law.

For the applicability of the substantive criminal norm, the relevant territorial boundaries are those recognized in the domestic law, not necessarily those recognized in international law, because the essence of the substantive criminal law is legal social control. The legal social control embodied in the substantive criminal law is a domestic one and not derived from international. Legal social control may be global or widespread, but it does not derive from the norms of international law, as discussed above.[107] The domestic criminal law may embrace specific norms from international law and transform them into domestic ones, but these still depend on the domestic sovereign.[108]

As a result, it is the domestic state that determines its territorial boundaries for the applicability of the substantive criminal law. These territorial boundaries should relate to the borders on land, sea, air, outer space, and transport crafts, as discussed below.

Territorial boundaries on land are legally determined by the domestic state through its sovereign actions of legislation, administration, and judicial rulings. In most legal systems, this determination has to do with constitutional law, international law, and the substantive criminal law. In the dynamic modern political reality, new states are created (e.g., the new countries formed out of the former Yugoslavia and the Soviet Union) and borders changed, wars and peace processes around the world result in territorial changes, and lands are purchased by states and incorporated into their territory. All these changes must be considered by the domestic state when determining its territorial borders on land.

---

[106] JAMES CRAWFORD, THE CREATION OF STATES IN INTERNATIONAL LAW 42 (1979); IAN BROWNLIE, PRINCIPLES OF INTERNATIONAL LAW 138–145 (4th ed., 1990).

[107] Above at Sect. 2.2.2.

[108] See e.g. the offense of piracy in Dawson, (1696) 13 St.Tr. 451; The Magellan Pirates, (1853) 1 Sp.Ecc.&Ad. 81, 164 E.R. 47; Harmony v. United States, 43 U.S. 210, 11 L.Ed. 239 (1844); Athens Maritime Enterprises Corporation v. Hellenic Mutual War Risks Association (Bermuda) Ltd., [1983] Q.B. 647, [1983] 1 All E.R. 590, [1983] 2 W.L.R. 425.

The territorial sea boundaries are legally determined by the domestic state through its sovereign actions of legislation, administration, and judicial rulings. In most legal systems, this determination has to do with international law and the substantive criminal law. Since the sixteenth century, the generally accepted width of the strip of the territorial sea has been three nautical miles (5,556 m) from the coast.[109] Article 3 of the United Nations Convention on the Law of the Sea, 1982, expanded the width of the territorial sea to twelve nautical miles (22,224 m).[110] Most modern states accepted the change and amended their domestic laws accordingly.[111] The method used to measure the territorial sea has been standardized internationally, and the standard has also been accepted worldwide.[112]

The twelve nautical miles territorial sea strip falls under the actual sovereignty of the domestic state. All of the legal norms of the domestic state are applicable within its territorial sea, including the substantive criminal norms.[113] Over the years, this realm has been recognized as the international custom, although the coastal state must enable innocent passage to foreign ships within its territorial sea, as long as the passage is direct and continuous.[114] When a foreign ship threatens the coastal state, the passage is not considered to be innocent. The domestic substantive criminal norms, however, are applicable aboard foreign ships in the course of an innocent passage if criminal offenses are committed on them, and if these offenses affect the domestic state (e.g., drug offenses, water pollution offenses, etc.), or if the ship asks for the assistance of the coastal state.[115]

The domestic coastal state may apply its substantive criminal norms to enforce tax, customs, fiscal, immigration, or sanitary laws not only within its territorial sea but also in the contiguous zone, which includes another strip of twelve nautical miles beyond the territorial sea strip.[116] Some states apply their domestic

---

[109]Keyn, (1876) 2 Q.B.D. 90, 2 Ex.D. 65.

[110]Article 3 of the United Nations Convention on the Law of the Sea, 1982, United Nations Publications Sales, E.83 V.5 (1983) states that "Every State has the right to establish the breadth of its territorial sea up to a limit not exceeding 12 nautical miles, measured from baselines determined in accordance with this Convention".

[111]Article 1(1)(a) of the Territorial Sea Act, 1987, c.49 states that "the breadth of the territorial sea adjacent to the United Kingdom shall for all purposes be 12 nautical miles".

[112]Article 5 of the United Nations Convention on the Law of the Sea, 1982, United Nations Publications Sales, E.83 V.5 (1983) states that "Except where otherwise provided in this Convention, the normal baseline for measuring the breadth of the territorial sea is the low-water line along the coast as marked on large-scale charts officially recognized by the coastal State"; See more in Kent Justices, [1967] 2 Q.B. 153, [1967] 1 All E.R. 560, [1967] 2 W.L.R. 765, 131 J.P. 212; Post Office v. Estuary Radio Ltd., [1968] 2 Q.B. 740, [1967] 3 All E.R. 663, [1967] 1 W.L.R. 1396.

[113]Anglo-Norwegian Fisheries, [1951] I.C.J. Rep. 116, 160.

[114]Corfu Channel, [1949] I.C.J. Rep. 1.

[115]Pianka v. The Queen, [1979] A.C. 107.

[116]Article 33 of the United Nations Convention on the Law of the Sea, 1982, United Nations Publications Sales, E.83 V.5 (1983) states that "(1) In a zone contiguous to its territorial sea, described as the contiguous zone, the coastal State may exercise the control necessary to: (a) prevent infringement of its customs, fiscal, immigration or sanitary laws and regulations within its

substantive criminal norms in national security and drug matters within the entire contiguous zone.[117] Beyond the contiguous zone, including the exclusive economic zone, the domestic substantive criminal norms of the coastal state are not applicable through territoriality.[118] The territorial and contiguous zone strips include the undersea as well, at any depth.[119]

The territorial boundaries of airspace are legally determined by the domestic state through its sovereign actions of legislation, administration, and judicial rulings. In most legal systems, this determination has to do with international law and the substantive criminal law. Most legal systems accepted and embraced the aeronautical legal regime that has been agreed internationally at the Chicago Convention on Civil Aviation in 1944,[120] based on the principles of the Paris convention of 1919 — the first convention in this field.[121] The dominant legal approach is defined in Article 1 of the Covenant, which decrees that "the contracting States recognize that every State has complete and exclusive sovereignty over the airspace above its territory."[122] The airspace above the domestic territory includes also the airspace above the territorial sea strip and the contiguous zone.[123] The maximum altitude considered as the territorial airspace is the minimal altitude of the outer space.

For the applicability of the substantive criminal norm, **the territorial boundary in outer space** is affected by the boundaries of the territorial airspace. According to English common law, the territorial airspace of the domestic state is not limited by altitude (*usque ad coelum*), and may include the outer space if accessible.[124] On December 20, 1961, the United Nations General Assembly accepted the principle that the outer space may not be under sovereignty of any state, and on January 27, 1967 the General Assembly accepted the international convention "Treaty on Principles Governing the Activities of States in the Exploration and Use of Outer Space including the Moon and other Celestial Bodies."[125]

According to the Treaty on Principles, no state may apply its domestic substantive criminal law in outer space. As a result, the question of the borderline between

---

territory or territorial sea; (b) punish infringement of the above laws and regulations committed within its territory or territorial sea. (2) The contiguous zone may not extend beyond 24 nautical miles from the baselines from which the breadth of the territorial sea is measured".

[117] Ibid.

[118] See in Part V of the United Nations Convention on the Law of the Sea, 1982, United Nations Publications Sales, E.83 V.5 (1983).

[119] MALCOLM N. SHAW, INTERNATIONAL LAW 418–422 (4th ed., 1997).

[120] Chicago Convention on Civil Aviation, 1944, 295 U.N.T.S. 15.

[121] Convention for the Regulation of Aerial Navigation, 1919, 173 L.N.T.S. 11.

[122] At p. 2 of the convention.

[123] Hirst, *supra* note 3, at pp. 104–106.

[124] J. F. McMahon, *Legal Aspects of Outer Space*, 38 BRITISH YEARBOOK OF INTERNATIONAL LAW 339 (1962).

[125] Treaty on Principles Governing the Activities of States in the Exploration and Use of Outer Space including the Moon and other Celestial Bodies, 1967, 610 U.N.T.S. 206.

the airspace of the domestic state (which is under its full sovereignty) and outer space (which is not under any sovereignty) becomes highly significant. Although it has not been formally recognized worldwide, the most accepted borderline between the airspace and outer space is at an altitude of 100 km above the sea.[126] From that altitude upward the domestic substantive criminal norm does not apply.

The territorial boundaries on transport crafts are affected by the type of the individual craft. The territoriality of **land transport crafts** is determined by its physical location at the time an offense is committed (*lex loci delicti*). For example, when an offense is committed in a car situated on French territory, the domestic substantive criminal norms of France are in force through territorial applicability, regardless of the nationality of the parties or the state in which the car is registered.

The territoriality of **maritime**, **undersea**, **air,** and **space crafts** differs depending on one of two possible situations. In the first situation, the territoriality of the craft is determined through territorial applicability (*lex loci delicti*). When a ship docks on German territory, German domestic substantive criminal law is applicable to any offense committed on it. In this situation, the craft is not different from land transport crafts.[127] In the second situation, the determining factor is the state in which the craft is registered. By their nature, when these crafts are in operation, they are not located within the domestic territory, but in a foreign territory or outside any domestic or foreign territory (e.g., a ship cruising on the high sea, an airplane in a transcontinental flight, or a spacecraft on its way to Mars).

Most legal systems have accepted that for these crafts the registry state is the relevant factor of territoriality when they are outside domestic territory, regardless of the ownership (or possession) of the craft.[128] To summarize, when these crafts are outside any territorial zone (domestic or foreign), the applicable criminal law is that of the registry state of the craft; when the crafts are in any given territory (domestic or foreign), the applicable criminal law is that of the relevant territory

[126]HENRI A. WASSENBERGH, PRINCIPLES OF OUTER SPACE IN HINDSIGHT 18 (1991).

[127]Mali v. Keeper of the Common Jail, 120 U.S. 1, 7 S.Ct. 385, 30 L.Ed. 565 (1887): "It is beneficial to commerce if the local government abstains from interfering with the ship's internal discipline, and the general regulation of the rights and duties of the officers and crew towards the vessel or among themselves"; See more in Lauritzen v. Larsen, 345 U.S. 571, 73 S.Ct. 921, 97 L. Ed. 1254 (1953); United States v. One Big Six Wheel, 166 F.3d 498 (2nd Cir.1999).

[128]United States v. Keller, 451 F.Supp. 631 (1978); Article 4 of the German penal code provides: "Das deutsche Strafrecht gilt, unabhängig vom Recht des Tatorts, für Taten, die auf einem Schiff oder Luftfahrzeug begangen werden, das berechtigt ist, die Bundesflagge oder das Staatszugehörigkeitszeichen der Bundesrepublik Deutschland zu führen"; Article 113-3 of the French penal code provides in relation to ships that "La loi pénale française est applicable aux infractions commises à bord des navires battant un pavillon français, ou à l'encontre de tels navires, en quelque lieu qu'ils se trouvent. Elle est seule applicable aux infractions commises à bord des navires de la marine nationale, ou à l'encontre de tels navires, en quelque lieu qu'ils se trouvent"; and in relation to aircrafts article 113-4 of the French penal code provides that "La loi pénale française est applicable aux infractions commises à bord des aéronefs immatriculés en France, ou à l'encontre de tels aéronefs, en quelque lieu qu'ils se trouvent. Elle est seule applicable aux infractions commises à bord des aéronefs militaires français, ou à l'encontre de tels aéronefs, en quelque lieu qu'ils se trouvent".

and the criminal law of the registry state of the craft.[129] In case of conflict of laws between several criminal norms, the general rules of conflict of laws based on applicability of the criminal norm in place are in force, as discussed below.[130]

4.3.3 Extraterritorial Application of the General Rule

4.3.3.1 General Interests of Extraterritoriality

Because of the territorial concept of sovereignty, the applicability of the domestic substantive criminal norm to foreign events is never taken for granted. Based on this, the domestic state is regarded as the one ultimately responsible for public order within its territorial boundaries. Applicability of a state's substantive criminal norms to factual events that took place in a foreign state may damage the territorial concept of sovereignty, which has precedence in the applicability of the substantive criminal norm.[131] Adequate justification is needed to establish extraterritorial applicability of the criminal norm.

Although the international law has recognized four types of extraterritoriality of the domestic substantive criminal norms for foreign events (protective, passive personality, active personality, and universal),[132] international law alone is not considered to be a legitimate source of the criminal law. Therefore, even if there are justifications for the extraterritorial applicability of the domestic substantive criminal law within international law, the domestic sovereignty still needs to provide appropriate justification.[133] International law can justify the extraterritorial applicability of the domestic substantive criminal norm by the rapid development of the international delinquency, the global desire to fight against international delinquency, and the globalization trends in economy, delinquency, and law enforcement.

[129]Anderson, [1861–1873] All E.R. 999, (1868) 11 Cox C.C. 198; United States v. Holmes, 18 U. S. 412, 5 L.Ed. 122 (1820); United States v. Rodgers, 150 U.S. 249, 14 S.Ct. 109, 37 L.Ed. 1071 (1893); United States v. Flores, 289 U.S. 137, 53 S.Ct. 580, 77 L.Ed. 1086 (1933); Hoopengarner v. United States, 270 F.2d 465 (6th Cir.1959); United States v. Reagan, 453 F.2d 165 (6th Cir.1971); United States v. Ross, 439 F.2d 1355 (9th Cir.1971); United States v. Allied Towing Corp., 602 F.2d 612 (4th Cir.1979); United States v. Arra, 630 F.2d 836 (1st Cir.1980); Marsh v. State, 95 N.M. 224, 620 P.2d 878 (1980); United States v. Ricker, 670 F.2d 987 (11th Cir.1982).

[130]Hereinafter at Sect. 4.4.1.

[131]Above at Sect. 4.3.2.1.

[132]Christopher L. Blakesley, *A Conceptual Framework for Extradition and Jurisdiction over Extraterritorial Crimes*, 1984 UTAH L. REV. 685 (1984); Mark A. Weisburd, *Due Process Limits on Federal Extraterritorial Legislation*, 35 COLUM. J. TRANSNAT'L L. 379 (1997); Frank Tuerkheimer, *Globalization of U.S. Law Enforcement: Does The Constitution Come Along?*, 39 HOUSTON L. REV. 307, 315 (2002).

[133]United States v. Bowman, 260 U.S. 94, 43 S.Ct. 39, 67 L.Ed. 149 (1922).

Nevertheless, these justifications may serve only as the background for justifying the extraterritorial applicability of the domestic substantive criminal norm.[134] Two major assumptions have been developed to examine the interaction between international law and the criminal law in this context:

(1) The territoriality assumption
(2) The matching assumption

The territoriality assumption argues against the extraterritorial applicability of the domestic substantive criminal norm[135] and determines the senior status of territoriality, as discussed above.[136] According to this assumption, the domestic court must apply the domestic substantive criminal norm on any domestic event, without the need for any justification,[137] but to apply it to a foreign event, a clear and explicit justification is required.[138] Although this assumption has been criticized in view of the globalization of the modern delinquency and its international sway, the assumption continues to govern the applicability of the substantive criminal norm in place, upholding the senior status of territoriality.[139]

The matching assumption determines that the domestic substantive criminal norm should not contradict any cogent international custom (*jus cogens*) derived from international conventions on criminal affairs (*jus gentium*) as long as there is no acute necessity to contradict it.[140] The matching assumption functions as a quasi-subsidiary principle, so that a cogent international custom can be contradicted only if there is no other alternative.[141] Thus, under certain circumstances the *jus gentium* allows the extraterritorial applicability of the domestic substantive criminal norm, but because such applicability is not mandatory, to make the domestic criminal law applicable extraterritorially, the state must do it in its domestic interest.

---

[134] Curtis A. Bradley, *Universal Jurisdiction and U.S. Law*, 2001 U. CHI. LEGAL F. 323, 330 (2001).

[135] William S. Dodge, *Understanding the Presumption Against Extraterritoriality*, 16 BERKELEY J. INT'L L. 85 (1998).

[136] Above at Sect. 4.3.2.1.

[137] American Banana Co. v. United Fruit Co., 213 U.S. 347, 29 S.Ct. 511, 53 L.Ed. 826 (1909): "The general and almost universal rule is that the character of an act as lawful or unlawful must be determined wholly by the law of the country where the act is done".

[138] E.E.O.C. v. Arabian American Oil Co., 499 U.S. 244, 111 S.Ct. 1227, 113 L.Ed.2d 274 (1991); Sale v. Haitian Centers Council, Inc., 509 U.S. 155, 113 S.Ct. 2549, 125 L.Ed.2d 128 (1993); Smith v. United States, 507 U.S. 197, 113 S.Ct. 1178, 122 L.Ed.2d 548 (1993); Argentine Republic v. Amerada Hess Shipping Corp., 488 U.S. 428, 109 S.Ct. 683, 102 L.Ed.2d 818 (1989); but see Hartford Fire Insurance Co. v. California, 509 U.S. 764, 113 S.Ct. 2891, 125 L.Ed.2d 612 (1993).

[139] Gary B. Born, *A Reappraisal of the Extraterritorial Reach of U.S. Law*, 24 LAW & POL'Y INT'L BUS. 1 (1992); Larry Kramer, *Vestiges of Beale: Extraterritorial Application of American Law*, 1991 SUP. CT. REV. 179 (1991).

[140] Murray v. The Schooner Charming Betsy, 6 U.S. 64, 2 L.Ed. 208 (1804): "an act of Congress ought never to be construed to violate the law of nations if any other possible construction remains".

[141] Chew Heong v. United States, 112 U.S. 536, 5 S.Ct. 255, 28 L.Ed. 770 (1884).

The domestic interest of the state in the matter of the extraterritoriality of its domestic criminal norms may be *in abstracto* and included in the general terms of extraterritorial applicability, which reflect the domestic interest of the state. Additionally, they may also be *in concreto*, embodied in specific considerations of state authorities to apply the domestic substantive criminal norm extraterritorially. Interests *in abstracto* are part of the basic conditions for extraterritorial applicability, as recognized by the state. Thus, a state may protect a persecuted population even if it is persecuted outside its territorial boundaries. Such protection expresses the domestic interests of the state with regard to a particular issue.

If the interests *in abstracto* match the international *jus gentium* or *jus cogens*, there is no legal problem, but if they contradict each other, the state can apply its domestic substantive criminal norms extraterritorially if it has no alternative and is justified in doing so. For example, if the international *jus gentium* does not condemn persecution of homosexuals, but the state wishes to protect this population, it may do so in its domestic interest. The international *jus gentium* and *jus cogens* accept the extraterritoriality of protective applicability, the passive personality applicability, the active personality applicability, and the universal applicability as a realization of the matching assumption.

The domestic interest of the state *in concreto* refers to the discretion of state authorities to apply a criminal norm to a factual foreign event. The ability to apply the norm in the interests *in abstracto* is not sufficient for actual application. The state can initiate the application, if desired. The most significant manifestation of such desire is the public interest, which serves as the basic motive for activating the domestic criminal process (different in this point from the civil process). The public interest can trigger the domestic criminal process even in the case of a foreign factual event.

As noted above, the domestic interests of the state *in abstracto* are embodied in four types of extraterritorial applicability, accepted by the international *jus gentium* and *jus cogens*. The interactions between the four types are subject to the conflict of laws based on the applicability of the criminal norm in place.[142] The four types of extraterritorial applicability are:

(1) Extraterritorial protective applicability
(2) Extraterritorial passive personality applicability
(3) Extraterritorial active personality applicability
(4) Extraterritorial universal applicability

The four types of extraterritorial applicability are discussed below.

4.3.3.2 Extraterritorial Protective Applicability

The extraterritorial protective applicability of the domestic substantive criminal norm to foreign factual events that are judged in the domestic instance is based on

[142] As discussed hereinafter at Sect. 4.4.1.

the general concept that the state can protect its interests. The concept originates in the principle of state protection (Staatsschutzprinzip) of the European-Continental legal systems.[143] In the middle of the twentieth century, this principle has also been accepted by the Anglo-American legal systems.[144] After the terror attacks at the end of the twentieth century and the beginning of the twenty-first, the principle was recognized in most of the western world and played a major role in the legal fight against terrorism.

Protection of interests identified with the state itself is considered to be a matter of first priority for the state. Even if the harm to these interests has been done (or it is intended to be done) outside the territory of the state, it is still considered a matter of first priority. For example, causing harm to state property outside the territory of the state is considered to be causing harm to the interests of the state. When its interests are harmed or intended to be, the state has the authority to protect them. It is not necessary that these interests be physically located within the domestic territory of the state, but they should be identified with the state itself, so that causing harm to these interests can be considered as causing harm to the domestic state itself.

The domestic state determines *in abstracto* what the relevant interests are. The decision is guided by its domestic concepts about society, the state, morals, the economy, etc. In most legal systems, the recognized interests are related to the national security of the state, and are embodied in offenses such as causing harm to the national security or to democracy, forging the coin or the official seal of the state, causing harm to symbols of the state, or even dealing in drugs.[145] Naturally, various states identify different interests under protective applicability, and although the extraterritorial protective applicability is recognized by international law, there is no uniformity among the various states with respect to the interests included in this applicability.[146]

---

[143]BGH 30, 1.

[144]United States v. Rodriguez, 182 F.Supp. 479 (S.D.Cal.1960); Joyce v. Director of Public Prosecutions, [1946] A.C. 347, [1946] 1 All E.R. 186, 174 L.T. 206, 62 T.L.R. 208, 31 Cr. App. Rep. 57, [1946] W.N. 31: "No principle of comity demands that a State should ignore the crime of treason committed against it outside its territory. On the contrary a proper regard for its own security requires that all those who commit that crime, whether they commit it within or without the realm should be amenable to its laws".

[145]Article 113-10 of the French penal code provides that "La loi pénale française s'applique aux crimes et délits qualifiés d'atteintes aux intérêts fondamentaux de la nation et réprimés par le titre Ier du livre IV, à la falsification et à la contrefaçon du sceau de l'Etat, de pièces de monnaie, de billets de banque ou d'effets publics réprimées par les articles 442-1, 442-2, 442-5, 442-15, 443-1 et 444-1 et à tout crime ou délit contre les agents ou les locaux diplomatiques ou consulaires français, commis hors du territoire de la République"; See more in the United States at United States v. Gonzalez, 776 F.2d 931 (11th Cir.1985); United States v. Peterson, 812 F.2d 486 (9th Cir.1987); United States v. Felix-Gutierrez, 940 F.2d 1200 (9th Cir.1991); United States v. Vasquez-Valesco, 15 F.3d 833 (9th Cir.1994); United States v. Cardales, 168 F.3d 548 (1st Cir.1999); and in Germany article 5 of the German penal code.

[146]Shaw, *supra* note 119, at pp. 468–469.

The core of the interests protected by extraterritorial applicability has to do with causing harm to the sovereignty of the domestic state. The harm may be symbolic, not necessarily physical or injurious to some substantial interest. At times it is the image of the state that is the interest being harmed, which is also grounds for establishing extraterritorial protective applicability. For example, using diplomatic mail to smuggle drugs causes harm to the image of the state and to its reputation, and it can therefore establish an adequate basis for extraterritorial protective applicability.

Extraterritorial protective applicability expresses most widely the internal interests of the domestic sovereignty through the applicability of the domestic substantive criminal norm to foreign factual events. This broad expression creates the most extensive harm to the territoriality assumption.[147] Nevertheless, the harm is recognized worldwide and internationally as part of the authorized actions the state can take to protect its domestic interests, and it does not harm the matching assumption.[148]

The domestic state is authorized to determine the interests and legal entities the harming of which is considered to be causing harm to the state itself. These legal entities represent and symbolize the state internally or externally. For example, causing harm to a diplomat of a state on assignment in a foreign state is considered to be causing harm to the state itself. This consideration is not limited to diplomats; causing harm to any official of the domestic state can be considered as causing harm to the state itself, even if the event occurred on foreign territory.[149]

If the domestic state considers harm caused to an entity as causing harm to itself, it is necessary to examine the function of the entity in relation to the harm, to accurately identify the harmed interest. If the function of the specific entity is incidental to the harm, the extraterritorial protective applicability is not appropriate, as for example in the case of an assault on an ambassador by an attacker who is not aware that the victim functions as an ambassador. In this case, the function of the ambassador is incidental to the assault, as the attacker did not intend to assault the ambassador for being an ambassador. In this case, therefore, the extraterritorial protective applicability is not appropriate.

If the ambassador of Germany in Turkey is attacked in Turkey by a Turkish resident because the German ambassador symbolizes Germany in the eyes of the attacker, the function of the ambassador is not incidental to the attack. The attacker wished to attack Germany itself by attacking the German ambassador. In this case, Germany has the authority to exercise its domestic substantive criminal norm with respect to this factual event through extraterritorial protective applicability. In sum, only if the legal entity is harmed because its relation with the state is the dominant motive for the harm, the extraterritorial protective applicability can be considered

---

[147]Above at Sect. 4.3.3.1.

[148]Shaw, *supra* note 119, at pp. 468–469.

[149]United States v. Lopez-Alvarez, 970 F.2d 583 (9th Cir.1992); United States v. Benitez, 741 F.2d 1312 (11th Cir.1984).

as the appropriate applicability of the domestic substantive criminal law to the factual event.

4.3.3.3 Extraterritorial Passive Personality Applicability

The extraterritorial passive personality applicability of the domestic substantive criminal norm to foreign factual events that are judged in a domestic instance is based on the general concept that the individual is entitled to be protected by the state from serious harm anywhere, even outside the state's territory. This applicability is called "passive personality" because two types of personalities are involved in a typical criminal event. The active personality is the offender, the passive personality is the victim the offense. Extraterritorial passive personality applicability focuses on the linkage between the victim and the state of origin, whereas extraterritorial active personality applicability, discussed below,[150] focuses on the linkage between the offender and the state of origin.

For example, when a French national is assaulted outside France, French courts may consider extraterritorial *passive* personality applicability. By contrast, when a French national assaults another person outside France, French courts may consider extraterritorial *active* personality applicability.

The concept whereby individuals are entitled to be protected by the state from serious harm anywhere, even outside the state's territory, originated in the protection of the individual principle (Individualschutzprinzip) of the European-Continental legal systems.[151] This principle has been accepted by the Anglo-American legal systems in the late twentieth century,[152] and has been recognized in international law.[153] According to this principle, the residence of the individual in a specific state is incidental to the harm. For example, if a German resident is assaulted outside Germany because of his German residence, the appropriate protective applicability in the case is the extraterritorial, and not the passive personality one. But, if a person is assaulted outside Germany and happens to have German residence unbeknownst to the attacker, whose attack was not motivated by the German residence, the appropriate applicability is extraterritorial passive personality and not the protective one.

---

[150] Hereinafter at Sect. 4.3.3.4.

[151] Article 7(1) of the German penal code provides that "Das deutsche Strafrecht gilt für Taten, die im Ausland gegen einen Deutschen begangen werden, wenn die Tat am Tatort mit Strafe bedroht ist oder der Tatort keiner Strafgewalt unterliegt"; Article 113-7 of the French penal code provides that "La loi pénale française est applicable à tout crime, ainsi qu'à tout délit puni d'emprisonnement, commis par un Français ou par un étranger hors du territoire de la République lorsque la victime est de nationalité française au moment de l'infraction".

[152] Hirst, *supra* note 3, at pp. 51–52; Finta, [1994] 1 S.C.R. 701.

[153] Shaw, *supra* note 119, at pp. 467–468.

The Anglo-American legal systems consider the protection of the individual principle (Individualschutzprinzip) to be most harmful to the territoriality assumption, as discussed above.[154] For a long time, these legal systems tended not to accept this extraterritorial applicability, despite its acceptance by the European-Continental legal systems. Three major factors were mentioned for rejecting the extraterritorial passive personality applicability in the Anglo-American legal systems.[155] First, the harm to the sovereignty of the foreign state has been regarded as unjustified, because the linkage of the foreign state with the factual event (territorial linkage of *lex loci delicti*) has been regarded as being much more relevant to the factual event than the residence or nationality of the victim (personal linkage of *lex patriae*).

Second, the harm to the fair notice requirement has been regarded as unjustified because the offender is assumed to be subject to the domestic territorial norms regardless of the residence or nationality of the victim, which is incidental to the offense. If the offender is ignorant of the nationality of the victim, which is incidental to the offense, it is regarded as unjustified to subject the offender to the domestic laws of the victim.[156]

Third, this extraterritorial applicability is not likely to be practical because most extradition covenants do not allow the extradition of an offender on such grounds to a foreign state that happens to be the state of residence of an incidental victim.

As a result, most of the Anglo-American legal systems objected to extraterritorial applicability and rejected it.[157] In the United States, a legal opinion of the Secretary of State from 1887 advised that the American government does not recognize or accept an extradition request from Mexico in order to indict and sentence a person who caused harm to Mexican residents.[158] But this approach has changed at the end of the twentieth and the beginning of the twenty-first centuries, since western countries must fight terrorism. To increase the effectiveness of the worldwide fight against terrorism, the Anglo-American legal systems had to accept the European-Continental approach and accept extraterritorial passive personality applicability because most victims of terrorism are not of a specific nationality.[159]

Within a short time, the American courts accepted extraterritorial passive personality applicability as part of the legal fight against terrorism.[160] British courts,

---

[154]Above at Sect. 4.3.3.1.

[155]Geoffrey R. Watson, *The Passive Personality Principle*, 28 TEX. INT'L L. J. 1 (1993).

[156]Ibid, at pp. 14–15.

[157]United States v. Davis, 25 F.Cas. 786 (C.C.D.Mass.1837).

[158]DEPARTMENT OF STATE, REPORT ON EXTRATERRITORIAL CRIME AND THE CUTTING CASE, IN FOREIGN RELATIONS LAW OF THE UNITED STATES 751, 762 (1887).

[159]United States v. Yunis, 681 F.Supp. 896 (D.D.C.1988); United States v. Yunis, 924 F.2d 1086 (D.C.Cir.1991).

[160]Abraham Abramovsky, *Extraterritorial Jurisdiction: The United States Unwarranted Attempt to Alter International Law in United States v. Yunis*, 15 YALE J. INT'L L. 121 (1990).

however, refused to accept it,[161] and in some instances the legislature had to intervene to enable extraterritorial passive personality applicability.[162]

4.3.3.4 Extraterritorial Active Personality Applicability

The extraterritorial active personality applicability of the domestic substantive criminal norm to foreign factual events that are judged in a domestic instance is based on the general concept that the individual is subject to the state of origin when committing offenses anywhere, even outside the state's territory. This applicability is called "active personality" because two types of personalities are involved in a typical criminal event. The active personality is the offender, the passive personality is the victim the offense. Extraterritorial active personality applicability is focused on the linkage between the offender and the state of origin, whereas the extraterritorial passive personality applicability, discussed above,[163] focuses on the linkage between the victim and the state of origin.

For example, when a Greek person is assaulted outside Greece, Greek courts may consider extraterritorial *passive* personality applicability. But when a Greek person assaults another person outside Greece, Greek courts may consider extraterritorial *active* personality applicability.

The concept, in which individuals are subject to the state of origin when committing offenses anywhere, even outside the state's territory, originated in the active personality principle (Aktiven Personalitätprinzip) of the European-Continental legal **systems.**[164] The principle has been regarded as a basic principle

---

[161]Rees v. Secretary of State for the Home Department, [1986] 1 A.C. 937, [1986] 2 All E.R. 321, [1986] 2 W.L.R. 1024, 83 Cr. App. Rep. 128.

[162]Counter-Terrorism Act, 2008, c.28; Terrorism (Northern Ireland) Act, 2006, c.4; Terrorism Act, 2006, c.11; Prevention of Terrorism Act, 2005, c.2; Anti-Terrorism, Crime and Security Act, 2001, c. 24; Terrorism Act, 2006, c.11; Terrorism Act, 2000, c.11; Criminal Justice (Terrorism and Conspiracy) Act, 1998, c.40; Prevention of Terrorism (Additional Powers) Act, 1996, c.7; Suppression of Terrorism Act, 1978, c.26; in Canada: Criminal Code, c.46, part II.1; Regulations Implementing the United Nations Resolutions on the Suppression of Terrorism, Under the United Nations Act, 2001; in New Zealand: International Terrorism (Emergency Powers) Act, 1987 No. 179; Terrorism Suppression Act, 2002 No. 34; Anti-Money Laundering and Countering Financing of Terrorism Act, 2009 No. 35.

[163]Above at Sect. 4.3.3.3.

[164]In the German law article 7(2)(1) of the German penal code provides that "(2) Für andere Taten, die im Ausland begangen werden, gilt das deutsche Strafrecht, wenn die Tat am Tatort mit Strafe bedroht ist oder der Tatort keiner Strafgewalt unterliegt und wenn der Täter (1) zur Zeit der Tat Deutscher war oder es nach der Tat geworden ist,. . ." and article 5(12) of the German penal code provides that "Das deutsche Strafrecht gilt, unabhängig vom Recht des Tatorts, für folgende Taten, die im Ausland begangen werden:. . . (12) Taten, die ein deutscher Amtsträger oder für den öffentlichen Dienst besonders Verpflichteter während eines dienstlichen Aufenthalts oder in Beziehung auf den Dienst begeht"; In the French law article 113-6 of the French penal code provides that "La loi pénale française est applicable à tout crime commis par un Français hors du territoire de la République. Elle est applicable aux délits commis par des Français hors du territoire

in all monotheistic religious legal systems, which are not territorial but personal. For example, a Christian is bound to Christian duties anywhere, including outer space, because Christian duties are relevant and applicable anywhere to persons of Christian faith.

The active personality principle assumes fiduciary relations between the individual and the state of origin, whether the individual is on the state's territory or outside it.[165] Thus, the extraterritorial active personality applicability of domestic norms to the domestic residents is in force even if the offense was committed outside the domestic state. The linkage with the domestic state is personal, embodied in the residence of the offender. The responsibility of the state is to enforce public order not only within its territorial borders, but also in its personal realm by enforcing the criminal law on its residents.

According to the assumed fiduciary relations between the individual and the state of origin, the extraterritorial active personality applicability is not exclusive to citizens of the state but includes all legal entities with such fiduciary relations. Thus, citizens, residents, and public workers are all subject to this applicability (Domizilprinzip).[166] The active personality principle has been accepted in international law.[167]

Whereas in the European-Continental legal systems the active personality principle has been widely accepted, in the Anglo-American legal systems it has been deemed harmful to the territoriality assumption, as discussed above,[168] and it has been necessary to justify the authority of the state to exercise its police powers outside its territorial borders.[169] Anglo-American courts acted differently than they did in the case of passive personality applicability, and enforced the domestic law through extraterritorial active personality applicability.[170] But such an application was rare and regarded as an exception.[171]

Until World War II, while this approach was dominant, only in rare and exceptional cases did the Anglo-American legal systems accept the extraterritorial

de la République si les faits sont punis par la législation du pays où ils ont été commis. Il est fait application du présent article lors même que le prévenu aurait acquis la nationalité française postérieurement au fait qui lui est imputé".

[165]Geoffrey R. Watson, *Offenders Abroad: The Case for Nationality-Based Criminal Jurisdiction*, 17 YALE J. INT'L L. 41 (1992).

[166]Article 5(13) of the German penal code provides that "Taten, die ein Ausländer als Amtsträger oder für den öffentlichen Dienst besonders Verpflichteter begeht".

[167]Shaw, *supra* note 119, at pp. 462–467.

[168]Above at Sect. 4.3.3.1.

[169]Perez v. Brownell, 356 U.S. 44, 78 S.Ct. 568, 2 L.Ed.2d 603 (1958).

[170]Bow Street Metropolitan Stipendiary Magistrate, [2000] 1 A.C. 147, [1999] 2 All E.R. 97, [1999] 2 W.L.R. 827.

[171]Blackmer v. United States, 284 U.S. 421, 52 S.Ct. 252, 76 L.Ed. 375 (1932); United States v. Bowman, 260 U.S. 94, 43 S.Ct. 39, 67 L.Ed. 149 (1922); Jones v. United States, 137 U.S. 202, 11 S.Ct. 80, 34 L.Ed. 691 (1890).

active personality applicability by explicit legislation[172] or court rulings.[173] After the end of World War II, it was necessary to determine extraterritorial active personality applicability in a more accurate and general manner because of the increasing mobility of domestic residents outside the domestic state and the emerging trend of globalization. In most cases, domestic states demanded to judge their own residents because they were concerned for the safety of their residents at the hands of foreign courts. There were constitutional objections against the right to judge and sentence a state's residents extraterritorially,[174] but eventually the extraterritorial active personality applicability become legitimate through legislation[175] and court rulings.[176] As a result, since the end of World War II the extraterritorial active personality applicability has been common in most legal systems around the world.

4.3.3.5 Extraterritorial Universal Applicability

The extraterritorial universal applicability of the domestic substantive criminal norm on foreign factual events that are judged in the domestic instance is based on the general concept that all states are part of the international community and of human society. As a result, all states are bound to combat delinquency aimed against humanity wherever it takes place, even if it occurs outside its territorial borders. This general concept emphasizes the commitment of all states and societies to human society in general.

The concept whereby all states are part of the international community and of human society, and are bound to combat delinquency aimed against humanity,

---

[172]See e.g. 18 U.S.C.A. §1203; 18 U.S.C.A. §1956; 18 U.S.C.A. §2332A; 18 U.S.C.A. §2339C.

[173]United States v. Hill, 279 F.3d 731 (9th Cir.2002); United States v. Plummer, 221 F.3d 1298 (11th Cir.2000); United States v. Thomas, 893 F.2d 1066 (9th Cir.1990); United States v. Walczak, 783 F.2d 852 (9th Cir.1986).

[174]United States v. Quarles, 350 U.S. 11, 76 S.Ct. 1, 100 L.Ed. 8 (1955); Reid v. Covert, 354 U.S. 1, 77 S.Ct. 1222, 1 L.Ed.2d 1148 (1957); Kinsella v. United States, 361 U.S. 234, 80 S.Ct. 297, 4 L. Ed.2d 268 (1960); Grisham v. Hagan, 361 U.S. 278, 80 S.Ct. 310, 4 L.Ed.2d 279 (1960); McElroy v. United States, 361 U.S. 281, 80 S.Ct. 305, 4 L.Ed.2d 282 (1960).

[175]See e.g. 18 U.S.C.A. §§3261-3267; War Crimes Act, 1991, c.13; Article 21 of the Antarctic Act, 1994, c.15 provides that "Where a United Kingdom national does or omits to do anything on any land lying south of 60 degrees South latitude and between 150 degrees West longitude and 90 degrees West longitude and that act or omission would have constituted an offence under the law of any part of the United Kingdom if it had occurred in that part, he shall be guilty of the like offence as if the act or omission had taken place in that part, and shall be liable to be proceeded against and punished accordingly".

[176]See e.g. People v. Weeren, 26 Cal.3d 654, 163 Cal.Rptr. 255, 607 P.2d 1279 (1980); Livings v. Davis, 465 So.2d 507 (Fla.1985); Commonwealth v. Gaines, 4 Va. 172 (1819); State v. Main, 16 Wis. 398 (1863); Strouther v. Commonwealth, 92 Va. 789, 22 S.E. 852 (1895); Al-Fawwaz, [2002] 1 All E.R. 545, [2002] 1 A.C. 556, [2002] 2 W.L.R. 101, [2001] U.K.H.L. 69; Sanders, [2006] E. W.C.A. Crim. 1842.

wherever it takes place originated in the principle of universality (Universalitätsprinzip)[177] of the European-Continental legal systems in conjunction with the development of the modern cogent international customs (*jus cogens*).[178]

The principle of universality does not refer to every type of offense but only to specific types that are aimed against humanity or human society. The harm to human society should be sufficiently serious so that all states would have the obligation to indict, judge, and sentence the offenders, regardless of the place or territory where offense was committed, and regardless of the national identity of the victims or the offenders. In this type of applicability the entire human society is considered to be one entity, committed to the fight against this type of delinquency. An individual state that enforces its domestic criminal norm through extraterritorial universal applicability is considered to be the representative of the entire human society.[179]

Development of the principle of universality in its modern form contributed to weakening the concept of the state as an atomistic sovereign, a concept that was traditional in international law and international relations until World War II. The principle of universality enables the domestic sovereign to apply its domestic substantive criminal norm to factual events occurring outside its territorial boundaries. In certain cases, it not only enables the sovereign to do that but compels it to apply its domestic substantive criminal norm to factual events occurring outside its territorial boundaries.[180]

As part of the general character, the principle of universality may be relevant only to certain specific offenses aimed at harming humanity *per se*. These offenses have been identified internationally as part of the cogent international custom (*jus cogens*). Most of the specific offenses have been inscribed in international declarative covenants, which are not constitutive because they do not create new offenses, but only declare the reality of existing offenses. Through worldwide acceptance of the cogent international customs (*jus cogens*), the principle of universality has been accepted also by the Anglo-American legal systems.[181]

The core of these offenses, which have been recognized as aimed against humanity and human society, are the offenses of piracy,[182] war crimes, crimes

---

[177]BGH 27, 30.

[178]FIONA MCKAY, UNIVERSAL JURISDICTION IN EUROPE (1999).

[179]Cherif M. Bassiouni, *Universal Jurisdiction for International Crimes: Historical Perspectives and Contemporary Practice*, 42 VA. J. INT'L L. 81, 88 (2001).

[180]Kenneth C. Randall, *Universal Jurisdiction under International Law*, 66 TEX. L. REV. 785 (1988); Bartram S. Brown, *The Evolving Concept of Universal Jurisdiction*, 35 NEW ENG. L. REV. 383 (2001).

[181]United States v. Smith, 18 U.S. 153, 5 L.Ed. 57 (1820); Bow Street Metropolitan Stipendiary Magistrate, [2000] 1 A.C. 147, [1999] 2 All E.R. 97, [1999] 2 W.L.R. 827.

[182]Dawson, (1696) 13 St.Tr. 451; The Magellan Pirates, (1853) 1 Sp.Ecc.&Ad. 81, 164 E.R. 47; Harmony v. United States, 43 U.S. 210, 11 L.Ed. 239 (1844); Athens Maritime Enterprises Corporation v. Hellenic Mutual War Risks Association (Bermuda) Ltd., [1983] Q.B. 647, [1983] 1 All E.R. 590, [1983] 2 W.L.R. 425.

against humanity, and crimes against peace.[183] Later, international covenants have added to the core offenses several less serious offenses, including slave trade,[184] drug trade,[185] torture by the state,[186] air terrorism,[187] maritime terrorism,[188] and the use of unconventional weapons.[189] These offenses are deemed to cause harm to humanity, human society, and its way of life. The list of offenses is not permanent and changes according to the dynamic development of international delinquency.

4.4 Conflict of Laws Based on the Applicability of the Criminal Norm in Place

4.4.1 The General Rule

It is almost inevitable that the various options of applicability of the criminal norm in place would create situations in which laws are in conflict with each other and given norms contradict others (conflict of laws). The relevant question in these situations is which norm governs and should be followed.[190] The principle of legality in criminal law accommodates four types of situations in which laws conflict, one type for every secondary principle. As far as the applicability of the criminal norm in place is concerned (the third secondary principle), conflicting laws have to do with norms of different applicability in place that contradict one another, i.e., when a domestic criminal norm contradicts a foreign criminal norm, and both may be applicable to a specific case.

The relevant question about conflicting laws based on applicability of the criminal norm in place concerns situations in which several criminal norms (some domestic and some foreign) are applicable to the same case (factual event

[183] Sawoniuk, [2000] 2 Cr. App. Rep. 220, [2000] Crim. L.R. 506; Convention on the Prevention and Punishment of the Crime of Genocide, 1948; Hague Convention (IV) respecting the Laws and Customs of War on Land and its annex: Regulations concerning the Laws and Customs of War on Land, 1907.

[184] Hirst, *supra* note 3, at pp. 246–247.

[185] United States v. Martinez-Hidalgo, 993 F.2d 1052 (3rd Cir.1993); United States v. Cardales, 168 F.3d 548 (1st Cir.1999).

[186] Bow Street Metropolitan Stipendiary Magistrate, [2000] 1 A.C. 147, [1999] 2 All E.R. 97, [1999] 2 W.L.R. 827.

[187] Martin, [1956] 2 Q.B. 272, [1956] 2 All E.R. 86, [1956] 2 W.L.R. 975, 120 J.P. 255, 40 Cr. App. Rep. 68; Naylor, [1962] 2 Q.B. 527, [1961] 2 All E.R. 932, [1961] 3 W.L.R. 898, 45 Cr. App. Rep. 69, 125 J.P. 603; Moussa, [1983] Crim. L.R. 618; Hindawi, (1988) 10 Cr. App. Rep. 104; Hussain, [1999] Crim. L.R. 570.

[188] Malvina Halberstam, *Terrorism on the High Seas: The Achille Lauro, Piracy and the IMO Convention on Maritime Safety*, 82 AM. J. INT'L L. 269 (1988).

[189] Hirst, *supra* note 119, at pp. 250–254.

[190] LAWRENCE COLLINS, DICEY AND MORRIS THE CONFLICT OF LAWS I 32 (13th ed., 2000).

or judicial decision). In these situations the question is which of the several norms should be applied to the case at hand. The answer is given in two stages. In the first stage we eliminate all the irrelevant criminal norms that do not apply in place to the event. In the second stage we decide which of the remaining criminal norms is the correct one that should be applied to the event.

In the first stage, irrelevant criminal norms are eliminated based on the following three questions about the exact type of the criminal norm:

(1) Is the criminal norm procedural or substantive?
(2) Is the criminal norm domestic or foreign?
(3) Is the criminal norm locally restricted or not restricted?

The answers to the three questions are essential for choosing the correct rule of applicability in place, as discussed above.[191] When several criminal norms appear to apply to a given case, each criminal norm is characterized by a certain applicability in place. The rule that determines which criminal norm must be applied in this situation, and which one rejected, can be stated in Latin as follows:

lex interior derogat exteriori

In English translation this means that domestic law prevails over foreign law.[192] Thus, for a domestic court, the domestic criminal norm always receives high priority for its application. Foreign criminal norms are not applicable in the domestic court, and the court may consider these norms only if it is allowed or obligated by domestic law to do so.[193] Naturally, in different domestic courts the relevant applicable criminal norm is different, albeit related to the same factual event.

For example, a Turkish resident murders his wife, also a Turkish resident, in Germany, in the name of "family honor." Because the factual event of homicide occurred in Germany, German domestic substantive criminal norm is applicable

[191] Above at Sects. 4.2.1 and 4.3.1.

[192] Ogden v. Folliot, (1790) 3 T.R. 726; Lynch v. Paraguay Provisional Government, [1861–1873] All E.R. 934, [1861–73] All E.R. 934; Huntington v. Attrill, [1893] A.C. 150; Attorney General for Canada v. Schulze, (1901) 9 S.L.T. 4; Raulin v. Fischer, [1911] 2 K.B. 93; Banco De Vizcaya v. Don Alfonso De Borbon Y Austria, [1934] All E.R. 555, [1935] 1 K.B. 140; 104 L.J.K.B. 46;151 L.T. 499; 50 T.L.R. 284; 78 Sol.Jo. 224; Frankfurter v. W. L. Exner Ltd., [1947] Ch. 629; Novello v. Hinrischen Edition Ltd., [1951] Ch. 595; Schemmer v. Property Resources Ltd., [1975] Ch. 273; Attorney General of New Zealand v. Ortiz, [1984] 1 A.C. 1, [1983] 2 W.L.R. 809, [1983] 2 All E. R. 93; United States of America v. Inkley, [1989] Q.B. 255, [1988] 3 W.L.R. 304, [1988] 3 All E. R. 144; Larkins v. N.U.M., [1985] I.R. 671; Bank of Ireland v. Meeneghan, [1994] 3 I.R. 111.

[193] *In re* The Antelope, (1825) 10 Wheat. 66: "The common law considers crimes as altogether local, and cognisable and punishable exclusively in the country where they are committed… The courts of no country execute the penal laws of another"; State v. Pelican Insurance Co., 127 U.S. 265, 8 S.Ct. 1370, 32 L.Ed. 239 (1888); SA Consortium General Textiles v. Sun & Sand Agencies Ltd., [1978] Q.B. 279, [1978] 2 All E.R. 339, [1978] 2 W.L.R. 1.

through territorial applicability in German courts. But because the victim is a Turkish resident, Turkish law is applicable in Turkish courts through extraterritorial passive personality applicability, and because the offender is a Turkish resident, Turkish law is applicable in Turkish courts through extraterritorial active personality applicability. If the criminal norms differ in their relation to the issue of "family honor" (accepting or rejecting it as a cultural defense), the question of applicability can be crucial.

In this case, because of the senior status of territoriality,[194] the German courts and German laws have the high priority in applying the German domestic criminal norm. If the defendant demands the application of the Turkish criminal norm, the general rule of *lex interior derogat exteriori* leads to rejection of the claim. But when the territorial applicability is irrelevant, and the only relevant types of applicability in place are extraterritorial, the most relevant extraterritorial applicability is the one with the highest linkage to the relevant state. The extraterritorial protective applicability has the highest linkage, followed by the extraterritorial passive personality applicability, the extraterritorial active personality applicability, and at last the extraterritorial universal applicability, which has the lowest linkage in the given context.

For example, a Turkish resident marries a German resident and kills her in the name of "family honor" in Antarctica, which is not within the territorial borders of any state. The Turkish criminal norm may be applicable through extraterritorial active personality applicability because the offender is a Turkish resident. But the German criminal norm may also be applicable through extraterritorial passive personality applicability, because the victim is a German resident. In this case, the more appropriate criminal norm is the German norm, because the extraterritorial passive personality applicability has a higher linkage to the state (Germany) than does the extraterritorial active personality applicability (Turkey).

Nevertheless, if the case is tried in a Turkish court (because the indictment was issued there, or the offender was apprehended there and not extradited to Germany), the Turkish court applies the Turkish criminal norm (substantive and procedural) as a domestic norm. Germany cannot prohibit Turkey from deciding judicially in this case, because the international law does not provide for such prohibition. Practically, therefore, the first state to indict the offender determines the criminal norm that applies in a given case.

4.4.2 International Cooperation and the Extraterritorial Vicarious Applicability

Conflict of laws in the applicability of the criminal norm in place can be resolved by international cooperation and extraterritorial vicarious applicability. Under a

[194] Above at Sect. 4.3.2.1.

mutual international consent between the relevant states, the domestic state can give up its jurisdiction over the case in favor of another state. Which state gives up jurisdiction is determined by various factors having to do with the effectiveness of indictment in a given state, the necessity for extradition, its chance to succeed, and so on.[195]

Such international cooperation between the states enables a foreign state to indict, judge, and sentence an offender *for* the domestic state, creating a situation of extraterritorial vicarious applicability. International cooperation between states is not an obligation, and it is entirely voluntary. International cooperation in matters of this type is settled by international covenants, whether bilateral or multilateral, depending on the interests of the states involved. Most states use extraterritorial vicarious applicability for their mutual benefit.[196]

For example, a British resident has committed an offense in the UK and escapes to Belgium. The offender is caught in Belgium, and the UK begins international proceedings of extradition. These proceedings, however, may last a long time and could restrict British authorities in the indictment, judging, and sentencing of the offender. As a result, the UK may give up its jurisdiction over the case in favor of Belgium, and enable Belgium to indict, judge, and sentence the offender under the domestic Belgian criminal norm (procedural and substantive). Such extraterritorial vicarious applicability, in which Belgium functions as the long arm of the UK, can be made possible through international cooperation.

---

[195]Compare with article 7(2)(2) of the German penal code that provides: "(2) Für andere Taten, die im Ausland begangen werden, gilt das deutsche Strafrecht, wenn die Tat am Tatort mit Strafe bedroht ist oder der Tatort keiner Strafgewalt unterliegt und wenn der Täter (1)...; (2) zur Zeit der Tat Ausländer war, im Inland betroffen und, obwohl das Auslieferungsgesetz seine Auslieferung nach der Art der Tat zuließe, nicht ausgeliefert wird, weil ein Auslieferungsersuchen innerhalb angemessener Frist nicht gestellt oder abgelehnt wird oder die Auslieferung nicht ausführbar ist".

[196]See e.g. European Convention on the Supervision of Conditionally Sentenced or Conditionally Released Offenders, [1964] European Treaty Series No. 51; European Convention on the Punishment of Road Traffic Offences, [1964] European Treaty Series No. 52; European Convention on the International Validity of Criminal Judgments, [1970] European Treaty Series No. 70; European Convention on the Transfer of Proceedings in Criminal Matters, [1972] European Treaty Series No. 73; European Convention on Mutual Assistance in Criminal Matters.

Chapter 5
Interpretation of the Criminal Norm

Contents

The fourth secondary principle of the principle of legality in criminal law concerns the interpretation of the criminal norm, which is required for its legitimacy as a legal social control. This secondary principle refers to criminal norms as verbal formulations and addresses the issues of their application through interpretation.

5.1 Structure of Interpretation of the Criminal Norm

The interpretation of the criminal norm takes place in two stages. The first stage involves the formulation of the criminal norm *ex ante* by the relevant authority. In most legal systems it is the legislator who formulates the criminal norm according to certain standards embodied in the first stage of interpretation. This is an *ex ante* stage because the legislator must consider the standards while formulating the criminal norm. These are substantive standards, related to the interpretation of the

G. Hallevy, *A Modern Treatise on the Principle of Legality in Criminal Law*,
DOI 10.1007/978-3-642-13714-3_5, © Springer-Verlag Berlin Heidelberg 2010

criminal norm (we discussed earlier the non-substantive standards having to do with the structure of the criminal norm).[1]

There are four substantive standards of formulation of the criminal norm applicable at the first stage of interpretation and functioning as substantive rules:

(1) Generality
(2) Feasibility
(3) Clarity and precision
(4) Relevance of external non-criminal norms

The four rules are discussed below.[2]

The second stage of interpretation involves the application of the criminal norm (*ex post*) by the relevant authority. In most legal systems the relevant authority for the application of the criminal law is the court. The *ex post* stage of interpretation is the stage of implementation. After the specific criminal norm has been formulated, enacted, and validated, it is applied to relevant cases by the courts. To properly implement the legal social control over individuals, the courts that apply the criminal norm must interpret it.

The second stage of interpretation (*ex post*) is relevant to the applicability of the norm to specific cases. Consider a criminal norm that aggravates the punishment of a civil servant convicted for theft, compared with the punishment imposed on a non-civil servant for the same offense. Now consider a case brought before the court in which an employee of a private corporation that is working for a government ministry is convicted of theft committed on the premises of the ministry, while the employee was at work. Is the employee considered to be a civil servant for the purposes of the applicability of this criminal norm? This is a question of interpretation, part of the second (*ex post*) stage.

The two stages of interpretation of the criminal norm govern the structure of interpretation embodied in the fourth secondary principle of the principle of legality, as described schematically in Fig. 5.1 below.

The two stages are discussed below.

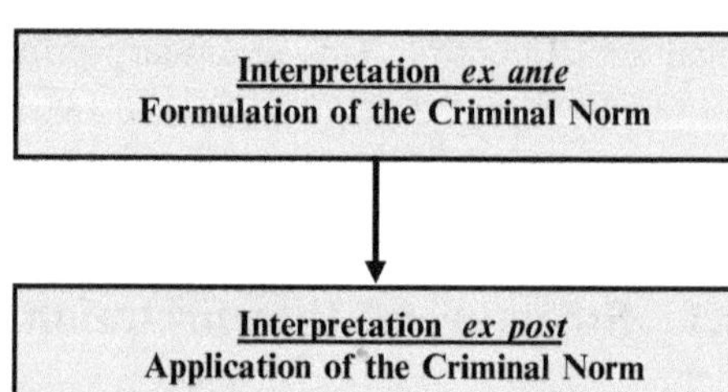

Fig. 5.1 Structure of interpretation of the criminal norm

[1]See above at Sects. 2.1.1 and 2.1.2.

[2]Hereinafter at Sects. 5.2.1–5.2.4.

5.2 Rules of Formulation of the Criminal Norm

When we examined the structure of the substantive criminal norm, we found that it consisted of **a valid conditional clause the result of which was a criminal sanction.**[3] The rules of formulation of the criminal norm examine the criminal norm substantively. The rules form the first stage of interpretation of the criminal norm, which includes four *ex ante* rules of interpretation: generality, feasibility, clarity and precision, and the relevance of external non-criminal norms.

5.2.1 Generality

The formulation rule of generality is not exclusive to the criminal norm, and may relate to any legal norm, but for criminal norms it is a mandatory rule because it has a special significance in preventing the persecution of specific individuals and minorities through application of the criminal norm. The rule of generality may be stated as follows:

The criminal norm must be in a general manner and must not refer to specific individuals.

There are two reasons for the rule of generality. First is modern society's commitment to equality among all individuals. A generally formulated criminal norm creates one law for all and prevents discrimination of specific individuals in the exercise of legal social control.[4] The second reason is that a general formulation of the criminal norm requires broad examination of all relevant considerations in order to define a policy upon which the criminal norm is based and which the norm reflects. Observing the rule of generality for these two reasons enables society to judge the characters of its criminal norms fairly.[5]

Examination of the generality of a norm is a substantive one based on the content of the criminal norm, and not a technical examination of its formulation. When a criminal norm is formulated using general definitions but in reality these are addressed to specific individuals or portions of the public, the norm is not considered to be a legitimately general one. For example, if in a given state lives a person

[3]Above at Sects. 2.1.1 and 2.1.2.

[4]Thomas P. Lewis, *The Sit-In Cases: Great Expectations*, 1963 Supreme Court Rev. 101, 110 (1963).

[5]Michael A. Fitts, *Can Ignorance Be Bliss? Imperfect Information as a Positive Influence in Political Institutions*, 88 Mich. L. Rev. 917 (1990); Adrian Vermeule, *Veil of Ignorance Rules in Constitutional Law*, 111 Yale L. J. 399 (2001).

(and only one) who is responsible for the death of more than a thousand people in a terror attack, and a criminal norm enacted after the terror attack decrees that "whoever commits a terror attack that causes the death of more than one thousand people shall not be entitled to amnesty," such a norm cannot be considered to be a general one because when the norm was enacted it could be applied to only one person. Although the name of the individual is not explicitly mentioned, there is no doubt that the norm is aimed specifically at this specific person. Such a criminal norm cannot be considered a legitimate general criminal norm. The criminal content of the norm must be examined from the point of view of its substance and not its technical linguistic formulation.

In general, when a criminal norm is aimed at an unspecified portion of the public, the rule of generality is not an issue. For example, when a criminal norm is defined as "whoever steals, shall be punished..." it is aimed at an unspecified portion of the public, because anyone can steal, regardless of any individual characteristics. A criminal norm of this type cannot be considered as discriminatory against anyone. But when a criminal norm is aimed at a specified portion of the public, the relevant question is whether specification of a given portion of the public contradicts the rule of generality.

For example, in some legal systems there is an explicit prohibition against infanticide during a short period after the birth of the infant, aimed at mothers: if the mother kills her newborn within a certain time after birth, she is not indicted for murder or manslaughter but for infanticide, which carries a lower maximum penalty than do murder or manslaughter. The reason for mitigating punishment in the case of infanticide lies with the recognition of the widespread symptom of postpartum depression. Because infanticide is aimed only at mothers and only for a short period of time after birth, it is not a general criminal norm.

Despite not being a general criminal norm, infanticide is considered to be a legitimate criminal norm in these legal systems. This type of legal provision reflects a social policy that treats a portion of the public differently based on a relevant criterion. It may not be fair to judge a mother suffering from postpartum depression as if she were a hired professional assassin. This is the reason for the recognition of such defenses *in personam* as infancy and insanity.[6] Naturally, the criterion used in the discrimination should be relevant to the criminal liability in question in a given society. If the criterion is not relevant, the legal provision is not legitimate. For example, the following formulation of an offense would not be legitimate: "A person who commits a robbery shall be punished by up to ten years of

[6]See e.g. Frederick Woodbridge, *Physical and Mental Infancy in the Criminal Law*, 87 U. Pa. L. Rev. 426 (1939); A.W.G. Kean, *The History of the Criminal Liability of Children*, 53 L. Q. Rev. 364 (1937); Benjamin B. Sendor, *Crime as Communication: An Interpretive Theory of the Insanity Defense and the Mental Elements of Crime*, 74 Geo. L. J. 1371, 1380 (1986); Joseph H. Rodriguez, Laura M. LeWinn and Michael L. Perlin, *The Insanity Defense Under Siege: Legislative Assaults and Legal Rejoinders*, 14 Rutgers L. J. 397, 406–407 (1983); Homer D. Crotty, *The History of Insanity as a Defence to Crime in English Common Law*, 12 Cal. L. Rev. 105 (1924).

imprisonment, but if the offender is Catholic, he shall be punished by up to twenty years of imprisonment."

A criminal norm that contradicts the rule of generality is not considered legitimate or valid, the court is not allowed to apply it, and the social legal control cannot be implemented through such a criminal norm. Legislators, therefore, have an incentive to formulate criminal norms in a general manner, with equal treatment of all individuals, and after considering all relevant factors for the formulation of an appropriate social policy.

5.2.2 *Feasibility*

The formulation rule of feasibility refers to the practicability and physical possibility of implementing the criminal norm. Society should not demand, through criminal norms, that individuals do the impossible or the impractical.[7] Although the formulation rule of feasibility is not exclusive to the criminal norm, this rule is crucial in criminal law because as part of the implementation of the legal social control, the individual is punished for breaching a criminal norm.

The major question for the formulation rule of feasibility is what is considered possible and impossible in a criminal norm. The question is not a simple one because of differences in the physical and mental capabilities of individuals. For example, the prohibition against drug use can be regarded as possible and reasonable for most people, but for persons addicted to drugs it may be considered to be impossible to observe.

There may be criminal norms that are not suitable for *all* individuals in a given society, therefore feasibility cannot be examined based on the capabilities of the entire population. In most cases, a norm is sufficiently appropriate if most of the population considers that the criminal norm contains a possible prohibition. Thus, although in the eyes of a person addicted to drugs the prohibition against drug use is impossible to observe, for most individuals the prohibition is possible to observe, and most individuals have no difficulty abiding by it.

A criminal norm can be considered feasible not only if the public is already implementing it, but based on the potential of the public to implement it. At times, the standard of examination is an objective one, taking into account the abilities of a "reasonable person" or of an "average person," but the potential for implementing a norm is examined not necessarily based on its existing implementation. In this way, it is possible to examine not only existing prohibitions within the criminal norm, but new ones as well. Furthermore, to fulfill its educational function of directing the daily social behavior of the public, the criminal law must embody a criminal norm to which the public can potentially adhere, so that the criminal norm can fulfill its mission.

---

[7]Lon L. Fuller, The Morality of Law 46–91 (1964).

Within a given society the potential for adhering to various types of criminal norms differs. In some totalitarian societies, individuals were forced to report on their relatives' political opinions to the authorities, if these opinions were in conflict with the official ideology.[8] If most individuals in society regard their loyalty to the state to take precedence over their loyalty to their families, this type of norm can be regarded as possible and reasonable, but in societies in which individuals consider their families to take precedence over the state, the same norm is regarded as impossible, and therefore illegitimate.

An impossible criminal norm cannot implement the legal social control efficiently, and it is likely that individuals will attempt to breach the prohibition without being discovered. In these societies, a delinquent sub-culture is likely to develop, with individuals losing their trust in the authorities and the regime. Thus, the social consequences of an impossible criminal norm are opposite to those that society hoped to achieve. Criminal norms should therefore be examined with respect to the formulation rule of feasibility by taking into account the physical and mental capabilities of the individuals subject to the criminal norm.

5.2.3 Clarity and Precision

Western legal systems have developed a formulation rule of clarity and precision of the criminal norm consistent with the Latin maxim of *nullum crimen sine lege certa* (there is no crime without a precise law). In the European-Continental legal systems the requirement of clarity and precision in the formulation of the criminal norm has been imposed on the legislator with respect to the content of criminal norms (Bestimmtheitsgebot). If a criminal norm had been formulated vaguely, the preferred interpretation was the one most lenient for the individual.[9] In rare cases, when a criminal norm was too vague to be applied, it was abolished.[10] In the Anglo-American legal systems, the praxis is that vague criminal norms are not implemented.[11] The discretion in the implementation of vague norms in the Anglo-American legal systems is granted to the judicial authorities, as part of the power of judicial review.[12]

---

[8]Herbert L.A. Hart, *Positivism and the Separation of Law and Morals*, 71 Harv. L. Rev. 593 (1958).

[9]BVerfGE 26, 41, 43; BVerfGE 48, 48, 56; BGH St 30, 285, 287.

[10]BayVGH 4 (1951) II 194: "...gegen die öffentliche Ordnung verstößt oder gegen die Interessen der alliierten Streitkräfte oder eines ihrer Mitglieder handelt".

[11]Ralph W. Aigler, *Legislation in Vague or General Terms*, 21 Mich. L. Rev. 831 (1923); United States v. Brewer, 139 U.S. 278, 11 S.Ct. 538, 35 L.Ed. 190 (1891).

[12]United States v. Reese, 92 U.S. 214, 23 L.Ed. 563 (1876); James v. Bowman, 190 U.S. 127, 23 S. Ct. 678, 47 L.Ed. 979 (1903); United States v. Evans, 333 U.S. 483, 68 S.Ct. 634, 92 L.Ed. 823 (1948).

The American judicial review produced the doctrine of **void-for-vagueness**, which directed courts to declare vague criminal norms as void.[13] The legal reason for this doctrine is that vague criminal norms, that a reasonable person cannot understand,[14] contradict the American constitution.[15] The vagueness of the criminal norm refers to three aspects in American law:

(1) Vagueness in the definition of the perpetrators[16]
(2) Vagueness of the conduct included in the criminal norm[17]
(3) Vagueness of the penalties included in the criminal norm[18]

The doctrine of void-for-vagueness has been applied in American criminal law to various types of criminal norms from all legitimate sources, including legislation.[19] The underlying ruling in American criminal law is that an individual's life, freedom, or property cannot taken by the state on the basis of speculations about the meaning of the criminal norm.[20]

The dominant rationale of modern criminal law in the formulation rule of clarity and precision refers to the fair notice requirement necessary for the efficient implementation of the criminal norm. A vague criminal norm does not provide fair notice to the individual in the planning of future conduct. When a criminal norm is vague, unclear, and not sufficiently precise, the discretion of state authorities in

[13]Ernst Freund, *The Use of Indefinite Terms in Statutes*, 30 Yale L. J. 437 (1921); Rex A. Collings Jr., *Unconstitutional Uncertainty – An Appraisal*, 40 Cornell L. Q. 195 (1955); Robert Batey, *Vagueness and the Construction of Criminal Statutes – Balancing Acts*, 5 Va. J. Soc. Pol'y & L. 1 (1997).

[14]Connally v. General Constr. Co., 269 U.S. 385, 46 S.Ct. 126, 70 L.Ed. 322 (1926).

[15]The contradiction is to the sixth amendment of the American constitution which provides that "[i]n all criminal prosecutions, the accused shall enjoy the right to a speedy and public trial, by an impartial jury of the State and district wherein the crime shall have been committed, which district shall have been previously ascertained by law, and **to be informed of the nature and cause of the accusation**; to be confronted with the witnesses against him; to have compulsory process for obtaining witnesses in his favor, and to have the Assistance of Counsel for his defense" (emphasis not in original); See more in Yu Cong Eng v. Trinidad, 271 U.S. 500, 46 S.Ct. 619, 70 L.Ed. 1059 (1926); United States v. L. Cohen Grocery Co., 255 U.S. 81, 41 S.Ct. 298, 65 L.Ed. 516 (1921).

[16]Lanzetta v. New Jersey, 306 U.S. 451, 59 S.Ct. 618, 83 L.Ed. 888 (1939).

[17]Winters v. New York, 333 U.S. 507, 68 S.Ct. 665, 92 L.Ed. 840 (1948); Interstate Circuit, Inc. v. City of Dallas, 390 U.S. 676, 88 S.Ct. 1298, 20 L.Ed.2d 225 (1968); Colautti v. Franklin, 439 U.S. 379, 99 S.Ct. 675, 58 L.Ed.2d 596 (1979).

[18]United States v. Evans, 333 U.S. 483, 68 S.Ct. 634, 92 L.Ed. 823 (1948).

[19]Winters v. New York, 333 U.S. 507, 68 S.Ct. 665, 92 L.Ed. 840 (1948); Ashton v. Kentucky, 384 U.S. 195, 86 S.Ct. 1407, 16 L.Ed.2d 469 (1966); M. Kraus & Bros. v. United States, 327 U.S. 614, 66 S.Ct. 705, 90 L.Ed. 894 (1946); United States v. Mersky, 361 U.S. 431, 80 S.Ct. 459, 4 L.Ed.2d 423 (1960).

[20]In *Lanzetta*, *supra* note 16, the court ruled that "[n]o one may be required at peril of life, liberty or property to speculate as to the meaning of penal statutes. All are entitled to be informed as to what the State commands or forbids".

its implementation is too wide – an undesirable situation in modern society.[21] The criminal norm should be formulated with sufficient clarity and precision for the average individual to be able to understand and follow it.[22]

Nevertheless, in the course of the development of criminal law in modern times, the use of legal terminology has become widespread and legitimate despite the fact that the average person is not familiar with it. In most legal systems, the professional legal terminology has been accepted as legitimate in the formulation of criminal norms, even if the average person is not familiar with certain legal terms.[23] But if the courts still considered given norms to be vague, they abolished criminal norms and exonerated defendants. Abolition of criminal norms is common especially in Anglo-American courts, whereas exoneration is preferred by European-Continental courts.

Occasionally, clarity and precision in the formulation of a criminal norm is a question of degree. Modern legal systems recognize the fact that it is impossible to achieve absolute precision through common, everyday language, and that there are few words of mathematical precision.[24] For example, the term "aircraft" can refer to many types of crafts and devices that are widely different from one another. To "decode" specific terms and apply them to individual cases, the courts must conduct processes of induction and deduction.[25] At times, the judicial decision is not guided by mere linguistic interpretation, but must take into account legal and social considerations as well.[26]

Furthermore, it is assumed that the legislator of the criminal norm cannot predict *all* possible situations that may be subjected to a given criminal norm, *ex ante*. Courts do not abolish or ignore criminal norms merely because the individual case brought before them falls in the gray area of the norm.[27] But when a criminal norm is too broad in its definition of a prohibition, its formulation may be wrong

[21]City of Chicago v. Morales, 527 U.S. 41, 119 S.Ct. 1849, 144 L.Ed.2d 67 (1999); Kolender v. Lawson, 461 U.S. 352, 103 S.Ct. 1855, 75 L.Ed.2d 903 (1983); Palmer v. City of Euclid, 402 U.S. 544, 91 S.Ct. 1563, 29 L.Ed.2d 98 (1971); Shuttlesworth v. City of Birmingham, 382 U.S. 87, 86 S. Ct. 211, 15 L.Ed.2d 176 (1965); BVerfGE 25, 269, 285; BVerfGE 26, 42; BVerfGE 37, 207; BVerfGE 57, 250, 262; Volker Krey, Deutsches Strafrecht Allgemeiner Teil, Teil I: Grundlagen 92–93 (2002); Hans-Heinrich Jescheck und Thomas Weigend, Lehrbuch des Strafrechts – Allgemeiner Teil 136–137 (Auf., 1996).

[22]Cline v. Frink Dairy Co., 274 U.S. 445, 47 S.Ct. 681, 71 L.Ed. 1146 (1927).

[23]United States v. Lanier, 520 U.S. 259, 117 S.Ct. 1219, 137 L.Ed.2d 432 (1997); Screws v. United States, 325 U.S. 91, 65 S.Ct. 1031, 89 L.Ed. 1495 (1945); Omaechevarria v. Idaho, 246 U.S. 343, 38 S.Ct. 323, 62 L.Ed. 763 (1918).

[24]In Grayned v. City of Rockford, 408 U.S. 104, 92 S.Ct. 2294, 33 L.Ed.2d 222 (1972) the court ruled that "[c]ondemned to the use of words, we can never expect mathematical certainty from our language".

[25]Hereinafter at Sect. 5.3.3.

[26]McBoyle v. United States, 283 U.S. 25, 51 S.Ct. 340, 75 L.Ed. 816 (1931).

[27]United States v. National Dairy Products Corp., 372 U.S. 29, 83 S.Ct. 594, 9 L.Ed.2d 561 (1963); United States v. Harriss, 347 U.S. 612, 74 S.Ct. 808, 98 L.Ed. 989 (1954).

according to modern concepts of the liberal state, whereby the state should limit itself to enacting criminal norms only when necessary.

As a result, the clarity and precision of a criminal norm are not examined only at the linguistic level but also by applying legal and social considerations with respect to the purpose and function of the criminal norm. For example, if the criminal norm is formulated as "whoever causes a person's death..." it is sufficiently clear and precise as long as the exact way in which the death occurred is irrelevant. But if the method by which death was caused is significant, this formulation is vague. A specific issue may or may not be significant for the imposition of criminal liability, according to the purpose of the given norm.

5.2.4 Relevance of Non-Criminal Norms

In many cases the criminal norm is independent and does not require any non-criminal norm for its application or implementation. In most legal systems, the criminal norms of homicide do not require any non-criminal norms in order to impose criminal liability. But there are two types of criminal norms that rely on non-criminal norms for the imposition of criminal liability. In one type, a criminal clause is added to a non-criminal norm to make the entire norm more effective under a criminal sanction. In this type of criminal norm, the non-criminal norm is absorbed into the criminal norm and becomes part of it.[28]

In the second type, the criminal norm refers to a non-criminal norm explicitly or implicitly. For example, in most legal systems the definition of an omission refers to a breach of duty imposed by the law or by a contract.[29] The term "law" in this definition is not restricted to criminal law, and of course "contract" is not necessarily a criminal contract. Therefore, the criminal norm references a non-criminal term. Another example is the use of the term "unlawfully" in the definition of specific offenses,[30] with reference to both criminal and non-criminal norms violated by the offensive conduct. In this type of criminal norm as well, the non-criminal norm is absorbed into the criminal norm and becomes part of it.

In all other cases, the non-criminal norm is irrelevant to criminal law in general and to specific criminal norms. Even if the non-criminal norm could simplify the

[28]See e.g. article 23 of the Private Security Industry Act, 2001, c.12.

[29]See e.g. in Smith, (1869) 11 Cox C.C. 210; State v. Harrison, 107 N.J.L. 213, 152 A. 867 (1931); State v. Benton, 38 Del. 1, 187 A. 609 (1936); Davis v. Commonwealth, 230 Va. 201, 335 S.E.2d 375 (1985); People v. Wong, 182 A.D.2d 98, 588 N.Y.S.2d 119 (1992); Commonwealth v. Pestinikas, 421 Pa.Super. 371, 617 A.2d 1339 (1992); State v. O'Brian, 32 N.J.L. 169 (1867); Anderson v. State, 27 Tex.App. 177, 11 S.W. 33, 3 L.R.A. 644, 11 Am.St.Rep. 189 (1889).

[30]See e.g. 228(2) of the Marine and Coastal Access Act, 2009, c.23 that provides: "A person who **unlawfully** takes or destroys, or attempts to take or destroy, any fish in water which is private property or in which there is any private right of fishery shall on summary conviction be liable to a fine not exceeding level 5 on the standard scale" (emphasis not in original).

understanding and implementation of the criminal norm, it is external to criminal law and cannot be exercised within it. The reason for this separation lies in the difference between criminal law and all other spheres of law with respect to the implementation of the legal social control. For a non-criminal norm to become relevant in criminal law, a criminal provision must explicitly reference the non-criminal norm.

The possible references in criminal norms to non-criminal norms raise two questions about place and time:

(1) Is the reference restricted to the domestic legal system, or can the criminal norm refer to non-criminal foreign norms as well?
(2) Is the reference restricted to current and valid norms in their current form, to current and valid norms including future amendments, or can the criminal norm refer to past non-criminal norms that are no longer valid?

The question of **place** has arisen especially in the Anglo-American legal systems that were based on English common law. In the current criminal norms of these legal systems there are many references to English common law as well as to other legal frameworks. For example, when the administration of Colorado was established, the legislators referred to the criminal code of Illinois, and "imported" it as the criminal code of Colorado.[31] In most legal systems legislators of the criminal norm can refer to all types of criminal norms, domestic or foreign, and "import" them into the domestic criminal norm.[32]

Moreover, it was recognized that acceptance of a foreign criminal norm includes the "importation" of the foreign interpretation relevant to the norm,[33] unless explicitly prohibited by the domestic sovereign.[34] Acceptance of foreign criminal norms is not restricted to final judicial decisions or statutes, but all sources may be considered. For example, the American model of the penal code has been accepted as an interpretive legal source in several states, even if the criminal norm had been enacted before the model penal code, and even if the model penal code is formally not more than a bill.[35] This has also been accepted with respect to the working papers of the foreign criminal norm.[36]

The question of **time** has arisen especially in cases in which the external norm has been amended, and the amendment is significant to the criminal liability defined by the referring criminal norm. This question has been answered in several cases of private international law, where a reference to a foreign or domestic law includes all

---

[31] WAYNE R. LAFAVE, CRIMINAL LAW 100 (4th ed., 2003).

[32] Commonwealth v. Mumma, 489 Pa. 547, 414 A.2d 1026 (1980); State v. Bautista, 86 Hawaii 207, 948 P.2d 1048 (1997); Hines v. State, 40 S.W.3d 705 (Tex.App.2001).

[33] State v. Elliot, 177 Conn. 1, 411 A.2d 3 (1979); State v. Chew, 150 N.J. 30, 695 A.2d 1301 (1997); State v. Willy, 155 Or.App. 279, 963 P.2d 739 (1998).

[34] State v. Chaplain, 101 Kan. 413, 166 P. 238 (1917).

[35] State v. Ross, 573 N.W.2d 906 (Iowa 1998); State v. Olsen, 618 N.W.2d 346 (Iowa 2000).

[36] People v. Frysig, 628 P.2d 1004 (Colo.1981); State v. Burger, 590 N.W.2d 197 (N.D.1999).

future amendments unless explicitly prohibited or unless a revolutionary amendment (as opposed to a reform or even a radical amendment) has been enacted.[37] For example, the Bolshevik revolution of 1917 has been accepted as a revolutionary amendment with regard to property and contract law.

The rationale of the above solution is that amendments to the external (referenced) norm can affect the criminal (referring) norm if it is based on the external norm. When social changes amend the external norm, they should affect all norms based on it. If the domestic legislator supposes that a given criminal norm is beyond any social change, and that no social change should affect it, it must state explicitly that no amendment shall affect the criminal norm. But the dynamics of modern social life and the desire that criminal law should reflect the legal social control do affect the criminal norm, making it accept relevant social amendments.

5.3 Rules of Application of the Criminal Norm

The rules of formulation of the criminal norm, as discussed above,[38] represent the first (*ex ante*) stage of interpretation. These rules are intended for the legislator of the criminal norm, but can also affect its implementation by the courts. The second (*ex post*) stage, however, refers to the implementation of the criminal norm after the formulation has been completed. Implementation must follow certain rules aimed at ensuring that the criminal norm is applied in a way that serves as an effective legal social control.

These rules of application are intended for the authority that implements the criminal norm, which in most legal systems is the court. But the rules can affect also the legislative process and the formulation of the criminal norm *ex ante*, because the legislators are also interested in making the criminal norm most effectively applicable as a legal social control. The general structure of the second (*ex post*) stage of interpretation of the criminal norm may be described as shown in Fig. 5.2.

According to the general structure of the interpretation of the criminal norm *ex post*, there are three stages of interpretation. The first stage is one of strict interpretation that focuses on the verbal logic (*ratio verborum*) of the criminal norm and on its plain meaning. This stage incorporates the application of both the specific criminal norm and of the general principles of criminal law.[39] The *ex post* interpretation of most criminal norms ends with the first stage. In rare cases, when the verbal logic of the criminal norm is not consistent with the legal logic, it is necessary to proceed to the second stage.

In the second stage, the criminal norm is interpreted with reference to its purpose. The purpose of the criminal norm is the major criterion used to understand

---

[37] Lawrence Collins, Dicey and Morris The Conflict of Laws I I 1216, 1236 (13th ed., 2000).

[38] Above at Sect. 5.2.

[39] The first stage is discussed hereinafter at Sects. 5.3.1–5.3.4.

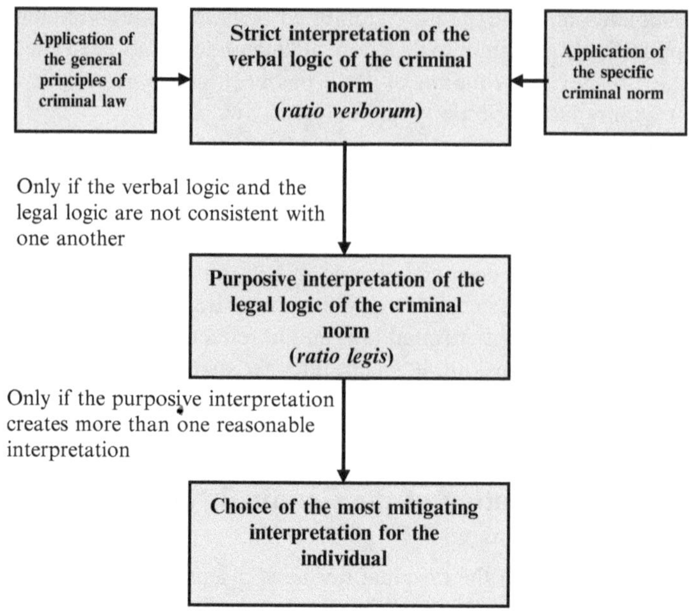

Fig. 5.2 The general structure of the interpretation of the criminal norm *ex post*

its legal logic (*ratio legis*). In the second stage, the *ratio legis* supersedes the *ratio verborum*, and if the two contradict each other, the criminal norm is interpreted according to the *ratio legis*.[40] Most criminal norms that have undergone two stages of interpretation do not proceed to the third stage. But when interpretation based on *ratio legis* creates more than one reasonable interpretation, it is necessary to proceed to the third stage, where the reasonable interpretation that is most mitigating for the individual is chosen.[41] The stages of the general structure of interpretation of the criminal norm *ex post* are discussed below.

5.3.1 Applicability of the General Principles of Criminal Law

Criminal law distinguishes between the general principles of criminal law and specific offenses. The general principles of criminal law relate to the principles of criminal liability in a general manner, and not to specific offenses. They relate to the principle of legality, the factual element requirement, the mental element requirement, the derivative criminal liability (attempt, complicity, and criminal liability of corporations), general defenses, and sentencing. The specific offenses are the

[40] The second stage is discussed hereinafter at Sect. 5.3.4.

[41] The third stage is discussed hereinafter at Sect. 5.3.6.

concrete implementation of the legal social control with respect to various issues. Together, the general principles of criminal law and the specific offenses form the criminal law.[42]

The relation between the specific offenses and the general principles of criminal law can be described as follows: the general principles of criminal law form the template into which the content of the specific offenses is flowed. The general principles of criminal law form a barrier against over-criminalization by specific offenses, because these principles require offenses to meet certain standards to be able to impose criminal liability. Offenses that do not meet the requirements of the principle of legality (the factual or the mental element requirements) are considered illegitimate, and no criminal liability can be imposed through them.

Because the general principles of criminal law are common to all offenses, it was convenient to separate the modern criminal codex into general and specific parts, with the general part containing the general principles of criminal law and the specific part the specific offenses. In this way, the general principles of criminal law are applicable to all specific offenses. In this way, the general principles of criminal law are applicable to all specific offenses, regardless of their legal source, and not only to provisions of the same criminal codex.

The legislator can indicate explicitly that portions of the general principles of criminal law are not applicable for certain offenses. Naturally, a determination of this type requires special reasoning. Deviations from the general principles of criminal law can cause legal harm to basic human rights embodied in these principles. If the legislator renounces the factual element requirement of an offense, this offense becomes a status offense that infringes on the basic human right of not being persecuted.[43] Therefore, a special argument is needed to justify such a deviation. In most cases, all offenses are subject to the general principles of criminal law.

5.3.2 *Specific and General Criminal Norms*

The Latin maxim *lex specialis derogat generali* expresses a well-known rule of interpretation in all spheres of law and in all legal systems worldwide.[44] The maxim

---

[42]LaFave, *supra* note 31, at pp. 8–9.

[43]A status offense is an offense that requires no conduct element within its factual element requirement. The offender becomes an offender not because of a certain behavior but for being in a certain status, which the individual does not necessarily control. For instance, a specific offense of "whoever **is** a catholic, shall. . ." is a status offense. This platform of offenses enables the regime persecuting individuals for what they are and not for what they do. See e.g. in *Ex Parte* Smith, 135 Mo. 223, 36 S.W. 628 (1896); Proctor v. State, 15 Okl.Cr. 338, 176 P. 771 (1918); State v. Labato, 7 N.J. 137, 80 A.2d 617 (1951); Robinson v. California, 370 U.S. 660, 82 S.Ct. 1417, 8 L.Ed.2d 758 (1962); *In re* Leory, 285 Md. 508, 403 A.2d 1226 (1979).

[44]State v. Collins, 55 Wash.2d 469, 348 P.2d 214 (1960).

states that **a special (specific) norm supersedes a general norm**. The rationale of this maxim is that general norms function as default when the law has not specified a specific norm, but when a specific norm has been formulated, the general norm is not required. The question is, how should a specific norm be defined in relation to the general norm.

Usually, a specific norm relates to a narrower legal aspect than the general norm. Naturally, "narrow" and "wide," and "specific" and "general" are relative terms. It is possible to consider a certain norm "narrow" or "specific" in relation to one norm, and "wide" or "general" in relation to another. The external elements of a special criminal norm are usually additional terms and conditions that are not part of the general criminal norm. Without these additional terms, it is the general norm that is applicable, not the special norm. The following comparison between two specific offenses illustrates this distinction:[45]

Theft	"A person who steals shall be punished..."
Theft by an employee	"An employee who steals from his employer shall be punished..."

The two offenses share the common element of stealing (conduct), but the circumstances are different. The second offense (theft by an employee) contains additional terms and conditions necessary to impose criminal liability on the individual (the individual must be an employee and the direct victim of the offense must be his employer). If these conditions are not fully met, the first offense becomes the applicable criminal norm, so that the first norm is considered to be the general norm and the second the special norm. If the norms have no element in common, neither of them may be considered to be general or special relative to each other. The specific offenses of manslaughter and theft by an employee illustrate this point:[46]

Manslaughter	"A person who kills shall be punished..."
Theft by an employee	"An employee who steals from his employer shall be punished..."

There is nothing in common between these two specific offenses, and therefore they cannot be considered as having a general vs. special relationship, and therefore *lex specialis derogat generali* does not apply to them. Legislators make use of special norms to indicate their preference for special social treatment in given cases. If no special social treatment is required, the general norm suffices.

Two specific norms can have a dual mutual relationship, in which they can alternately function as general and special norms for each other. The specific offenses of cattle theft and theft by an employee illustrate this point:

[45]See e.g. in articles 242 and 243 of the German penal code.

[46]See e.g. in article 212 of the German penal code.

Cattle theft	"A person who steals cattle shall be punished..."
Theft by an employee	"An employee who steals from his employer shall be punished..."

As far as the identity of the stolen goods is concerned, the first offense (cattle theft) is special (only cattle) and the second (theft by an employee) is general (any item). But as far as the identity of the offender is concerned, the second offense is specific (employee only) and the first is general (any person). In this case, the question is which of the norms should be considered special and which one general: for example, which of these offenses is relevant (and supersedes the other) if an employee steals cattle from his employer. The relevant authority (in most legal systems the court) would have to decide which are the dominant relevant circumstances in the case, the identity of the stolen goods or the identity of the offender, based on the factual description of the case.

If the court determines that the relevant dominant circumstances are the identity of the offender, the first offense (cattle theft) is considered general (any person) and the second one is considered special (employee only). If the court decides that the relevant dominant circumstances are the identity of the stolen goods, the first offense is considered special (only cattle) and the second one is general (any item).

5.3.3 Analogy

A common rule of interpretation of the criminal norm *ex post* is the rule against analogy, which has been accepted in most legal systems and is identified with the constitutional concepts of the rule of law and the separation of powers.[47] The rule against analogy has been developed initially in the European-Continental legal systems (Analogieverbot). It was identified with the rule of law and adhered to strictly.[48] Eventually, the Anglo-American legal systems accepted the rule as well.[49] To apply this rule, the basic term of analogy must be clarified in the context of the criminal norm.

Analogy is an interpretative method, in which a rule is applied to a case because its application to another case, based on some similarity between the cases. For example, according to the criminal norm underlying the specific offense of theft by an employee, the court punishes employees who steal from their employers in a certain way. If a case comes before the court, in which a contractor has stolen from his client, and the court exercises the analogy method, the contractor may be

[47]BGH St 35, 390, 395; BVerfGE 73, 206, 234.

[48]BVerfGE 71, 108; BGH 18, 136, 140; RG 32, 165; RG 68, 65; BGH 2, 317, 319; BGH 3, 259, 262; BGH 5, 129; BGH 7, 256; BGH 10, 375; BGH 11, 117; BGH 14, 116; BGH 23, 40; BGH 29, 129; BGH 33, 244; Jescheck und Weigend, *supra* note 21, at pp. 134–135.

[49]Jerome Hall, General Principles of Criminal Law 36–38 (2nd ed., 1960, 2005).

considered as an employee for this specific offense. If the court does not use the analogy, the specific offense is not considered to be applicable in this case. To exercise the analogy method, the court must indicate the similarity that exists between an employee and a contractor in this context.

The dilemma associated with this method of interpretation is not a trivial one. On one hand, the binding precedent praxis (*stare decisis*), which is acceptable in the Anglo-American legal systems,[50] is based on analogies. The legal ruling, which is accepted as a binding precedent, is applicable to similar cases, which are not necessarily identical.[51] On the other hand, exercising analogy as an interpretative method creates in practice a new criminal norm that applies retroactively and that has never been accepted explicitly by the legislator. The norm is applied retroactively because the court ruling relates to an existing factual event, that has already occurred, as opposed to future events which may take place from the point of the ruling onward.[52] In the example above, a new criminal norm is created in which the prohibition intended initially for employees becomes applicable to contractors as well. Most legal systems recognize the limited ability of legislators to predict *all* possible factual events and include them in relevant norms, and therefore rely on analogy to cover new situations.

The resolution of the dilemma is based on the understanding of the logical mechanism of the analogy. Application of the relevant legal rule depends on the similarity between the cases, which can be similar but not necessarily identical. Identification of the points of similarity between the cases is carried out in two separate and consecutive logical processes: induction and deduction. First, the case is redefined by induction, generalizing its relevant characteristics. Second, it is redefined by deduction, with reference to the specific characteristics of the case.

We can use the above example of the employee vs. the contractor to illustrate the mechanism at work. In this example, the problematic relevant characteristic is that of the contractor, who is not an employee. As a result, the first process (induction) redefines the term "employee" for the specific offense as a "person who has a commercial relation" or a "person who has a contractual relation" with an employer, client, etc. Next, in the complimentary process of deduction, the new term is shown to apply to a "contractor" as well because a contractor is a "person who has a commercial relation" or "person who has a contractual relation," etc. If the analogy is accepted, the specific offense becomes applicable to contractors as well as to employees. The processes are shown schematically in Fig. 5.3.

The above is a convenient example. But induction of the term "employee" does not necessarily result in the term "person who has a commercial relation," and may also produce a more general term of "person," because an employee is also a person. This raises the question of the boundaries of induction. Similarly, deduction of the term "person who has a commercial relation" does not necessarily lead to the

[50]See above at Sect. 2.2.2.4.

[51]LaBarge v. State, 74 Wis.2d 327, 246 N.W.2d 794 (1976).

[52]McCord v. People, 46 N.Y. 470 (1871); People v. Tompkins, 186 N.Y. 413, 79 N.E. 326 (1906).

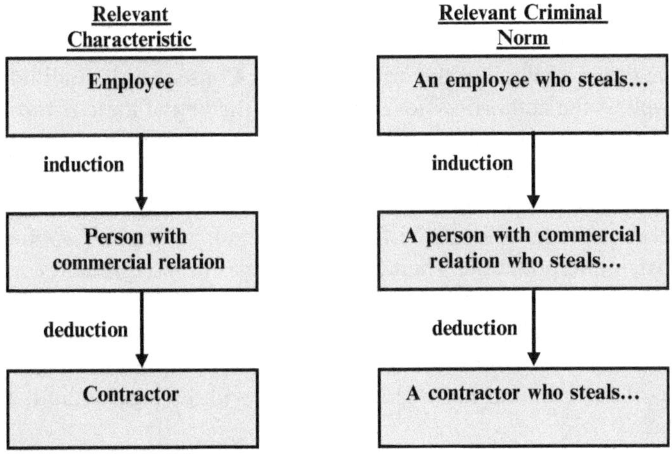

Fig. 5.3 The logical mechanism of analogy

term "contractor," and can also produce other, more removed terms such as "lessee in a rental contract," etc. The possible results of the deductive process may lead us far away from the original idea of the specific criminal norm, raising also the question of the boundaries of deduction.[53]

Most modern legal systems use strict and purposive interpretation to circumscribe the boundaries of the logical process of analogy in the interpretation of the criminal norm. According to this method, the verbal logic (*ratio verborum*) of the criminal norm is an expression of its legal logic (*ratio legis*). Therefore, the boundaries of the interpretation of the criminal norm are within the legal logic of the relevant criminal norm.[54] This solution is not exclusive to the question of analogy, induction, and deduction, and it is relevant to other questions of interpretation. Strict and purposive interpretations are discussed below.

5.3.4 Strict and Purposive Interpretations

The common approach to interpretation of the criminal norm in most legal systems worldwide combines strict and purposive interpretations.[55] According to this approach, the legal logic (*ratio legis*) of every criminal norm reflects the legal

[53]In most cases the question of deduction is wider, since there are very many general terms in which the process of deduction may be too wide for their original meaning and interpretation. E.g. the term "thing" as discussed in RG 32, 165.

[54]Krey, *supra* note 21, at pp. 72–73; ZStW 1964, 13.

[55]BVerfGE 71, 108; BGH 18, 136, 140; Jescheck und Weigend, *supra* note 21, at pp. 134–136; ACP 10987/07 State v. Cohen (unreported, March 2, 2009).

and social purposes of that norm. The author of the criminal norm must publish it, and therefore must formulate these objectives verbally, so that the verbal formulation matches the legal logic of the criminal norm. Consequently, individuals in the society as well as the authorities act according to the verbal logic (*ratio verborum*) of the criminal norm, and apply it based on its verbal logic. This is the strict interpretation.

In some rare cases, when the verbal logic does not strictly reflect the legal logic, the latter takes precedence over the former and the legal logic is applied directly, using purposive interpretation. Therefore, two stages of interpretation are involved in this approach: the first stage is that of the strict interpretation of the criminal norm based on the verbal logic; the second stage is that of the purposive interpretation based on the legal logic. In most cases, the first stage is sufficient, and only if the verbal logic of the criminal norm is inconsistent with its legal logic is the second stage needed.

In the second stage of interpretation, the legal logic of the criminal norm takes precedence over the verbal logic and it is applied in order to repair the error in the verbal formulation of the norm. In this method of interpretation, the rare application of the legal logic is not considered to be retroactive judicial legislation because the legal logic of the criminal norm has existed since its inception, albeit its verbal formulation may have been inadequate.[56]

In the first stage of interpretation of the criminal norm its verbal logic (*ratio verborum*) is examined in a strict manner, based on the plain meaning of the words that make up the relevant clause. In some legal systems this is known as the plain meaning, or literal rule.[57] Most criminal norms do not require more than the examination of the verbal logic to be applied.[58] When the verbal formulation of the criminal norm is simple, clear, and unequivocal, the courts must adhere to the plain formulation and implement it,[59] even if the court does not accept the rationale of the criminal norm or its social values.[60]

When the court does not accept the rationale of a criminal norm, it can notify the legislator through an *obiter dictum*, but it cannot reject the norm. The court must implement and apply criminal norms legitimately enacted by the legislator, and until the legislator abolishes the criminal norm, it remains valid and the court

---

[56]Walter V. Schaefer, *The Control of 'Sunbursts': Techniques of Prospective Overruling*, 42 N.Y.U. L. Rev. 631 (1967); Great Northern Ry. v. Sunburst Oil & Ref. Co., 287 U.S. 358, 53 S.Ct. 145, 77 L.Ed. 360 (1932); Mutual Life Ins. Co. v. Bryant, 296 Ky. 815, 177 S.W.2d 588 (1943); Durham v. United States, 214 F.2d 862 (D.C.Cir.1954).

[57]Stephen F. Ross, *The Limited Relevance of Plain Meaning*, 73 Wash. U. L. Q. 1057 (1995); Michael S. Moore, *Plain Meaning and Linguistics – A Case Study*, 73 Wash. U. L. Q. 1253 (1995); David A. Strauss, *Why Plain Meaning?*, 72 Notre Dame L. Rev. 1565 (1997).

[58]Article 111-4 of the French penal code provides that "La loi pénale est d'interprétation stricte".

[59]Caminetti v. United States, 242 U.S. 470, 37 S.Ct. 192, 61 L.Ed. 442 (1917); Smith v. United States, 508 U.S. 223, 113 S.Ct. 2050, 124 L.Ed.2d 138 (1993); Bailey v. United States, 516 U.S. 137, 116 S.Ct. 501, 133 L.Ed.2d 472 (1995).

[60]Reed F. Dickerson, The Interpretation and Application of Statutes 229–233 (1975).

cannot ignore it. This is the strict interpretation approach, in which the judicial discretion of the court is limited to the manner of implementation of the norm: verifying that all requirements of the offense have been met and that criminal liability must be imposed, and weighing punishment and sentencing considerations.

The court may declare that the verbal logic of the criminal norm is inconsistent with its legal logic. This is not necessarily a criticism of the legislator, and it may indicate an inconsistency that interferes with the plain implementation of the criminal norm based on the strict interpretation method. In these rare cases, the court must compare the verbal logic of the criminal norm with its legal logic and examine the nature of the inconsistency. If the court finds that the two are after all consistent, it must implement the criminal norm based on its verbal formulation and plain meaning. But if the verbal and legal logic are indeed inconsistent, the court proceeds to the second stage of interpretation, where it must prefer the legal logic over the verbal one.[61]

The question that arises in the second stage of interpretation is how to reveal the legal logic of the criminal norm. The most appropriate way to do it is by revealing its purpose. Criminal norms are enacted for a purpose, which is the reason and rationale for the enactment. The verbal formulation of the purpose may not always be consistent with the purpose because of errors, misunderstandings, or the absence of an appropriate vocabulary at the time of enactment. Although the verbal formulation may change from time to time, the purpose of the norm remains constant. It is this purpose that forms the legal logic (*ratio legis*) of the criminal norm.[62]

When the court finds an inconsistency between the verbal and the legal logic, and prefers the legal logic, the question of retroactivity arises. Examination of the legal logic is carried out in the process of the legal discussion in court, long after the factual event has occurred. Application of the purposive interpretation through the legal logic of the criminal norm is the application of an interpretation of which the public did not receive fair notice because it is different from the plain meaning of the words that make up the criminal norm. Indeed, this inconsistency is the very reason for applying the purposive interpretation. As a result, it may be argued that the purposive interpretation is being exercised in the given judicial decision for the first time (long after the occurrence of the factual event), and therefore it is applied retroactively to that factual event.[63]

---

[61]Church of the Holy Trinity v. United States, 143 U.S. 457, 12 S.Ct. 511, 36 L.Ed. 226 (1892); People v. Clark, 242 N.Y. 313, 151 N.E. 631 (1926); United States v. X-Citement Video, Inc., 513 U.S. 64, 115 S.Ct. 464, 130 L.Ed.2d 372 (1994); Veronica M. Dougherty, *Absurdity and the Limits of Literalism: Defining the Absurd Result Principle in Statutory Interpretation*, 44 Am. U. L. Rev. 127 (1994).

[62]See e.g. Sullens, 1 Mood. 129, 168 E.R. 1212 (1826); Commonwealth v. Ryan, 155 Mass. 523, 30 N.E. 364 (1892); Ker v. People, 110 Ill. 627 (1884); Ker v. Illinois, 119 U.S. 436, 7 S.Ct. 225, 30 L.Ed. 421 (1886); Bismarck v. State, 45 Tex.Crim. 54, 73 S.W. 965 (1903); United States v. Whitlock, 663 F.2d 1094 (D.C.Cir.1980).

[63]See State v. Mellenberger, 163 Or. 233, 95 P.2d 709 (1939) in relation to State v. Alexander, 76 Or. 329, 148 P. 1136 (1915).

Nevertheless, despite the fact that the court declares the legal logic of the said criminal norm for the first time when it issues the judicial decision, this is not considered to be a retroactive application to the factual event primarily because the legal logic of the criminal norm has always been present, even if its verbal formulation may have been inconsistent. The court merely states what the legal logic is, it does not invent it. In some legal systems, however, the verbal formulation of the criminal norm is considered to represent fair notice, and therefore articulation of the legal logic is considered to be a new interpretation and as such a retroactive application of a new criminal norm. In these legal systems, "retroactive" applicability can be avoided in two ways:

(1) Acquit the defendant in the case at hand and declare that from that point onward persons in the same circumstances will be convicted and punished. This declaration serves as proper fair notice.[64]
(2) Accept a "mistake of law" or "ignorance of the law"[65] defense and acquit the defendant in the case at hand, because it is not just to expect the defendant to have knowledge of a "new" law. Subsequently, "mistake of law" and "ignorance of the law" arguments in future cases will be rejected.[66]

In both solutions the defendant is acquitted but the legal logic is in force from that point onward. This approach has not been universally accepted, however. In most legal systems, the defendant is not acquitted in these circumstances, but the punishment may be reduced.

This two-stage method of interpretation makes it possible to implement the legal logic (*ratio legis*) directly, in the rare cases when it is necessary to do so. The two stages of interpretation, and especially the second one, assume that the criminal norm is characterized by a single clear, unequivocal legal logic. But when the purposive interpretation leads to more than one reasonable outcome, it is necessary to choose the most appropriate interpretation. This choice is guided by mitigating interpretation, as discussed below.

*5.3.5 Assisting Legal Measures for Revealing the Legal Logic (*Ratio Legis*) Through the Purposive Interpretation*

When the verbal logic (*ratio verborum*) and legal logic (*ratio legis*) of a criminal norm are inconsistent with each other, the court prefers the legal logic, which it reveals through purposive interpretation. The questions that arise at this stage are

---

[64]State v. Bell, 136 N.C. 674, 49 S.E. 163 (1904); State v. Jones, 44 N.M. 623, 107 P.2d 324 (1940).

[65]See above at Sect. 2.2.1.4.

[66]State v. O'Neil, 147 Iowa 513, 126 N.W. 454 (1910); State v. Longino, 109 Miss. 125, 67 So. 902 (1915).

how to determine the exact legal logic of the criminal norm and what its exact legal purpose is. If the courts are unable to answer these questions they cannot determine that the verbal formulation of the specific criminal norm is inconsistent with the legal logic.

Discovering the purpose of a norm without restrictions can lead to a legal logic that is far removed from the original formulation. As a result, the following seven assisting legal measures have been developed to find the legal logic (*ratio legis*) within the purposive interpretation of a criminal norm:

(1) Legal history of the criminal norm
(2) Titles of the criminal norm
(3) Various meanings of the legal terms separately and in the context of the criminal norm
(4) *Ejusdem generis*
(5) *Expressio unius est exclusio alterius*
(6) Errors in the verbal formulation of the criminal norm
(7) *Lacuna juris*

The seven assisting legal measures function as restrictions on judicial discretion in the process of finding the legal logic of a criminal norm through purposive interpretation. The assisting measures are described below.

5.3.5.1 Legal History of the Criminal Norm

Examination of the legal history of the criminal norm enables examination of its legal development in order to reveal the legal logic and purposes of the norm. This measure is acceptable both in the Anglo-American[67] and European-Continental[68] legal systems in the second stage of interpretation.[69] In rare cases, this measure can also help in understanding the verbal logic of the criminal norm.[70]

Examination of the legal history of the criminal norm can vary in different legal systems because different rules of creation of the criminal norm can affect its history. In general, this examination includes all historical aspects of the creation

[67] Bernard W. Bell, *Legislative History without Legislative Intent: The Public Justification Approach to Statutory Interpretation*, 60 Ohio St. L. J. 1 (1999); Edward Heath, *How Federal Judges Use Legislative History*, 25 J. Legis. 95 (1999); Jonathan R. Siegel, *The Use of Legislative History in a System of Seperated Powers*, 53 Vand. L. Rev. 1457 (2000); John F. Manning, *Putting Legislative History to a Vote: A Response to Professor Siegel*, 53 Vand. L. Rev. 1529 (2000).

[68] Jescheck und Weigend, *supra* note 21, at p. 90.

[69] State v. Partlow, 91 N.C. 550 (1884); Perrin v. United States, 444 U.S. 37, 100 S.Ct. 311, 62 L. Ed.2d 199 (1979).

[70] Ratzlaf v. United States, 510 U.S. 135, 114 S.Ct. 655, 126 L.Ed.2d 615 (1994): "...we do not resort to legislative history to cloud a statutory text that is clear"; Brogan v. United States, 522 U.S. 398, 118 S.Ct. 805, 139 L.Ed.2d 830 (1998); Carter v. United States, 530 U.S. 255, 120 S.Ct. 2159, 147 L.Ed.2d 203 (2000).

of the criminal norm, considerations of verbal formulation, the discussions in the relevant forums in the course of the verbal formulation, the reasons adduced, and the implications,[71] including auxiliary decisions that various legal and social forums reached in the course of the creation of the specific norm. For example, a detailed recommendation of a committee why to amend or not to amend the criminal norm, which has been accepted by parliament, can be relevant to the examination.[72]

Comparing previous drafts of the formulation of the criminal norm and analyzing the factors that contributed to the amendments is an acceptable method of examination of the legal history of the norm. The method has been used repeatedly since the nineteenth century in the Anglo-American legal systems,[73] although the practice is much more common in civil law than in criminal law.[74]

5.3.5.2 Titles of the Criminal Norm

Most criminal norms are enacted with titles. The titles may be those of the statute, of a chapter, of a specific article, etc. In some criminal norms, the titles are incorporated clearly within the text of the specific norm, but others have no titles, in which case this assisting measure is not relevant.[75] For example, some criminal norms created by common law through case law are not organized as statutes and have no formal titles, except perhaps the names of the parties in the relevant case. Some international customs may also lack formal titles.

According to the most accepted approach, the titles of the criminal norm have no independent legal status but may function as an interpretive measure to reveal the right meaning of the norm.[76] The primary reason for this approach is that the titles of the norm are intended to ease the administrative organization associated with the norm, and that this organization may reflect the legal logic of the norm. If the content of the norm is clear, but it contradicts its title, the clear content governs. The assistance of the title is sought only when the verbal formulation of the content of the criminal norm is vague or unclear.

Vague and unclear content of the criminal norm is the only adequate reason for interpreting the legal logic (*ratio legis*) of the norm based on its title.[77] Reliance on

---

[71] S.E.C. v. Robert Collier & Co., 76 F.2d 939 (2nd Cir.1935); Holloway v. United States, 526 U.S. 1, 119 S.Ct. 966, 143 L.Ed.2d 1 (1999).

[72] Gossnell v. Spang, 84 F.2d 889 (3rd Cir.1936).

[73] Tolson, (1889) 23 Q.B.D. 168, [1889] All E.R. 26; Commonwealth v. Mash, 48 Mass. 472 (1844).

[74] Schwegmann Bros. v. Calvert Distillers Corp., 341 U.S. 384, 71 S.Ct. 745, 95 L.Ed. 1035 (1951).

[75] See e.g. article 1 of the Sexual Offences Act, 2003, c.42.

[76] Norman J. Singer, Sutherland on Statutory Construction sec. 47.03 (5th ed., 1992); United States v. Fisher, 6 U.S. 358, 2 L.Ed. 304 (1804).

[77] State v. Miller, 74 Kan. 667, 87 P. 723 (1906); State v. Wilchinski, 242 Conn. 211, 700 A.2d 1 (1997).

the title can also reflect a vague verbal formulation (*ratio verborum*) of the content of the criminal norm,[78] but it is never appropriate to rely on the title in order to contradict explicitly a clearly formulated content of the norm.

5.3.5.3 Various Meanings of Legal Terms Separately and in the Context of the Criminal Norm

When the relevant judicial instance examines the verbal formulation of the text of a criminal norm and finds some vague terms, it attempts to interpret the vague terms as separate legal terms, and again in the context of the criminal norm. This praxis has been developed in the English common law for the interpretation of legal documents in civil law (contracts, wills, etc.), and has been adopted for the interpretation of legal norms, including criminal norms.[79] If comparison of the meaning of the legal term when interpreted separately with the meaning of the same term when interpreted in the relevant context of the criminal norm reveals differences, this may be an indication of a different verbal logic (*ratio verborum*); if the difference is a deep and significant one, it may be an indication of a different legal logic (*ratio legis*) as well.[80]

This interpretative measure may be relevant only when the difference between the meanings does not derive strictly from the difference in time. If the legal term that had been used when the norm was enacted had a different meaning from its present one, and if this is the reason for the difference between the meanings (separately vs. in context), this interpretative measure is less relevant than the legal history of the criminal norm, which may better explain that the difference.[81]

This interpretative measure should be applied with caution. For example, when the verbal formulation of the criminal norm is the result of various amendments enacted at different times, using different terminology each time (following the accepted practice at the time when each amendment was enacted), the different meanings may not necessarily be related to verbal or legal logic but to different verbal or textual styles, or to developments in the legal or general vocabulary.[82] If the difference in the meanings of the legal term interpreted separately and in

---

[78]Carter v. United States, 530 U.S. 255, 120 S.Ct. 2159, 147 L.Ed.2d 203 (2000): "the title of a statute is of use only when it sheds light on some ambiguous word or phrase in the statute itself".

[79]United States v. Fisher, 6 U.S. 358, 2 L.Ed. 304 (1804): "It is undoubtedly a well established principle in the exposition of statutes, that every part is to be considered, and the intention of the legislature to be extracted from the whole. It is also true, that where great inconvenience will result from a particular construction, that construction is to be avoided, unless the meaning of the legislature be plain; in which case it must be obeyed".

[80]Bank of New South Wales v. Piper, [1897] A.C. 383; S.E.C. v. Robert Collier & Co., 76 F.2d 939 (2nd Cir.1935).

[81]See above at Sect. 5.3.5.1.

[82]State v. Gerhardt, 145 Ind. 439, 44 N.E. 469 (1896); State v. Johnston, 149 S.C. 195, 146 S.E. 657 (1929); State v. Dorby, 217 Iowa 858, 250 N.W. 702 (1933).

context follows from a substantive normative change, this implies an inconsistency in the legal logic of the criminal norm.

5.3.5.4 *Ejusdem Generis*

The term *ejusdem generis* (of the same type) refers to a verbal formulation of a criminal norm that uses examples that are not conclusive, and the text completes the list in the example with general terms that have the meaning of "etc." When the text explicitly defines the example as a non-conclusive example, it is not necessary to use such terms. The legal interpretive rule in this case is that additional examples must be of the same sort (*ejusdem generis*).[83]

Logically, the courts can define another example as being of the same sort only through a process of analogy, as discussed above.[84] In the first stage, a process of induction is carried out to generalize the existing example or examples. In the second stage, a process of deduction is performed to examine the compatibility of the case at hand with the existing examples. The case at hand functions as if it were another example that must be examined to verify whether it is of the same type as the other examples.

Using analogy to provide additional examples "of the same sort" is subject to the rules of the first stage of interpretation (strict interpretation of the verbal logic[85]).[86] The strict use of this interpretive measure is explained by the requirement of fair notice,[87] because the "new example" has not been explicitly listed in the text of the criminal norm.[88] Nevertheless, as part of the structure of the interpretation of the criminal norm (*ex post*),[89] when the verbal logic is not consistent with the legal logic, it is considered reasonable to include "new examples" that are consistent with the legal logic of the criminal norm but not necessarily with its verbal logic.

5.3.5.5 *Expressio Unius Est Exclusio Alterius*

The term *expressio unius est exclusio alterius* (the explicit mention of one thing excludes all others) refers to the use of a legal term in an exclusive manner, so that

[83]Singer, *supra* note 76, at paragraphs 47.17–47.22.

[84]Above at Sect. 5.3.3.

[85]State v. Brantley, 201 Or. 637, 271 P.2d 668 (1954); State v. Kahalewai, 56 Haw. 481, 541 P.2d 1020 (1975); Giant of Maryland, Inc. v. State's Attorney, 274 Md. 158, 334 A.2d 107 (1975).

[86]Above at Sect. 5.3.3.

[87]United States v. Alpers, 338 U.S. 680, 70 S.Ct. 352, 94 L.Ed. 457 (1950); United States v. Powell, 423 U.S. 87, 96 S.Ct. 316, 46 L.Ed.2d 228 (1975).

[88]La Barge v. State, 74 Wis.2d 327, 246 N.W.2d 794 (1976).

[89]Above at Sect. 5.3.

no other similar legal terms may be used, even when the other terms can be considered to be "of the same sort."[90] As an interpretative measure, *expressio unius est exclusio alterius* functions as the opposite of *ejusdem generis*. In general, *expressio unius est exclusio alterius* can be used with reference to the verbal logic (*ratio verborum*) of the criminal norm, but it is not restricted to such use, and may be used in relation to the legal logic (*ratio legis*) as well.

For example, in the traditional definition of "rape" the victim of the offense has been defined as a "woman," not as a "person."[91] Based on *expressio unius est exclusio alterius*, the traditional definition did not allow the inclusion of terms other than "woman." As a result, only women could be considered victims of rape; men could be considered victims of sodomy, but not of rape. If it had been possible to use *ejusdem generis*, the legal option of designating male victims of rape would have been available, but because the relevant interpretative measure was not *ejusdem generis* but *expressio unius est exclusio alterius*, legislators had to amend the verbal formulation of the offense of rape to make it consistent with the modern concept of rape, which includes both female and male victims.[92]

This interpretative measure is generally used at the level of the verbal logic of the criminal norm.[93] The choice between this interpretative measure and *ejusdem generis* depends on the exact verbal formulation of the text of the criminal norm. When the term "etc." is used, or when the example is inconclusive, there is no reasonable option of using *expressio unius est exclusio alterius* in interpreting the norm. But when no such terms are used, or when the reference is not to an example but to a conclusive rule, there is no reasonable option of using *ejusdem generis* in interpreting the norm.

---

[90]United States v. Davis, 978 F.2d 415 (8th Cir.1992).

[91]Gabriel Hallevy, *Victim's Complicity in Criminal Law*, 2 INT'L J. OF PUNISHMENT & SENTENCING 72 (2006).

[92]See e.g. in Britain article 1(1) of the Sexual Offences Act, 2003, c.42 which provides that "[a] person (A) commits an offence if- (a) he intentionally penetrates the vagina, anus or mouth of another person (B) with his penis, (b) B does not consent to the penetration, and (c) A does not reasonably believe that B consents"; in Germany article 177(1) of the German penal code which provides that "[w]er eine andere Person (1) mit Gewalt, (2) durch Drohung mit gegenwärtiger Gefahr für Leib oder Leben oder (3) unter Ausnutzung einer Lage, in der das Opfer der Einwirkung des Täters schutzlos ausgeliefert ist, nötigt, sexuelle Handlungen des Täters oder eines Dritten an sich zu dulden oder an dem Täter oder einem Dritten vorzunehmen, wird mit Freiheitsstrafe nicht unter einem Jahr bestraft"; in France article 222-23 of the French penal code which provides that "[t]out acte de pénétration sexuelle, de quelque nature qu'il soit, commis sur la personne d'autrui par violence, contrainte, menace ou surprise est un viol. Le viol est puni de quinze ans de réclusion criminelle".

[93]Tolson, (1889) 23 Q.B.D. 168, [1889] All E.R. 26; People v. Nichols, 3 Cal.3d 150, 89 Cal.Rptr. 721, 474 P.2d 673 (1970); Glisson v. State, 188 Ga.App. 152, 372 S.E.2d 462 (1988); Walt v. State, 727 A.2d 836 (Del.1999).

5.3.5.6 Errors in the Verbal Formulation of the Criminal Norm

When an error occurs in the verbal formulation of a criminal norm, the judicial instance is required to identify the error and later to consider its response to it. Identifying errors in the verbal formulation of a norm and choosing the proper legal response to it requires a distinction between two types of errors:

(1) Absurd errors
(2) Errors that have legal meaning

Absurd errors are textual-verbal errors that render the legal norm absurd. Spelling errors, the omission of words or letters, and the addition of unnecessary words or letters produce absurd errors, so that the relevant clause becomes meaningless or absurd. When the court identifies an absurd error it is authorized to ignore it and interpret the criminal norm as if it contained no errors.[94] This response is applicable also when the absurd error refers to a legal definition that is no longer relevant because it has been abolished or substantially amended.

Errors that have legal meaning are textual-verbal errors that do not render the legal norm absurd, so that the criminal norm could be applied and implemented with the error. In these cases, a distinction must be made between the various effects of such errors. Errors that have legal meaning can affect both verbal logic (*ratio verborum*) and legal logic (*ratio legis*). When the error affects the verbal logic but not the legal logic, the norm can be applied and implemented with the error, especially when the error is in favor of the individual.[95] Thus, an error that affects only the verbal logic is not necessarily considered an error, even if the judicial instance identifies it as such.

When the error affects the legal logic of the criminal norm, whether or not the verbal logic is also affected, the effect of the error must be examined carefully. If the legal logic of a criminal norm is affected in such a way that the correct legal logic and purpose of the criminal norm no longer exist, the error must be fixed by the court in order to restore the correct legal logic. Identification of errors that have legal meaning may be accomplished using the other interpretive measures. For example, at times an error may be identified as such only after examining the legal history of the criminal norm, which provides evidence that part of the amendment should be considered to be an error.

5.3.5.7 *Lacuna Juris*

The term *lacuna juris* (gap in the law) refers to situations in which the law is silent about a given type of cases. Within the general law, the silence of the law can be

---

[94]Haworth v. Chapman, 113 Fla. 591, 152 So. 663 (1933).

[95]United States v. Evans, 333 U.S. 483, 68 S.Ct. 634, 92 L.Ed. 823 (1948); State v. Archuletta, 526 P.2d 911 (Utah 1974).

interpreted in two ways. First, the silence can be regarded as a negative opinion of the law about the issue at hand, and second, it can be regarded as a legal gap (lacuna).

According to the first view, the law is assumed to have been asked for its opinion on a legal issue, and to have rejected it. For example, the English common law has formulated a rule of simultaneity.[96] In most Anglo-American codifications and recodifications of the criminal law, the rule of simultaneity is not mentioned at all. The common interpretation is that this represents a negative opinion of the legislator. As a result, no rule of simultaneity is required anymore to impose criminal liability.

According to the second view, the silence of the law is regarded as a legal gap, where the law neither accepted nor rejected a legal settlement. In such cases, the judicial instance can resort to complementary sources of the law in order to fill the lacuna. The second way can be relevant to most spheres of the law, but not to criminal law, where *lacuna juris* is interpreted as a negative opinion of the law and not as a legal gap that can be filled by the court. Whenever the law has not determined explicitly that a conduct is criminal, it is not; or that an element is required to impose criminal liability, it is not; or that a defense is applicable, it is not.

For example, in most modern societies there is no criminal liability for adultery because there is no specific offense of adultery. Could a court regard this *lacuna juris* as a gap, fill it with other complementary legal sources (e.g., religious ones), and convict a person for adultery? The answer is, of course, no. The interpretation of *lacuna juris* as a negative opinion and not as a legal lacuna is derived from the first secondary principle of the principle of legality, described by the Latin maxim of *nullum crimen sine lege*. To criminalize a certain conduct, an explicit criminal norm is required. If no such criminal norm exists, the conduct is permitted and not prohibited.

This measure does not necessarily interpret the criminal norm in favor of the individual. When the criminal law is silent about a certain defense, it is considered that the defense has not been accepted by the criminal law, although the acceptance of defenses is in favor of the individual. Similarly, when the criminal law is silent about the requirement that a certain element be present in order to impose criminal

[96]Fowler v. Padget, (1798) 7 T.R. 509, 101 E.R. 1103; Fagan v. Metropolitan Police Commissioner, [1969] 1 Q.B. 439, [1968] 3 All E.R. 442, [1968] 3 W.L.R. 1120, 52 Cr. App. Rep. 700, 133 J.P. 16; Miller, [1983] 2 A.C. 161, [1983] 1 All E.R. 978, [1983] 2 W.L.R. 539, 77 Cr. App. Rep. 17; Singh, [1974] 1 All E.R. 26, [1973] 1 W.L.R. 1444, 138 J.P. 85; Kaitamaki, [1985] 1 A.C. 147, [1984] 2 All E.R. 435, [1984] 3 W.L.R. 137, [1984] Crim. L.R. 564, 79 Cr. App. Rep. 251; Matthews, [1950] 1 All E.R. 137, 48 L.G.R. 190, 66 T.L.R. (Pt. 1) 153, 114 J.P. 73, 34 Cr. App. Rep. 55; People v. Decina, 2 N.Y.2d 133, 138 N.E.2d 799, 157 N.Y.S.2d 558 (1956); Hill v. Baxter, [1958] 1 Q.B. 277, [1958] 1 All E.R. 193, [1958] 2 W.L.R. 76, 56 L.G.R. 117, 42 Cr. App. Rep. 51; Thabo Meli, [1954] 1 All E.R. 373, [1954] 1 W.L.R. 228; Church, [1966] 1 Q.B. 59, [1965] 2 All E.R. 72, [1965] 2 W.L.R. 1220, 49 Cr. App. Rep. 206, 129 J.P. 366; Le Brun, [1992] Q.B. 61; Geoffrey Marston, *Contemporaneity of Act and Intention*, 86 LAW Q. REV. 208 (1970); A. R. White, *The Identity and Time of the* Actus Reus, [1977] CRIM. L. REV. 148 (1977); Ramsay, [1967] N.Z.L.R. 1005; Jackson v. Commonwealth, 100 Ky. 239, 38 S.W. 422 (1896); Masilela, 1968 (2) S.A. 558 (A.D.); Chiswibo, 1960 (2) S.A. 714; Scott, [1967] V.R. 276.

liability, it is considered that that element of criminal liability has not been accepted by the criminal law, although acceptance of more requirements for the imposition of criminal liability is also in favor of the individual.

5.3.6 Mitigating Interpretation

As mentioned above, following the legal logic (*ratio legis*) of a criminal norm in its interpretation may lead to more than one reasonable interpretation. If all the interpretations are consistent with the legal logic, the second stage of the interpretation cannot suggest a way of choosing between them. In these rare cases, the most mitigating interpretation is chosen. The most mitigating interpretation is the one that minimizes the criminal liability under the given criminal norm.[97]

In practice, the choice of the mitigating interpretation functions as a third stage of interpretation. The court is authorized to exercise the mitigating interpretation only after declaring that the verbal logic of the criminal norm is inconsistent with its legal logic, and that purposive interpretation of the legal logic leads to more than one reasonable interpretation.[98]

The origin of the third stage of the interpretation of the criminal norm lies in the English common law of the late Middle Ages. The purpose of the rule was to prevent the use of capital punishment as the main penalty. In England in the Middle Ages, a defendant who claimed to be part of the Christian clergy could be exempted from capital punishment on offenses of the English common law. To examine the seriousness of the claim, the court had to be convinced that the defendant was not illiterate. But as of the late fourteenth century, literacy became common in England, and more and more defendants claimed to belong to the clergy.[99]

The English authorities responded by legislating new offenses through statutes rather than through the case law of the English common law. In the new offenses, claiming to be part of the clergy was irrelevant, as explicitly stated in the definitions of these offenses.[100] As a result, capital punishment became common in England once again. Under the reign of Henry VIII, 72,000 executions of capital punishment were reported based on convictions under the new offenses,[101] a situation that continued through the reigns of Elizabeth I and James I.[102] In an attempt to regain their eroded judicial discretion, the English courts devised the rule of strict

---

[97]Commonwealth v. Wotan, 422 Mass. 740, 665 N.E.2d 976 (1996).

[98]See above Fig. 5.2.

[99]Livingston Hall, *Strict or Liberal Construction of Penal Statutes*, 48 HARV. L. REV. 748 (1935); LEONA CHRISTINE GABEL, BENEFIT OF CLERGY IN ENGLAND IN THE LATER MIDDLE AGES 14 (1928, 1969).

[100]JOHN LAURENCE, A HISTORY OF CAPITAL PUNISHMENT 8 (1932, 1960).

[101]See e.g. 4 Hen. VIII, c.2 (1512); 23 Hen. VIII, c.1 (1531); 25 Hen. VIII, c.3, c.6 (1533); 27 Hen. VIII, c.17 (1535); 28 Hen. VIII, c.1 (1536); 37 Hen. VIII, c.8 (1545).

[102]See e.g. 18 Eliz. c.7 (1576); 31 Eliz. c.12 (1589); 39 Eliz. c.9 (1597); 39 Eliz. c.15 (1597); 2 Jac. I, c.8 (1604); 21 Jac. I, c.27 (1623).

construction, also known as the rule of mitigating interpretation, which requires the exercise of mitigating interpretation of any criminal norm in favor of the defendant. As a consequence of this rule, defendants were being convicted for English common law offenses rather than for statute-legislated offenses, and defendants who claimed to belong to the clergy were exempt from capital punishment.[103] This rule has also been known as the interpretative rule in favor of life (*in favorem vitae*).

In the nineteenth century, capital punishment ceased to be a major penalty in the English legal system, and was replaced gradually by other penalties, especially imprisonment. Nevertheless, the mitigating interpretation rule continued to be a valid English common law rule and was absorbed into all Anglo-American legal systems (which are based on English common law).[104] Anglo-American courts apply this rule frequently, to the point where it has been regarded as a misuse of the courts' interpretive power because it can defeat the purpose of criminal norms.

Because of the broad application of the mitigating interpretation rule, it was necessary to restrict its use by the courts to cases in which the verbal formulation of the criminal norm is unclear. When the verbal formulation of the criminal norm is clear, the courts cannot apply the mitigating interpretation even if they criticize the norm in the *obiter dictum.*[105] In American law, the restriction on the mitigating interpretation rule has been justified further by the requirement not to violate the individual's right to fair notice,[106] as only the legislator is authorized to enact new offenses, not the courts.[107]

---

[103] Jerome Hall, Theft, Law and Society 79–81, 87–100 (1935); Harvey, (1747) 1 Wils. K.B. 164, 95 E.R. 551 (1747).

[104] Bell v. United States, 349 U.S. 81, 75 S.Ct. 620, 99 L.Ed. 905 (1955); Rewis v. United States, 401 U.S. 808, 91 S.Ct. 1056, 28 L.Ed.2d 493 (1971); United States v. Bass, 404 U.S. 336, 92 S.Ct. 515, 30 L.Ed.2d 488 (1971); McNally v. United States, 483 U.S. 350, 107 S.Ct. 2875, 97 L.Ed.2d 292 (1987); Jones v. United States, 529 U.S. 848, 120 S.Ct. 1904, 146 L.Ed.2d 902 (2000).

[105] In United States v. Wiltberger, 18 U.S. 76, 5 L.Ed. 37, 5 Wheat. 76, 95 (1820) the court ruled that "...though penal laws are to be construed strictly, they are not to be construed so strictly as to defeat the obvious intention of the legislature. The maxim is not to be so applied as to narrow the words of the statute to the exclusion of cases which those words, in their ordinary acceptation, or in that sense in which the legislature has obviously used them, would comprehend. The intention of the legislature is to be collected from the words they employ. Where there is no ambiguity in the words, there is no room for construction. The case must be a strong one indeed, which would justify a Court in departing from the plain meaning of words, especially in a penal act, in search of an intention which the words themselves did not suggest. To determine that a case is within the intention of a statute, its language must authorise us to say so. It would be dangerous, indeed, to carry the principle, that a case which is within the reason or mischief of a statute, is within its provisions, so far as to punish a crime not enumerated in the statute, because it is of equal atrocity, or of kindred character, with those which are enumerated. If this principle has ever been recognized in expounding criminal law, it has been in cases of considerable irritation, which it would be unsafe to consider as precedents forming a general rule for other cases".

[106] State v. Stockton, 97 Wash.2d 528, 647 P.2d 21 (1982); Crandon v. United States, 494 U.S. 152, 110 S.Ct. 997, 108 L.Ed.2d 132 (1990).

[107] United States v. Bass, 404 U.S. 336, 92 S.Ct. 515, 30 L.Ed.2d 488 (1971); State v. Jewell, 345 So.2d 1166 (La.1977).

Although the mitigating interpretation rule has been absorbed into most modern legal systems,[108] it functions as a third stage of interpretation of the criminal norm, not as a second stage. When the verbal formulation of the criminal norm is unclear, the mitigating interpretation is not applied immediately because it may defeat the social and legal purpose of the norm. Therefore, when the verbal formulation of the criminal norm is unclear, the legal logic (*ratio legis*) of the norm is examined, and if the court finds that the verbal logic (*ratio verborum*) and the legal logic are inconsistent, it applies the legal logic of the criminal norm. If the court recognizes only one reasonable interpretation based on the legal logic of the norm, this is the interpretation that it applies.

Only if the court recognizes more than one reasonable interpretation based on the legal logic of the norm does it proceed to the third stage of interpretation, where it chooses the most mitigating interpretation from all the reasonable interpretations based on the legal logic (purposive interpretation) of the criminal norm. This three-stage interpretation process may be described schematically as shown in Fig. 5.4.

This three-stage interpretation process makes it possible for the courts to resolve any doubt, if one exists, in favor of the defendant (*in dubio pro reo*) without preventing implementation of the legal and social purpose of the norm. The three-stage interpretation process has been accepted worldwide,[109] including the notion

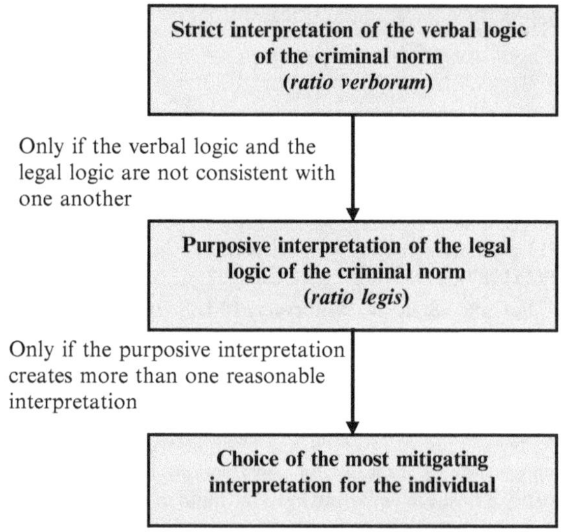

Fig. 5.4 Three stages of the interpretation

[108]See e.g. article 111-4 of the French penal code.

[109]Salinas v. United States, 522 U.S. 52, 118 S.Ct. 469, 139 L.Ed.2d 352 (1997); Bates v. United States, 522 U.S. 23, 118 S.Ct. 285, 139 L.Ed.2d 215 (1997); United States v. Wells, 519 U.S. 482, 117 S.Ct. 921, 137 L.Ed.2d 107 (1997); Caron v. United States, 524 U.S. 308, 118 S.Ct. 2007, 141 L.Ed.2d 303 (1998); Muscarello v. United States, 524 U.S. 125, 118 S.Ct. 1911, 141 L.Ed.2d 111 (1998); State v. Colvin, 645 N.W.2d 449 (Minn.2002); ACP 10987/07 State v. Cohen (unreported, March 2, 2009).

that the mitigating interpretation is not intended to prevent realization of the purpose[110] and legal logic of the criminal norm,[111] and that it is always the third stage of interpretation, after the previous two stages have been exhausted.[112]

5.4 Conflict of Laws Based on the Interpretation of the Criminal Norm

It is almost inevitable that the various options of applicability of the criminal norm in place would create situations in which laws are in conflict with each other and given norms contradict others (conflict of laws). The relevant question in these situations is which norm governs and should be followed.[113] The principle of legality in criminal law accommodates four types of situations in which laws conflict, one type for every secondary principle. As far as the interpretation of the criminal norm is concerned (the fourth secondary principle), conflicting laws have to do with differently interpreted norms that contradict one another, i.e., when a strictly interpreted criminal norm contradicts a purposive interpretation of that criminal norm, and both may be applicable to a specific case.

The relevant question about conflicting laws based on interpretation of the criminal norm concerns situations in which several criminal norms or several interpretations are applicable to the same case (factual event or judicial decision). In these situations the question is which of the several norms should be applied to the case at hand. The answer is given in two stages. In the first stage, we eliminate all the irrelevant criminal norms or interpretations that are not relevant to the event. In the second stage, we decide which of the remaining criminal norms or interpretations is the correct one and should be applied to the event.

Examination of the relevant criminal norms is carried out according to the structure of the second stage of interpretation, as described above,[114] because the conflict of laws is resolved at the second stage of interpretation, by the courts (*ex post*), and not at the first stage, by the legislator (*ex ante*). It is therefore necessary to check the applicability of the general principles of criminal law and of the relevant special criminal norm to the case at hand. As part of this examination, the special criminal norm supersedes the general norm. According to the

[110]Barrett v. United States, 423 U.S. 212, 96 S.Ct. 498, 46 L.Ed.2d 450 (1976); State v. Millett, 392 A.2d 521 (Me.1978); State v. Hobokin, 768 S.W.2d 76 (Mo.1989); Smith v. United States, 508 U. S. 223, 113 S.Ct. 2050, 124 L.Ed.2d 138 (1993).

[111]United States v. Moore, 423 U.S. 122, 96 S.Ct. 335, 46 L.Ed.2d 333 (1975); Dover v. State, 664 P.2d 536 (Wyo.1983); United States v. Sepulveda, 115 F.3d 882 (11th Cir.1997).

[112]State v. Carter, 89 Wash.2d 236, 570 P.2d 1218 (1977); Commonwealth v. Gordon, 511 Pa. 481, 515 A.2d 558 (1986).

[113]Lawrence Collins, Dicey and Morris The Conflict of Laws I 32 (13th ed., 2000).

[114]Above at Sect. 5.1.

general structure of the interpretation of the criminal norm *ex post*, there are three stages of interpretation.

The first stage of strict interpretation focuses on the verbal logic (*ratio verborum*) of the criminal norm based on its plain meaning. This stage addresses the application of both the specific criminal norm and of the general principles of criminal law. The interpretation of most criminal norms *ex post* ends with the first stage. In rare cases, the verbal and legal logic of the criminal norm are inconsistent and it becomes necessary to proceed to the second stage. When the plain meaning of the verbal formulation of the criminal norm is clear and unambiguous, there is no need for further stages of interpretation.

In the second stage, the criminal norm is interpreted with reference to its purpose, which is the principal guide to understanding the legal logic of the criminal norm (*ratio legis*). In these cases, the *ratio legis* governs the *ratio verborum*, and if the two contradict one another, the criminal norm is interpreted according to the *ratio legis*. Most criminal norms that reach the second stage of examination do not proceed to the third stage. But when interpretation based on the *ratio legis* produces more than one reasonable answer, it is necessary to proceed to the third stage, in which the reasonable interpretation that is most mitigating from the point of view of the individual is chosen.

The structure of interpretation of the criminal norm *ex post* incorporates the following rules of conflict of laws relevant to the interpretation of the criminal norm, in this order:

(1) The general principles of criminal law are applicable unless a different applicability is determined explicitly[115]
(2) *Lex specialis derogat generali*[116]
(3) The strict interpretation of the verbal logic (*ratio verborum*) of the criminal norm is superseded by a purposive interpretation of the legal logic (*ratio legis*) of that norm if the two interpretations are inconsistent[117]
(4) When several reasonable purposive interpretations of the legal logic (*ratio legis*) of the criminal norm are possible, the most mitigating interpretation is applied[118]

This order of rules in the interpretation of criminal norms is not accidental, and it reflects the structure of the interpretation of the criminal norm *ex post*. Naturally, the structure of interpretation *ex post* affects the formulation of the criminal norm *ex ante*, as noted above.[119] But the rules of the conflict of laws address the implementation and application of the criminal norm, and are therefore relevant to the interpretation *ex post* rather than to the formulation *ex ante* of the criminal norm.

---

[115]See above at Sect. 5.3.1.

[116]See above at Sect. 5.3.2.

[117]See above at Sects. 5.3.3–5.3.5.

[118]See above at Sect. 5.3.6.

[119]Above at Sect. 5.3.

Chapter 6
The Conflict of Laws Within the Conflicts of Laws in the Principle of Legality

As part of all secondary principles of the principle of legality in criminal law, certain rules are employed to govern the resolution of the conflict of laws. All secondary principles of the principle of legality face situations in which one criminal norm contradicts another, or one interpretation of a criminal norm contradicts another, with all the relevant criminal norms and interpretations applicable to case at hand. As discussed in Chaps. 2–5, the rules of conflict of laws provide solutions for solving these conflicts within each secondary principle. Thus, four sets of rules exist for solving the conflict of laws involving the principle of legality in criminal law, one set for each secondary principle:

(1) Rules based on the legitimate sources of the criminal norm, stating that a superior norm supersedes an inferior one (*lex superior derogat inferiori*)[1]
(2) Rules based on the applicability of the criminal norm in time, stating that a later norm supersedes an earlier one (*lex posterior derogat priori*)[2]
(3) Rules based on the applicability of the criminal norm in place, stating that an internal norm supersedes an external one (*lex interior derogat exteriori*)[3]
(4) Rules based on the interpretation of the criminal norm, stating the prevalence of the interpretation of the criminal norm *ex post*[4]

Each of the four sets of rules of each secondary principle appears to act separately from the other three, and this would be the legal situation if the conflict of laws occurred always within the same secondary principle. But this is not the prevailing legal situation. For example, none of the four sets of rules can solve a conflict of laws between a later regulation and an earlier statute. According to the first set of rules (*lex superior derogat inferiori*), the statute supersedes the regulation because it is a superior norm and the regulation an inferior one. But according

[1]See above at Sect. 2.3.
[2]See above at Sect. 3.4.
[3]See above at Sect. 4.4.
[4]See above at Sect. 5.4.

G. Hallevy, *A Modern Treatise on the Principle of Legality in Criminal Law*,
DOI 10.1007/978-3-642-13714-3_6,

to the second set of rules (*lex posterior derogat priori*), the later norm (regulation) supersedes the earlier one (statute).

The legal question in these cases is which *set of rules* takes precedence over the others. The answer lies in the solution to the conflict of laws *within* the conflicts of laws involving the principle of legality in criminal law. This solution addresses the conflict between the four sets of rules used to resolve the conflicts of laws, as described above. The solution to the conflict of laws within the conflicts of laws organizes the four sets of rules hierarchically. According to this hierarchy, when the conflict of laws is resolved based on the set of rules with the highest precedence among the relevant sets of rules, there is no need to proceed to the examination of any other set of rules. The hierarchical organization of the sets of rules of the conflict of laws is described schematically in Fig. 6.1.

The structure of the conflict of laws within the conflicts of laws is the conclusive solution to the multi-dimensional conflict of laws. The structure contains a preliminary stage and four major stages, one for each secondary principle of the principle of legality. The preliminary stage is exclusive to criminal law, and it is intended to eliminate foreign norms from becoming candidates for application in a domestic court. The reason for the preliminary stage is the determination of criminal law that

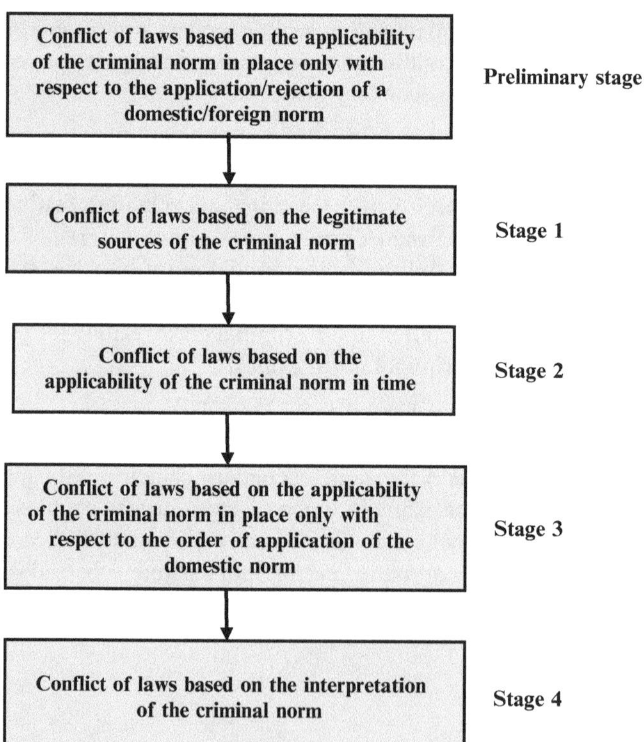

Fig. 6.1 The structure of the conflict of laws within the conflicts of laws

no foreign law is applicable in a domestic court.[5] In other spheres of law, where no such restriction exists, there is no need for such a preliminary stage.[6]

After the preliminary stage, all the remaining relevant norms are domestic. Within the domestic criminal norms, the order of precedence of the sets of rules for conflict resolution is the same as the order of secondary principles of the principle of legality, based on the same rationale. Thus, in the first stage, the governing rules of conflict resolution are based on the legitimate sources of the criminal norm, and therefore superior norms supersede inferior ones (*lex superior derogat inferiori*). If only one of the relevant norms is superior, the conflict of laws is resolved by applying that norm. But if more than one superior norm is derived from the same legitimate source, conflict resolution proceeds to the second stage.[7]

After the first stage, all the remaining relevant norms are domestic and superior. Within domestic and superior norms, the order of precedence for conflict resolution is based on the applicability of the criminal norm in time, and therefore later norms supersede earlier ones (*lex posterior derogat priori*). If one of the relevant norms is latest, the conflict of laws is resolved by applying that norm. But if several of the norms are equally recent, conflict resolution proceeds to the third stage.[8]

After the second stage, all the remaining relevant norms are domestic, superior, and recent. Within domestic, superior, and recent norms, the order of precedence for conflict resolution is based on the applicability of the criminal norm in place, and therefore norms with a stronger connection to the domestic sovereign supersede norms with a weaker connection (the wide application of *lex interior derogat exteriori*), for example, a norm that can be applied through the territorial applicability of the criminal norm supersedes a norm that can be applied through its protective applicability. If one of the relevant norms is found to have the strongest connection to the domestic sovereign, the conflict of laws is resolved by applying

[5]Ogden v. Folliot, (1790) 3 T.R. 726; Lynch v. Paraguay Provisional Government, [1861–1873] All E.R. 934, [1861–73] All E.R. 934; Huntington v. Attrill, [1893] A.C. 150; Attorney General for Canada v. Schulze, (1901) 9 S.L.T. 4; Raulin v. Fischer, [1911] 2 K.B. 93; Banco De Vizcaya v. Don Alfonso De Borbon Y Austria, [1934] All E.R. 555, [1935] 1 K.B. 140; 104 L.J.K.B. 46;151 L.T. 499; 50 T.L.R. 284; 78 Sol.Jo. 224; Frankfurter v. W. L. Exner Ltd., [1947] Ch. 629; Novello v. Hinrischen Edition Ltd., [1951] Ch. 595; Schemmer v. Property Resources Ltd., [1975] Ch. 273; Attorney General of New Zealand v. Ortiz, [1984] 1 A.C. 1, [1983] 2 W.L.R. 809, [1983] 2 All E. R. 93; United States of America v. Inkley, [1989] Q.B. 255, [1988] 3 W.L.R. 304, [1988] 3 All E. R. 144; Larkins v. N.U.M., [1985] I.R. 671; Bank of Ireland v. Meeneghan, [1994] 3 I.R. 111; *In re* The Antelope, (1825) 10 Wheat. 66; State v. Pelican Insurance Co., 127 U.S. 265, 8 S.Ct. 1370, 32 L.Ed. 239 (1888); SA Consortium General Textiles v. Sun & Sand Agencies Ltd., [1978] Q.B. 279, [1978] 2 All E.R. 339, [1978] 2 W.L.R. 1.

[6]LAWRENCE COLLINS, DICEY AND MORRIS THE CONFLICT OF LAWS II 1195–1283 (13th ed., 2000).

[7]For instance, when two statutes contradict one regulation. According to the first stage, the two statutes govern the regulation, but within the first stage the conflict of laws between these two statutes cannot be solved, and the second stage is required.

[8]For instance, when two posterior statutes contradict one prior statute. According to the second stage, the two posterior statutes govern the one prior statute, but within the second stage the conflict of laws between these two statutes cannot be solved, and the third stage is required.

that norm. But if there are several norms with equally strong connection to the local sovereign, conflict resolution proceeds to the fourth stage.[9]

After the third stage, all the remaining relevant norms are domestic, superior, recent, and with a strong connection to the local sovereign. Within these norms, the order of precedence for conflict resolution is based on the interpretation of the criminal norm, and therefore norms that are preferable to others from the point of view of their interpretation (e.g., specific vs. general norms), supersede the others. This is the final stage of conflict resolution, where all conflicts of laws are resolved.[10]

Thus, only when the conflict of laws has not been resolved at a given stage does it become necessary to proceed to the next stage. If conflict resolution comes down to the fourth and final stage, after the rules of this stage are applied only one relevant applicable criminal norm remains.

[9]For instance, when two norms, which are applicable through the protective applicability of the criminal norm, contradict one norm, which is applicable through the passive personality applicability. According to the third stage, the two norms, which are applicable through the protective applicability of the criminal norm, govern the one norm, which is applicable through the passive personality applicability, but within the third stage the conflict of laws between these two norms cannot be solved, and the fourth stage is required.

[10]State v. Collins, 55 Wash.2d 469, 348 P.2d 214 (1960); compare with Simpson v. United States, 435 U.S. 6, 98 S.Ct. 909, 55 L.Ed.2d 70 (1978); *Ex Parte* Chiapetto, 93 Cal.App.2d 497, 209 P.2d 154 (1949).

Cases

Anglo-American Cases

- A. v. The Secretary of State for the Home Department, [2005] 2 W.L.R. 87, [2004] U.K.H.L. 56
- Abbott, [1977] A.C. 755
- Al-Fawwaz, [2002] 1 All E.R. 545, [2002] 1 A.C. 556, [2002] 2 W.L.R. 101, [2001] U.K.H.L. 69
- Allday, (1837) 8 Car. & P. 136, 173 Eng. Rep. 431
- Allen v. State, 91 Md.App. 705, 605 A.2d 960 (1992)
- Almendarez-Torres v. United States, 523 U.S. 224, 118 S.Ct. 1219, 140 L.Ed.2d 350 (1998)
- American Banana Co. v. United Fruit Co., 213 U.S. 347, 29 S.Ct. 511, 53 L.Ed. 826 (1909)
- Anderson, [1861–1873] All E.R. 999, (1868) 11 Cox C.C. 198
- Anderson v. State, 27 Tex.App. 177, 11 S.W. 33, 3 L.R.A. 644, 11 Am.St.Rep. 189 (1889)
- Argentine Republic v. Amerada Hess Shipping Corp., 488 U.S. 428, 109 S.Ct. 683, 102 L.Ed.2d 818 (1989)
- Arrowsmith, [1975] Q.B. 678, [1975] 1 All E.R. 463, [1975] 2 W.L.R. 484, 60 Cr. App. Rep. 211, 139 J.P. 221
- Ashton v. Kentucky, 384 U.S. 195, 86 S.Ct. 1407, 16 L.Ed.2d 469 (1966)
- Athens Maritime Enterprises Corporation v. Hellenic Mutual War Risks Association (Bermuda) Ltd., [1983] Q.B. 647, [1983] 1 All E.R. 590, [1983] 2 W.L.R. 425
- Attorney General for Canada v. Schulze, (1901) 9 S.L.T. 4
- Attorney General of New Zealand v. Ortiz, [1984] 1 A.C. 1, [1983] 2 W.L.R. 809, [1983] 2 All E.R. 93
- Attorney General v. Nikolaiovitch, [1940] A.L.R. 3, (1940) 7 P.L.R. 1
- Aubert v. Maze, (1801) 2 Bos & Pul 371, 126 E.R. 1333
- Bacon, (1664) 1 Lev. 146, 1 Sid. 230, 1 Keble 809, 83 E.R. 341
- Bailey, (1818) Russ. & Ry. 341, 168 Eng. Rep. 835

- Bailey v. United States, 516 U.S. 137, 116 S.Ct. 501, 133 L.Ed.2d 472 (1995)
- Baker v. State, 377 So.2d 17 (Fla.1979)
- Banco De Vizcaya v. Don Alfonso De Borbon Y Austria, [1934] All E.R. 555, [1935] 1 K.B. 140; 104 L.J.K.B. 46;151 L.T. 499; 50 T.L.R. 284; 78 Sol.Jo. 224
- Bank of New South Wales v. Piper, [1897] A.C. 383
- Barker, [1924] N.Z.L.R. 865
- Barrett v. United States, 423 U.S. 212, 96 S.Ct. 498, 46 L.Ed.2d 450 (1976)
- Bates v. United States, 522 U.S. 23, 118 S.Ct. 285, 139 L.Ed.2d 215 (1997)
- Bell v. Maryland, 378 U.S. 226, 84 S.Ct. 1814, 12 L.Ed.2d 822 (1964)
- Bell v. State, 394 So.2d 979 (Fla. 1981)
- Bell v. United States, 349 U.S. 81, 75 S.Ct. 620, 99 L.Ed. 905 (1955)
- Bennet v. Hundred of Hartford, (1650) Style 233, 82 E.R. 671
- Bensley v. Bignold, (1822) 5 Barn and Ald 335, 106 E.R. 1214
- Bismarck v. State, 45 Tex.Crim. 54, 73 S.W. 965 (1903)
- Blackmer v. United States, 284 U.S. 421, 52 S.Ct. 252, 76 L.Ed. 375 (1932)
- Blackpool Corporation v. Locker, [1948] 1 K.B. 349, 361 [1948] 1 All E.R. 85, 46 L.G.R. 58, 112 J.P. 130, 150 E.G. 477, [1947] E.G.D. 155, [1948] W.N. 27
- Blue v. State, 716 So.2d 567 (Miss.1998)
- Bonham, (1610) 8 Co. Rep. 114
- Bouie v. Columbia, 378 U.S. 347, 84 S.Ct. 1697, 12 L.Ed.2d 894 (1964)
- Bow Street Metropolitan Stipendiary Magistrate, [2000] 1 A.C. 147, [1999] 2 All E.R. 97, [1999] 2 W.L.R. 827
- Brett v. Rigden, (1568) 1 Plowd. 340, 75 Eng. Rep. 516
- Brind v. Secretary of State for the Home Department, [1991] 1 A.C. 696, [1991] 1 All E.R. 720 [1991] 2 W.L.R. 588
- Brogan v. United States, 522 U.S. 398, 118 S.Ct. 805, 139 L.Ed.2d 830 (1998)
- Bsharah v. United States, 646 A.2d 993 (D.C.App.1994)
- Burnett, (1815) 4 M. & S. 272, 105 Eng. Rep. 835
- Butler, (1834) 6 Car. & P. 368, 172 E.R. 1280
- Button, [1900] All E.R. 1648, [1900] 2 Q.B. 597, 69 L.J.Q.B. 901, 83 L.T. 288, 64 J.P. 600, 48 W.R. 703, 16 T.L.R. 525, 44 Sol. Jo. 659, 19 Cox. C.C. 568
- Calder v. Bull, 3 U.S. 386, 1 L.Ed. 648 (1798)
- Cambridge and Isle of Ely County Council v. Rust, [1972] 2 Q.B. 426, [1972] 3 All E.R. 232, [1972] 3 W.L.R. 226
- Caminetti v. United States, 242 U.S. 470, 37 S.Ct. 192, 61 L.Ed. 442 (1917)
- Campbell and Bradley v. Ward, [1955] N.Z.L.R. 471
- Canal Bank v. Bank of Albany, 1 Hill. 287 (1841)
- Carass, [2002] 2 Cr. App. R. 77
- Caron v. United States, 524 U.S. 308, 118 S.Ct. 2007, 141 L.Ed.2d 303 (1998)
- Carter v. United States, 530 U.S. 255, 120 S.Ct. 2159, 147 L.Ed.2d 203 (2000)
- Casement, [1917] 1 K.B. 98
- Chan Chi-hung, [1996] A.C. 442
- Charles, (1976) 63 Cr. App. R. 252; Oxford v. Moss, (1978) 68 Cr. App. R. 183, [1979] Crim. L.R. 119
- Chevron International Oil Co. Ltd. v. A/S Sea Team, [1983] Lloyd's Rep. 356

- Chew Heong v. United States, 112 U.S. 536, 5 S.Ct. 255, 28 L.Ed. 770 (1884)
- Chiapetto, 93 Cal.App.2d 497, 209 P.2d 154 (1949)
- Chiswibo, 1960 (2) S.A. 714
- Christian, [2006] U.K.P.C. 47, [2007] 2 A.C. 400
- Church, [1966] 1 Q.B. 59, [1965] 2 All E.R. 72, [1965] 2 W.L.R. 1220, 49 Cr. App. Rep. 206, 129 J.P. 366
- Church of the Holy Trinity v. United States, 143 U.S. 457, 12 S.Ct. 511, 36 L.Ed. 226 (1892)
- City of Chicago v. Morales, 527 U.S. 41, 119 S.Ct. 1849, 144 L.Ed.2d 67 (1999)
- Clarence, (1888) 22 Q.B.D. 23, [1890] All E.R. 133
- Clark, [2003] 2 Cr. App. R. 363
- Cline v. Frink Dairy Co., 274 U.S. 445, 47 S.Ct. 681, 71 L.Ed. 1146 (1927)
- Coal & C.R. v. Conley, 67 W.Va. 129, 67 S.E. 613 (1910)
- Colautti v. Franklin, 439 U.S. 379, 99 S.Ct. 675, 58 L.Ed.2d 596 (1979)
- Collingwood, (1704) 6 Mod. 288, 87 E.R. 1029
- Commonwealth v. Adams, 114 Mass. 323, 19 Am.Rep. 362 (1873)
- Commonwealth v. Barsell, 424 Mass. 737, 678 N.E.2d 143 (1997)
- Commonwealth v. Boynton, 84 Mass. 160, 2 Allen 160 (1861)
- Commonwealth v. Diaz, 326 Mass. 525, 95 N.E.2d 666 (1950)
- Commonwealth v. Flagg, 135 Mass. 545 (1883)
- Commonwealth v. Gaines, 4 Va. 172 (1819)
- Commonwealth v. Goodman, 97 Mass. 117 (1867)
- Commonwealth v. Gordon, 511 Pa. 481, 515 A.2d 558 (1986)
- Commonwealth v. Guthrie, 420 Pa.Super. 372, 616 A.2d 1019 (1992)
- Commonwealth v. Hunt, 4 Metc. 111 (Mass.1842)
- Commonwealth v. Kimball, 38 Mass. 373, 21 Pick. 373 (1838)
- Commonwealth v. Kratsas, 564 Pa. 36, 764 A.2d 20 (2001)
- Commonwealth v. Mash, 48 Mass. 472 (1844)
- Commonwealth v. Mink, 123 Mass. 422, 25 Am.Rep. 109 (1877)
- Commonwealth v. Mumma, 489 Pa. 547, 414 A.2d 1026 (1980)
- Commonwealth v. Peaslee, 177 Mass. 267, 59 N.E. 55 (1901)
- Commonwealth v. Pestinikas, 421 Pa.Super. 371, 617 A.2d 1339 (1992)
- Commonwealth v. Rhodes, 920 S.W.2d 531 (Ky.App.1996)
- Commonwealth v. Ryan, 155 Mass. 523, 30 N.E. 364 (1892)
- Commonwealth v. Vaughn, 329 Mass. 333, 108 N.E.2d 559 (1952)
- Commonwealth v. Wotan, 422 Mass. 740, 665 N.E.2d 976 (1996)
- Connally v. General Constr. Co., 269 U.S. 385, 46 S.Ct. 126, 70 L.Ed. 322 (1926)
- Cotter, [2002] Crim. L.R. 824
- Cowper, (1696) 5 Mod. 206, 87 E.R. 611
- Cox v. Louisiana, 379 U.S. 559, 85 S.Ct. 476, 13 L.Ed.2d 487 (1965)
- Cox v. People, 82 Ill. 191 (1876)
- Crandon v. United States, 494 U.S. 152, 110 S.Ct. 997, 108 L.Ed.2d 132 (1990)
- Crawshaw, (1860) Bell. 303, 169 Eng. Rep. 1271
- Creel v. State, 186 Miss. 738, 191 So. 814 (1939)
- Crow Dog, 109 U.S. 556, 3 S.Ct. 396, 27 L.Ed. 1030 (1883)

- Cutter v. State, 36 N.J.L. 125 (1873)
- Daniell, (1704) 6 Mod. 99, 87 E.R. 856
- Davis v. Commonwealth, 230 Va. 201, 335 S.E.2d 375 (1985)
- Dawson, (1696) 13 St.Tr. 451
- De Nicols v. Curlier, [1900] A.C. 21, 69 L.J.Ch. 109, 81 L.T. 733, 16 T.L.R. 101, 48 W.R. 269
- Debardelaben v. State, 99 Tenn. 649, 42 S.W. 684 (1897)
- Director of Public Prosecutions v. Armstrong, (1999) 143 S.J. L.B. 279, [2000] Crim. L.R. 379
- District of Columbia v. Colts, 282 U.S. 63, 51 S.Ct. 52, 75 L.Ed. 177 (1930)
- Dixon, (1814) 3 M. & S. 11, 105 Eng. Rep. 516
- Dixon v. State, 104 Miss. 410, 61 So. 423 (1913)
- Dobbert v. Florida, 432 U.S. 282, 97 S.Ct. 2290, 53 L.Ed.2d 344 (1977)
- Donnelly v. United States, 228 U.S. 243, 33 S.Ct. 449, 57 L.Ed. 820 (1913)
- Dotson v. State, 6 Cold. 545 (1869)
- Dover v. State, 664 P.2d 536 (Wyo.1983)
- Draper v. United States, 164 U.S. 240, 17 S.Ct. 107, 41 L.Ed. 419 (1896)
- Dupleix v. De Roven, (1705) 2 Vern. 540, (1705) 23 E.R. 950
- Durham v. United States, 214 F.2d 862 (D.C.Cir.1954)
- E.E.O.C. v. Arabian American Oil Co., 499 U.S. 244, 111 S.Ct. 1227, 113 L. Ed.2d 274 (1991)
- Eagleton, [1855] 6 Cox C.C. 559
- Cr.App. 336/61 Eichmann v. Attorney General, 16 (3) PD 2032 (1962)
- Esop, (1836) 7 Car. & P. 456, 173 Eng. Rep. 203
- Estell v. State, 51 N.J.L. 182, 17 A. 118 (1889)
- Estrada, 63 Cal.2d 740, 408 P.2d 948, 48 Cal.Rptr. 172 (1965)
- Factortame Ltd., [1990] 2 A.C. 85
- Fagan v. Metropolitan Police Commissioner, [1969] 1 Q.B. 439, [1968] 3 All E. R. 442, [1968] 3 W.L.R. 1120, 52 Cr. App. Rep. 700, 133 J.P. 16
- Falk, 64 Cal. 2d 684, 414 P.2d 407, 51 Cal.Rptr. 279 (1966)
- Farmer v. People, 77 Ill. 322 (1875)
- Finta, [1994] 1 S.C.R. 701
- Flaherty v. Thomas, 94 Mass. 428 (1866)
- Forbes, (1835) 7 Car. & P. 224, 173 Eng. Rep. 99
- Fort Belknap Indian Community v. Mazurek, 43 F.3d 428 (9th Cir.1994)
- Fortescue v. Vestry of St. Mathew Bethnal Green, (1891) 2 Q.B. 170
- Fowler v. Padget, (1798) 7 T.R. 509, 101 E.R. 1103
- Frankfurter v. W. L. Exner Ltd., [1947] Ch. 629
- Galvan v. Press, 347 U.S. 522, 74 S.Ct. 737, 98 L.Ed. 911 (1954)
- Garland v. British Rail Engineering Ltd., [1983] 2 A.C. 751, [1982] 2 All E.R. 402, [1982] 2 W.L.R. 918
- Giant of Maryland, Inc. v. State's Attorney, 274 Md. 158, 334 A.2d 107 (1975)
- Gilgert v. Stockton Port Dist., 7 Cal.2d 384, 60 P.2d 847 (1936)
- Glisson v. State, 188 Ga.App. 152, 372 S.E.2d 462 (1988)
- Gold, [1987] Q.B. 1116, [1987] 3 All E.R. 618, [1987] 3 W.L.R. 803, [1988] A.C. 1063

- Goldman, [2001] Crim. L.R. 894
- Gomez, [1993] A.C. 442, [1993] 1 All E.R. 1, [1992] 3 W.L.R. 1067
- Gorman, 269 Ind. 236, 379 N.E.2d 970 (1978)
- Gossnell v. Spang, 84 F.2d 889 (3rd Cir.1936)
- Gouveia v. Vokes, 800 F.Supp. 241 (1992)
- Grant v. McAuliffe, 41 Cal.2d 859, 246 P.2d 944 (1953)
- Grayned v. City of Rockford, 408 U.S. 104, 92 S.Ct. 2294, 33 L.Ed.2d 222 (1972)
- Great Northern Ry. v. Sunburst Oil & Ref. Co., 287 U.S. 358, 53 S.Ct. 145, 77 L. Ed. 360 (1932)
- Gregory, (1867) 1 Crim. C.R. 77
- Gregory v. State, 259 Ind. 652, 291 N.E.2d 67 (1973)
- Grindstaff v. State, 214 Tenn. 58, 377 S.W.2d 921 (1964)
- Grisham v. Hagan, 361 U.S. 278, 80 S.Ct. 310, 4 L.Ed.2d 279 (1960)
- Grumbine v. State, 60 Md. 355 (1883)
- Gunter v. State, 499 S.W.2d 954 (Tenn.Crim.App. 1973)
- Hagen v. Utah, 510 U.S. 399, 114 S.Ct. 958, 127 L.Ed.2d 252 (1994)
- Hall, (1828) 3 Car. & P. 409, 172 Eng. Rep. 477
- Hansen v. Dixon, (1906) 96 L.T. 32, (1906) 23 T.L.R. 56
- Harmony v. United States, 43 U.S. 210, 11 L.Ed. 239 (1844)
- Hartford Fire Insurance Co. v. California, 509 U.S. 764, 113 S.Ct. 2891, 125 L. Ed.2d 612 (1993)
- Harvey, (1747) 1 Wils. K.B. 164, 95 E.R. 551 (1747)
- Haworth v. Chapman, 113 Fla. 591, 152 So. 663 (1933)
- Helvering v. Mitchell, 303 U.S. 391, 58 S.Ct. 630, 82 L.Ed.2d 917 (1938)
- Henderson, [1948] 91 C.C.C. 97
- Henderson v. Sherborne, (1837) 150 E.R. 743
- Henry, 15 Idaho 755, 99 P. 1054 (1909)
- Henry v. United States, 432 F.2d 114 (9th Cir.1970)
- Hentzner v. State, 613 P.2d 821 (Alaska.1980)
- Higgins, (1801) 2 East 5, 102 E.R. 269
- Hill v. Baxter, [1958] 1 Q.B. 277, [1958] 1 All E.R. 193, [1958] 2 W.L.R. 76, 56 L.G.R. 117, 42 Cr. App. Rep. 51
- Hindawi, (1988) 10 Cr. App. Rep. 104
- Hines v. State, 40 S.W.3d 705 (Tex.App.2001)
- Hinks, [2001] 2 A.C. 241, [2000] 3 W.L.R. 1590, [2000] 4 All E.R. 833
- Holloway v. United States, 526 U.S. 1, 119 S.Ct. 966, 143 L.Ed.2d 1 (1999)
- Hoopengarner v. United States, 270 F.2d 465 (6th Cir.1959)
- Huber v. Steiner, (1835) 2 Bing.N.C. 202, 210, [1835] All E.R. 159
- Hughes v. Holley, (1988) 86 Cr. App. R. 130
- Hunt, [1987] A.C. 352, [1987] 1 All E.R. 1, [1986] 3 W.L.R. 1115, 84 Cr. App. R. 163
- Huntington v. Attrill, [1893] A.C. 150
- Hurt v. State, 184 Tenn. 608, 201 S.W.2d 988 (1947)
- Hussain, [1999] Crim. L.R. 570
- Hutton v. Edgerton, 6 S.C. 485 (1876)

- Hyde v. United States, 225 U.S. 347, 32 S.Ct. 793, 56 L.Ed. 114 (1912)
- Interstate Circuit, Inc. v. City of Dallas, 390 U.S. 676, 88 S.Ct. 1298, 20 L.Ed.2d 225 (1968)
- Jackson v. Commonwealth, 100 Ky. 239, 38 S.W. 422 (1896)
- Jackson v. Harrison, (1978) 138 C.L.R. 438, 455
- James v. Bowman, 190 U.S. 127, 23 S.Ct. 678, 47 L.Ed. 979 (1903)
- Jellico Coal-Min. Co. v. Commonwealth, 96 Ky. 373, 29 S.W. 26 (1895)
- Johnson, (1678) 2 Shaw. K.B. 1, 89 E.R. 753
- Johnson v. State, 251 Ind. 17, 238 N.E.2d 651 (1968)
- Jones, (1832) 4 B. & Ad. 345, 110 E.R. 485
- Jones v. Randall, (1774) Lofft 383, 98 E.R. 706
- Jones v. State, 32 Tex.Crim. 533, 25 S.W. 124 (1894)
- Jones v. United States, 137 U.S. 202, 11 S.Ct. 80, 34 L.Ed. 691 (1890)
- Jones v. United States, 529 U.S. 848, 120 S.Ct. 1904, 146 L.Ed.2d 902 (2000)
- Jones v. United States, 529 U.S. 848, 120 S.Ct. 1904, 146 L.Ed.2d 902 (2000)
- Joyce v. Director of Public Prosecutions, [1946] A.C. 347, [1946] 1 All E.R. 186, 174 L.T. 206, 62 T.L.R. 208, 31 Cr. App. Rep. 57, [1946] W.N. 31
- Kaitamaki, [1985] 1 A.C. 147, [1984] 2 All E.R. 435, [1984] 3 W.L.R. 137, [1984] Crim. L.R. 564, 79 Cr. App. Rep. 251
- Kamara v. Director of Public Prosecutions, [1974] A.C. 104, [1973] 2 All E.R. 1242, [1973] 3 W.L.R. 198, 57 Cr. App. Rep. 880, 137 J.P. 714
- Kansas v. Hendricks, 521 U.S. 346, 117 S.Ct. 2072, 138 L.Ed.2d 501 (1997)
- Keeble v. United States, 412 U.S. 205, 93 S.Ct. 1993, 36 L.Ed.2d 844 (1973)
- Keller v. State, 155 Tenn. 633, 299 S.W.803 (1927)
- Kent Justices, [1967] 2 Q.B. 153, [1967] 1 All E.R. 560, [1967] 2 W.L.R. 765, 131 J.P. 212
- Ker v. Illinois, 119 U.S. 436, 7 S.Ct. 225, 30 L.Ed. 421 (1886)
- Ker v. People, 110 Ill. 627 (1884)
- Keyn, (1876) 2 Q.B.D. 90, 2 Ex.D. 65
- Kilberg v. Northeast Airlines Inc., 9 N.Y.2d 34, 172 N.E.2d 526, 211 N.Y.S.2d 133 (1961)
- King v. State, 157 Tenn. 635, 11 S.W.2d 904 (1928)
- Kingston, [1995] 2 A.C. 355, [1994] 3 All E.R. 353, [1994] 3 W.L.R. 519, [1994] Crim. L.R. 846, 99 Cr. App. Rep. 286, 158 J.P. 717
- Kinsella v. United States, 361 U.S. 234, 80 S.Ct. 297, 4 L.Ed.2d 268 (1960)
- Knuller (Publishing, Printing and Promotions) Ltd. v. Director of Public Prosecutions, [1973] A.C. 435, [1972] 2 All E.R. 898, [1972] 3 W.L.R. 143, 56 Cr. App. Rep. 633, 136 J.P. 728
- Kolender v. Lawson, 461 U.S. 352, 103 S.Ct. 1855, 75 L.Ed.2d 903 (1983)
- Kunkle v. State, 32 Ind. 220 (1869)
- LaBarge v. State, 74 Wis.2d 327, 246 N.W.2d 794 (1976)
- Lacy's Case, (1582) 1 Leon. 270
- Lambert, [2002] 2 A.C. 545, [2001] 3 W.L.R. 206, [2002] 1 All E.R. 2
- Langley, (1703) 2 Salk. 697, 91 E.R. 590
- Lanzetta v. New Jersey, 306 U.S. 451, 59 S.Ct. 618, 83 L.Ed. 888 (1939)

- Larkins v. N.U.M., [1985] I.R. 671; Bank of Ireland v. Meeneghan, [1994] 3 I.R. 111
- Larsen v. State, 86 Nev. 451, 470 P.2d 417 (1970)
- Lauritzen v. Larsen, 345 U.S. 571, 73 S.Ct. 921, 97 L.Ed. 1254 (1953)
- Lawrence v. Texas, 539 U.S. 558, 123 S.Ct. 2472, 156 L.Ed.2d 508 (2003)
- Le Brun, [1992] Q.B. 61
- Lemke v. United States, 14 Alaska 587, 211 F.2d 73 (9th Cir. 1954)
- Leory, 285 Md. 508, 403 A.2d 1226 (1979)
- Lewisham Borough Council v. Roberts, [1949] 2 K.B. 608, [1949] 1 All E.R. 815, 829, 47 L.G.R. 479, 153 E.G. 262, [1949] E.G.D. 187, 65 T.L.R. 423, 113 J. P. 260, 208 L.T. 23, 210 L.T. 322, [1949] W.N. 165, 100 L.Q.R. 588
- Lim Chin Aik, [1963] A.C. 160, 171 [1963] 1 All E.R. 223, [1963] 2 W.L.R. 42
- Lindsey v. Washington, 301 U.S. 397, 57 S.Ct. 797, 81 L.Ed. 1182 (1937)
- Liparota v. United States, 471 U.S. 419, 105 S.Ct. 2084, 85 L.Ed.2d 434 (1985)
- Livings v. Davis, 465 So.2d 507 (Fla.1985)
- Long v. State, 44 Del. 262, 65 A.2d 489 (1949)
- Lonschein v. Warden, 43 Misc.2d 109, 250 N.Y.S.2d 15 (1964)
- Lutwin v. State, 97 N.J.L. 67, 117 A. 164 (1922)
- Lynce v. Mathis, 519 U.S. 433, 117 S.Ct. 891, 137 L.Ed.2d 63 (1997)
- Lynch v. Paraguay Provisional Government, [1861–1873] All E.R. 934, [1861–73] All E.R. 934
- M. Kraus & Bros. v. United States, 327 U.S. 614, 66 S.Ct. 705, 90 L.Ed. 894 (1946)
- Macleod v. Attorney General for New South Wales, [1891] A.C. 455, 459
- Magellan Pirates, (1853) 1 Sp.Ecc.&Ad. 81, 164 E.R. 47
- Mali v. Keeper of the Common Jail, 120 U.S. 1, 7 S.Ct. 385, 30 L.Ed. 565 (1887)
- Manaca, 146 Mich. 697, 110 N.W. 75 (1906)
- Manley, [1933] 1 K.B. 529
- Manser, (1584) 2 Co. Rep. 3, 76 Eng. Rep. 392
- Marbury v. Madison, 5 U.S. 137, 2 L.Ed. 60, 1 Cranch 137 (1803)
- Marsh v. State, 95 N.M. 224, 620 P.2d 878 (1980)
- Martin, [1956] 2 Q.B. 272, [1956] 2 All E.R. 86, [1956] 2 W.L.R. 975, 120 J.P. 255, 40 Cr. App. Rep. 68; Naylor, [1962] 2 Q.B. 527, [1961] 2 All E.R. 932, [1961] 3 W.L.R. 898, 45 Cr. App. Rep. 69, 125 J.P. 603
- Masilela, 1968 (2) S.A. 558 (A.D.)
- Matthews, [1950] 1 All E.R. 137, 48 L.G.R. 190, 66 T.L.R. (Pt. 1) 153, 114 J.P. 73, 34 Cr. App. Rep. 55
- Mawgan, (1838) 112 E.R. 927
- McBoyle v. United States, 283 U.S. 25, 51 S.Ct. 340, 75 L.Ed. 816 (1931)
- McCord v. People, 46 N.Y. 470 (1871)
- McElroy v. United States, 361 U.S. 281, 80 S.Ct. 305, 4 L.Ed.2d 282 (1960)
- McGuire v. State, 76 Miss. 504, 25 So. 495 (1899)
- McKinley v. United States, 249 U.S. 397, 39 S.Ct. 324, 63 L.Ed. 668 (1919)
- McNally v. United States, 483 U.S. 350, 107 S.Ct. 2875, 97 L.Ed.2d 292 (1987)
- MH, [2004] W.L. 137 2419
- Michell v. Brown, (1858) 120 E.R. 909

- Mildmay, (1584) 1 Co. Rep. 175a, 76 Eng. Rep. 379
- Miller, [1983] 2 A.C. 161, [1983] 1 All E.R. 978, [1983] 2 W.L.R. 539, 77 Cr. App. Rep. 17
- Miller v. Commonwealth, 25 Va.App. 727, 492 S.E.2d 482 (1997)
- Miller v. Florida, 482 U.S. 423, 107 S.Ct. 2446, 96 L.Ed.2d 351 (1987)
- Mistretta v. United States, 488 U.S. 361, 109 S.Ct. 647, 102 L.Ed.2d 714 (1989)
- M'Kenzie, (1820) 168 E.R. 881
- Moreno, 58 Cal.App.3d 740, 130 Cal.Rptr. 78 (1976)
- Morgan, [1976] A.C. 182, [1975] 2 W.L.R. 913, [1975] 2 All E.R. 347
- Moskal v. United States, 498 U.S. 103, 111 S.Ct. 461, 112 L.Ed.2d 449 (1990)
- Moussa, [1983] Crim. L.R. 618
- Murray v. The Schooner Charming Betsy, 6 U.S. 64, 2 L.Ed. 208 (1804)
- Muscarello v. United States, 524 U.S. 125, 118 S.Ct. 1911, 141 L.Ed.2d 111 (1998)
- Mutual Life Ins. Co. v. Bryant, 296 Ky. 815, 177 S.W.2d 588 (1943)
- Novello v. Hinrischen Edition Ltd., [1951] Ch. 595
- O'Connor v. United States, 399 A.2d 21 (D.C.Cir.1979)
- Odekirk v. Ryan, 85 F.2d 313 (1936)
- Ogden v. Folliot, (1790) 3 T.R. 726
- Ogden v. Ogden, [1908] P. 46, 77 L.J.P. 34, 97 L.T. 827, 24 T.L.R. 94
- Omaechevarria v. Idaho, 246 U.S. 343, 38 S.Ct. 323, 62 L.Ed. 763 (1918)
- Page, [1954] 1 Q.B. 170, 175, [1953] 2 All E.R. 1355, [1953] 3 W.L.R. 895, 37 Cr. App. Rep. 189
- Palmer v. City of Euclid, 402 U.S. 544, 91 S.Ct. 1563, 29 L.Ed.2d 98 (1971)
- Paquete Habana, The Lola 175 U.S. 677, 20 S.Ct 290, 44 L.Ed 320 (1900)
- Parish, (1837) 8 Car. & P. 94, 173 Eng. Rep. 413
- Pattni, [2001] Crim. L.R. 570
- Pearce, 103 Utah 522, 136 P.2d 969 (1943)
- People v. Acosta, 80 N.Y.2d 665, 593 N.Y.S.2d 978, 609 N.E.2d 518 (1993)
- People v. Bracey, 41 N.Y.2d 296, 392 N.Y.S.2d 412, 360 N.E.2d 1094 (1977)
- People v. Brengard, 265 N.Y. 100, 191 N.E. 850 (1934)
- People v. Buffum, 40 Cal.2d 709, 256 P.2d 317 (1953)
- People v. Causley, 299 Mich. 340, 300 N.W. 111 (1941)
- People v. Clark, 242 N.Y. 313, 151 N.E. 631 (1926)
- People v. Decina, 2 N.Y.2d 133, 138 N.E.2d 799, 157 N.Y.S.2d 558 (1956)
- People v. Donovan, 53 Misc.2d 687, 279 N.Y.S.2d 404 (Ct.Spec.Sess.1967)
- People v. Downer, 57 Cal.2d 800, 22 Cal. Rptr. 347, 372 P.2d 107 (1962)
- People v. Edenburg, 88 Cal.App. 558, 263 P. 857 (1928)
- People v. Elmore, 128 Ill.App.2d 312, 261 N.E.2d 736 (1970)
- People v. Ferguson, 134 Cal.App. 41, 24 P.2d 965 (1933)
- People v. Fraser, 96 N.Y.2d 318, 728 N.Y.S.2d 115, 752 N.E.2d 244 (2001)
- People v. Frysig, 628 P.2d 1004 (Colo.1981)
- People v. Grant, 242 App.Div. 310, 275 N.Y.S. 74 (1934)
- People v. Hawkins, 311 Ill.App.3d 418, 243 Ill.Dec. 621, 723 N.E.2d 1222 (2000)
- People v. Mahboubian, 74 N.Y.2d 174, 544 N.Y.S.2d 769, 543 N.E.2d 34 (1989)

- People v. Marrero, 69 N.Y.2d 382, 515 N.Y.S.2d 212, 507 N.E.2d 1068 (1987)
- People v. McCalla, 63 Cal.App. 783, 220 P. 436 (1923)
- People v. Nichols, 3 Cal.3d 150, 89 Cal.Rptr. 721, 474 P.2d 673 (1970)
- People v. Oliver, 1 N.Y.2d 152, 134 N.E.2d 197, 151 N.Y.S.2d 367 (1956)
- People v. Stead, 845 P.2d 1156 (1993)
- People v. Tompkins, 186 N.Y. 413, 79 N.E. 326 (1906)
- People v. Townsend, 214 Mich. 267, 183 N.W. 177 (1921)
- People v. Warren, 66 N.Y.2d 831, 498 N.Y.S.2d 353, 489 N.E.2d 240 (1985)
- People v. Weeren, 26 Cal.3d 654, 163 Cal.Rptr. 255, 607 P.2d 1279 (1980)
- People v. Wong, 182 A.D.2d 98, 588 N.Y.S.2d 119 (1992)
- Peoples v. Commonwealth, 87 Ky. 487, 9 S.W. 509 (1888)
- Pepper v. Hart, [1993] A.C. 593
- Percy, [2002] Crim. L.R. 835, [2002] A.C.D. 24
- Perez v. Brownell, 356 U.S. 44, 78 S.Ct. 568, 2 L.Ed.2d 603 (1958)
- Perrin v. United States, 444 U.S. 37, 100 S.Ct. 311, 62 L.Ed.2d 199 (1979)
- Pettibone v. United States, 148 U.S. 197, 13 S.Ct. 542, 37 L.Ed. 419 (1893)
- Phillips v. Eyre, (1870) 6 K.B. 1
- Pianka v. The Queen, [1979] A.C. 107
- Pierce v. State, 96 Okl.Cr. 76, 248 P.2d 633 (1952)
- Pigot, (1707) Holt 758, 90 E.R. 1317
- Post Office v. Estuary Radio Ltd., [1968] 2 Q.B. 740, [1967] 3 All E.R. 663, [1967] 1 W.L.R. 1396
- Potter v. State, 162 Ind. 213, 70 N.E. 129 (1904)
- Poulterers' Case, (1611) 9 Coke Rep. 55b, 77 E.R. 813
- Preddy, [1996] A.C. 815, [1996] 3 All E.R. 481, [1996] 3 W.L.R. 255
- Prince, (1875) L.R. 2 C.C.R. 154
- Proctor v. State, 15 Okl.Cr. 338, 176 P. 771 (1918)
- R, [1992] 1 A.C. 599, [1991] 4 All E.R. 481, [1991] 3 W.L.R. 767, 94 Cr. App. Rep. 216, 155 J.P. 989, [1992] Crim. L.R. 207, [1992] 1 F.L.R. 217, [1992] Fam. Law 108
- Raley v. Ohio, 360 U.S. 423, 79 S.Ct. 1257, 3 L.Ed.2d 1344 (1959)
- Ramsay, [1967] N.Z.L.R. 1005
- Ratzlaf v. United States, 510 U.S. 135, 114 S.Ct. 655, 126 L.Ed.2d 615 (1994)
- Raulin v. Fischer, [1911] 2 K.B. 93
- Redmond v. State, 36 Ark. 58 (1880)
- Rees v. Secretary of State for the Home Department, [1986] 1 A.C. 937, [1986] 2 All E.R. 321, [1986] 2 W.L.R. 1024, 83 Cr. App. Rep. 128
- Reid v. Covert, 354 U.S. 1, 77 S.Ct. 1222, 1 L.Ed.2d 1148 (1957)
- Rewis v. United States, 401 U.S. 808, 91 S.Ct. 1056, 28 L.Ed.2d 493 (1971)
- Rice v. Rehner, 463 U.S. 713, 103 S.Ct. 3291, 77 L.Ed.2d 961 (1983)
- Rivett v. State, 578 P.2d 946 (Alaska, 1978)
- Robinson, [1915] 2 K.B. 342
- Robinson v. California, 370 U.S. 660, 82 S.Ct. 1417, 8 L.Ed.2d 758 (1962)
- Robinson v. State, 353 Md. 683, 728 A.2d 698 (1999)
- Roderick, (1837) 7 Car. & P. 795, 173 E.R. 347

- Rogers v. Tennessee, 532 U.S. 451, 121 S.Ct. 1693, 149 L.Ed.2d 697 (2001)
- Romer v. Evans, 517 U.S. 620, 116 S.Ct. 1620, 134 L.Ed.2d 855 (1996)
- Ross v. Oregon, 227 U.S. 150, 33 S.Ct. 220, 57 L.Ed. 458 (1913)
- S.E.C. v. Robert Collier & Co., 76 F.2d 939 (2nd Cir.1935)
- SA Consortium General Textiles v. Sun & Sand Agencies Ltd., [1978] Q.B. 279, [1978] 2 All E.R. 339, [1978] 2 W.L.R. 1
- Sale v. Haitian Centers Council, Inc., 509 U.S. 155, 113 S.Ct. 2549, 125 L.Ed.2d 128 (1993)
- Salinas v. United States, 522 U.S. 52, 118 S.Ct. 469, 139 L.Ed.2d 352 (1997)
- Salomon v. Commissioner of Customs and Excise, [1967] 2 Q.B. 116, [1966] 3 All E.R. 871, [1966] 3 W.L.R. 1223
- Sanders, [2006] E.W.C.A. Crim. 1842
- Sawoniuk, [2000] 2 Cr. App. Rep. 220, [2000] Crim. L.R. 506
- Schemmer v. Property Resources Ltd., [1975] Ch. 273
- Schlossman v. State, 105 Md.App. 277, 659 A.2d 371 (1995)
- Schuster v. State, 48 Ala. 199 (1872)
- Schwegmann Bros. v. Calvert Distillers Corp., 341 U.S. 384, 71 S.Ct. 745, 95 L. Ed. 1035 (1951)
- Scofield, (1784) Cald. Mag. Rep. 397
- Scott, [1967] V.R. 276
- Screws v. United States, 325 U.S. 91, 65 S.Ct. 1031, 89 L.Ed. 1495 (1945)
- Sedley, [1664] 1 Siderfin 168, 1 Keb. 620
- Seling v. Young, 531 U.S. 250, 121 S.Ct. 727, 148 L.Ed.2d 734 (2001)
- Shaw v. Director of Public Prosecutions, [1962] A.C. 220, [1961] 2 All E.R. 446, [1961] 2 W.L.R. 897, 45 Cr. App. Rep. 113, 125 J.P. 437
- Sheed v. State, 61 Okl.Cr. 96, 65 P.2d 1245 (1937)
- Sheldrake, [2005] 1 A.C. 264, [2005] 1 All E.R. 237, [2005] 1 Cr. App. R. 28
- Shuttlesworth v. City of Birmingham, 382 U.S. 87, 86 S.Ct. 211, 15 L.Ed.2d 176 (1965)
- Sidley, (1664) 1 Sid. 168, 1 Keble 620, 82 E.R. 1036
- Simpson v. United States, 435 U.S. 6, 98 S.Ct. 909, 55 L.Ed.2d 70 (1978)
- Singh, [1974] 1 All E.R. 26, [1973] 1 W.L.R. 1444, 138 J.P. 85
- Sizemore v. Commonwealth, 218 Va. 980, 243 S.E.2d 212 (1978)
- Smallwood v. District of Columbia, 17 F.2d 210 (D.C.Cir.1927)
- Smith, (1869) 11 Cox C.C. 210
- Smith, 135 Mo. 223, 36 S.W. 628 (1896)
- Smith v. Benabe, (1937) 1 All E.R. 523
- Smith v. Commonwealth, 54 Pa. 209 (1867)
- Smith v. Doe, 538 U.S. 84, 123 S.Ct. 1140, 155 L.Ed.2d 164 (2003)
- Smith v. Hern, 102 Kan. 373, 170 P. 990 (1918)
- Smith v. United States, 507 U.S. 197, 113 S.Ct. 1178, 122 L.Ed.2d 548 (1993)
- Société Anonyme Metellurgique de Prayon v. Koppel, (1933) 77 S.J. 800
- Sparks v. Commonwealth, 66 Ky. 111 (1868)
- Squire v. State, 46 Ind. 459 (1874)
- Starling, (1664) 1 Sid. 174, 82 E.R. 1039

- State v. Alexander, 76 Or. 329, 148 P. 1136 (1915)
- State v. Anderson, 94 Wash.App. 151, 971 P.2d 585 (1999)
- State v. Anthony, 179 Or. 282, 169 P.2d 587 (1946)
- State v. Archuletta, 526 P.2d 911 (Utah 1974)
- State v. Avery, 7 Conn. 266 (1828)
- State v. Bautista, 86 Hawaii 207, 948 P.2d 1048 (1997)
- State v. Beckwith, 135 Me. 423, 198 A. 739 (1938)
- State v. Bell, 136 N.C. 674, 49 S.E. 163 (1904)
- State v. Bellows, 596 N.W.2d 509 (Iowa 1999)
- State v. Benton, 38 Del. 1, 187 A. 609 (1936)
- State v. Blechman, 135 N.J.L. 99, 50 A.2d 152 (1946)
- State v. Brantley, 201 Or. 637, 271 P.2d 668 (1954)
- State v. Brewer, 932 S.W.2d 1 (Tenn.Cr.App.1996)
- State v. Budge, 126 Me. 223, 137 A. 244 (1927)
- State v. Burger, 590 N.W.2d 197 (N.D.1999)
- State v. Burnham, 15 N.H. 396 (1844)
- State v. Cain, 9 W. Va. 559 (1874)
- State v. Carter, 89 Wash.2d 236, 570 P.2d 1218 (1977)
- State v. Chaplain, 101 Kan. 413, 166 P. 238 (1917)
- State v. Chew, 150 N.J. 30, 695 A.2d 1301 (1997)
- State v. Chicago, M. & St.P.R. Co., 130 Minn. 144, 153 N.W. 320 (1915)
- State v. Click, 2 Ala. 26 (1841)
- State v. Clottu, 33 Ind. 409 (1870)
- ACP 10987/07 State v. Cohen (unreported, March 2, 2009)
- State v. Collins, 55 Wash.2d 469, 348 P.2d 214 (1960)
- State v. Colvin, 645 N.W.2d 449 (Minn.2002)
- State v. Curtis, 230 N.C. 169, 52 S.E.2d 364 (1949)
- State v. Dailey, 191 Ind. 678, 134 N.E. 481 (1922)
- State v. Daley, 29 Conn. 272 (1860)
- State v. Darchuck, 117 Mont. 15, 156 P.2d 173 (1945)
- State v. Davis, 63 Wis.2d 75, 216 N.W.2d 31 (1974)
- State v. De Wolfe, 67 Neb. 321, 93 N.W. 746 (1903)
- State v. DeCastro, 81 Haw. 147, 913 P.2d 558 (App.1996)
- State v. Detter, 298 N.C. 604, 260 S.E.2d 567 (1979)
- State v. Dorby, 217 Iowa 858, 250 N.W. 702 (1933)
- State v. Downs, 116 N.C. 1064, 21 S.E. 689 (1895)
- State v. Dube, 409 A.2d 1102 (Me.1979)
- State v. Dyer, 289 A.2d 693 (Me.1972)
- State v. Elliot, 177 Conn. 1, 411 A.2d 3 (1979)
- State v. Foster, 22 R.I. 163, 46 A. 833 (1900)
- State v. Foster, 379 A.2d 1219 (Me.1977)
- State v. Gallion, 572 P.2d 683 (Utah.1977)
- State v. Gerhardt, 145 Ind. 439, 44 N.E. 469 (1896)
- State v. Goodenow, 65 Me. 30 (1876)
- State v. Guzman, 89 Haw. 27, 968 P.2d 194 (App.1998)

- State v. Hampton, 210 N.C. 283, 186 S.E. 251 (1936)
- State v. Harrison, 107 N.J.L. 213, 152 A. 867 (1931)
- State v. Hartzog, 26 Wash.App. 576, 615 P.2d 480 (1980)
- State v. Hartzog, 96 Wash.2d 383, 635 P.2d 694 (1981)
- State v. Hobokin, 768 S.W.2d 76 (Mo.1989)
- State v. Hollyway, 41 Iowa 200 (1875)
- State v. Horton, 139 N.C. 588, 51 S.E. 945 (1905)
- State v. Huff, 89 Me. 521, 36 A. 1000 (1897)
- State v. Jewell, 345 So.2d 1166 (La.1977)
- State v. Johnston, 149 S.C. 195, 146 S.E. 657 (1929)
- State v. Jones, 44 N.M. 623, 107 P.2d 324 (1940)
- State v. Kahalewai, 56 Haw. 481, 541 P.2d 1020 (1975)
- State v. Kellison, 233 Iowa 1274, 11 N.W.2d 371 (1943)
- State v. King, 257 N.W.2d 693 (Minn.1977)
- State v. Labato, 7 N.J. 137, 80 A.2d 617 (1951)
- State v. Lampe, 131 Minn. 65, 154 N.W. 737 (1915)
- State v. Lawrence, 97 N.C. 492, 2 S.E. 367 (1887)
- State v. Longino, 109 Miss. 125, 67 So. 902 (1915)
- State v. Main, 16 Wis. 398 (1863)
- State v. Mandel, 78 Ariz. 226, 278 P.2d 413 (1954)
- State v. Mellenberger, 163 Or. 233, 95 P.2d 709 (1939)
- State v. Merrifield, 180 Kan. 267, 303 P.2d 155 (1956)
- State v. Miller, 74 Kan. 667, 87 P. 723 (1906)
- State v. Millett, 392 A.2d 521 (Me.1978)
- State v. Moore, 196 La. 617, 199 So. 661 (1940)
- State v. Nagel, 98 Idaho 129, 559 P.2d 308 (1977)
- State v. O'Brian, 32 N.J.L. 169 (1867)
- State v. Olsen, 618 N.W.2d 346 (Iowa 2000)
- State v. O'Neil, 147 Iowa 513, 126 N.W. 454 (1910)
- State v. Pardon, 272 N.C. 72, 157 S.E.2d 698 (1967)
- State v. Partlow, 91 N.C. 550 (1884)
- State v. Patten, 353 N.W.2d 30 (N.D.1984)
- State v. Pelican Insurance Co., 127 U.S. 265, 8 S.Ct. 1370, 32 L.Ed. 239 (1888)
- State v. Potts, 75 Ariz. 211, 254 P.2d 1023 (1953)
- State v. Redmon, 121 S.C. 139, 113 S.E. 467 (1922)
- State v. Ross, 573 N.W.2d 906 (Iowa 1998)
- State v. Sasse, 6 S.D. 212, 60 N.W. 853 (1894)
- State v. Sheedy, 125 N.H. 108, 480 A.2d 887 (1984)
- State v. Simmons, 143 N.C. 613, 56 S.E. 701 (1907)
- State v. Smith, 262 N.J.Super. 487, 621 A.2d 493 (1993)
- State v. Smith, 539 P.2d 754 (Okl.Crim.App.1975)
- State v. Stewart, 143 Wis.2d 28, 420 N.W.2d 44 (1988)
- State v. Stockton, 97 Wash.2d 528, 647 P.2d 21 (1982)
- State v. Striggles, 202 Iowa 1318, 210 N.W. 137 (1926)
- State v. Sullivan, 110 Mo.App. 75, 84 S.W. 105 (1904)

- State v. Tapp, 26 Utah.2d 392, 490 P.2d 334 (1971)
- State v. Tuttle, 730 P.2d 630 (Utah 1986)
- State v. Waterman, 190 N.W.2d 809 (Iowa.1971)
- State v. Western Union Tel. Co., 12 N.J. 468, 97 A.2d 480 (1953)
- State v. Whitman, 116 Fla. 196, 156 So. 705 (1934)
- State v. Whitoomb, 52 Iowa 85, 2 N.W. 970 (1879)
- State v. Wilchinski, 242 Conn. 211, 700 A.2d 1 (1997)
- State v. Willy, 155 Or.App. 279, 963 P.2d 739 (1998)
- Stinnett v. Commonwealth, 55 F.2d 644 (4th Cir.1932)
- Stone v. United States, 506 F.2d 561 (8th Cir.1974)
- Strassheim v. Daily, 221 U.S. 280, 31 S.Ct. 558, 55 L.Ed. 735 (1911)
- Strouther v. Commonwealth, 92 Va. 789, 22 S.E. 852 (1895)
- Sullens, 1 Mood. 129, 168 E.R. 1212 (1826)
- Sutton, (1736) Cas. T. Hard. 370, 95 E.R. 240
- Swan v. Moore, 14 La.Ann. 833 (1859)
- Sweet v. Parsley, [1970] A.C. 132, [1969] 1 All E.R. 347, [1969] 2 W.L.R. 470, 133 J.P. 188, 53 Cr. App. Rep. 221, 209 E.G. 703, [1969] E.G.D. 123
- Tan, [1983] Q.B. 1053
- Taylor, [1950] 2 K.B. 368
- Thabo Meli, [1954] 1 All E.R. 373, [1954] 1 W.L.R. 228
- The Antelope, (1825) 10 Wheat. 66
- The Colorado, [1923] All E.R. 531, [1923] P. 102, 92 L.J.P. 100, 128 L.T. 759, 16 Asp. M.L.C. 145
- Thurston, (1663) 1 Lev. 91, 83 E.R. 312
- Timberley, (1663) 1 Sid. 68, 1 Keble 203, 82 E.R. 974, 83 E.R. 900
- Tolson, (1889) 23 Q.B.D. 168, [1889] All E.R. 26
- Tosti, [1997] Crim. L.R. 746
- Touby v. United States, 500 U.S. 160, 111 S.Ct. 1752, 114 L.Ed.2d 219 (1991)
- Treacy v. Director of Public Prosecutions, [1971] A.C. 537, 559, [1971] 1 All E. R. 110, [1971] 2 W.L.R. 112, 55 Cr. App. Rep. 113, 135 J.P. 112
- Turner v. State, 1 Ohio St. 422 (1853)
- United States of America v. Inkley, [1989] Q.B. 255, [1988] 3 W.L.R. 304, [1988] 3 All E.R. 144
- United States v. Achter, 52 F.3d 753 (8th Cir.1995)
- United States v. Albertini, 830 F.2d 985 (9th Cir.1987)
- United States v. Allied Towing Corp., 602 F.2d 612 (4th Cir.1979)
- United States v. Alpers, 338 U.S. 680, 70 S.Ct. 352, 94 L.Ed. 457 (1950)
- United States v. Antelope, 430 U.S. 641, 97 S.Ct. 1395, 51 L.Ed.2d 701 (1977)
- United States v. Arra, 630 F.2d 836 (1st Cir.1980)
- United States v. Austin, 915 F.2d 363 (8th Cir.1990)
- United States v. Barker, 546 F.2d 940 (D.C.Cir.1976)
- United States v. Bass, 404 U.S. 336, 92 S.Ct. 515, 30 L.Ed.2d 488 (1971)
- United States v. Batchelder, 442 U.S. 114, 99 S.Ct. 2198, 60 L.Ed.2d 755 (1979)
- United States v. Benitez, 741 F.2d 1312 (11th Cir.1984)
- United States v. Blue, 722 F.2d 383 (8th Cir.1983)

- United States v. Bowman, 260 U.S. 94, 43 S.Ct. 39, 67 L.Ed. 149 (1922)
- United States v. Brewer, 139 U.S. 278, 11 S.Ct. 538, 35 L.Ed. 190 (1891)
- United States v. Burns, 529 F.2d 114 (9th Cir.1975)
- United States v. Cardales, 168 F.3d 548 (1st Cir.1999)
- United States v. Casson, 434 F.2d 415 (D.C.Cir.1970)
- United States v. Clegg, 846 F.2d 1221 (9th Cir.1988)
- United States v. Colpon, 185 F.2d 629 (1950)
- United States v. Coolidge, 14 U.S. 415, 4 L.Ed. 124 (1816)
- United States v. Crawford, 115 F.3d 1397 (1997)
- United States v. Cruz-Jiminez, 977 F.2d 95 (3rd Cir. 1992)
- United States v. Davis, 167 F.2d 228 (D.C.Cir.1948)
- United States v. Davis, 25 F.Cas. 786 (C.C.D.Mass.1837)
- United States v. Davis, 978 F.2d 415 (8th Cir.1992)
- United States v. Desena, 287 F.3d 170 (2nd Cir.2002)
- United States v. Doyon, 194 F.3d 207 (1st Cir.1999)
- United States v. Duggan, 743 F.2d 59 (2nd Cir.1984)
- United States v. Evans, 333 U.S. 483, 68 S.Ct. 634, 92 L.Ed. 823 (1948)
- United States v. Everett, 700 F.2d 900 (3rd Cir. 1983)
- United States v. Felix-Gutierrez, 940 F.2d 1200 (9th Cir.1991)
- United States v. Fisher, 6 U.S. 358, 2 L.Ed. 304 (1804)
- United States v. Flores, 289 U.S. 137, 53 S.Ct. 580, 77 L.Ed. 1086 (1993)
- United States v. Gonzalez, 776 F.2d 931 (11th Cir.1985)
- United States v. Grimaud, 220 U.S. 506, 31 S.Ct. 480, 55 L.Ed. 563 (1911)
- United States v. Guiteau, 12 D.C. 498 (1882)
- United States v. Gutierrez-Gonzalez, 184 F.3d 1160 (10th Cir.1999)
- United States v. Hancock, 231 F.3d 557 (9th Cir.2000)
- United States v. Harriss, 347 U.S. 612, 74 S.Ct. 808, 98 L.Ed. 989 (1954)
- United States v. Hill, 279 F.3d 731 (9th Cir.2002)
- United States v. Holmes, 18 U.S. 412, 5 L.Ed. 122 (1820)
- United States v. Hudson, 11 U.S. 32, 3 L.Ed. 259 (1812)
- United States v. International Minerals & Chemical Corp., 402 U.S. 558, 91 S. Ct. 1697, 29 L.Ed.2d 178 (1971)
- United States v. Keller, 451 F.Supp. 631 (1978)
- United States v. L. Cohen Grocery Co., 255 U.S. 81, 41 S.Ct. 298, 65 L.Ed. 516 (1921)
- United States v. Lanier, 520 U.S. 259, 117 S.Ct. 1219, 137 L.Ed.2d 432 (1997)
- United States v. Lee, 886 F.2d 998 (1989)
- United States v. Lopez, 514 U.S. 549, 115 S.Ct. 1624, 131 L.Ed.2d. 626 (1995); United States v. Bell, 70 F.3d 495 (7th Cir.1995)
- United States v. Lopez-Alvarez, 970 F.2d 583 (9th Cir.1992)
- United States v. Lyles, 4 Cranch C.C. 469, Fed.Cas.No. 15,646 (1834)
- United States v. Mancuso, 139 F.2d 90 (3rd Cir.1943)
- United States v. Martinez-Hidalgo, 993 F.2d 1052 (3rd Cir.1993)
- United States v. McBratney, 104 U.S. 621, 26 L.Ed. 869 (1881)
- United States v. McDowell, 714 F.2d 106 (11th Cir. 1983)

- United States v. McKenzie, 922 F.2d 1323 (1991)
- United States v. Mersky, 361 U.S. 431, 80 S.Ct. 459, 4 L.Ed.2d 423 (1960)
- United States v. Moore, 423 U.S. 122, 96 S.Ct. 335, 46 L.Ed.2d 333 (1975)
- United States v. National Dairy Products Corp., 372 U.S. 29, 83 S.Ct. 594, 9 L. Ed.2d 561 (1963)
- United States v. One Big Six Wheel, 166 F.3d 498 (2nd Cir.1999)
- United States v. Ormsby, 252 F.3d 844 (6th Cir.2001)
- United States v. Pace, 898 F.2d 1218 (1990)
- United States v. Parker, 622 F.2d 298 (8th Cir.1980)
- United States v. Paskow, 11 F.3d 873 (1993)
- United States v. Peggy, 5 U.S. 103, 2 L.Ed. 49, 1 Cranch 103 (1801)
- United States v. Pennsylvania Industrial Chemical Corp., 411 U.S. 655, 93 S.Ct. 1804, 36 L.Ed.2d 567 (1973)
- United States v. Peterson, 812 F.2d 486 (9th Cir.1987)
- United States v. Plummer, 221 F.3d 1298 (11th Cir.2000)
- United States v. Poludniak, 657 F.2d 948 (8th Cir.1981)
- United States v. Postal, 589 F.2d 862 (5th Cir.1979)
- United States v. Powell, 423 U.S. 87, 96 S.Ct. 316, 46 L.Ed.2d 228 (1975)
- United States v. Quarles, 350 U.S. 11, 76 S.Ct. 1, 100 L.Ed. 8 (1955)
- United States v. Ramirez-Valencia, 202 F.3d 1106 (9th Cir.2000)
- United States v. Ramos, 179 F.3d 1333 (11th Cir.1999)
- United States v. Reagan, 453 F.2d 165 (6th Cir.1971)
- United States v. Reese, 92 U.S. 214, 23 L.Ed. 563 (1876)
- United States v. Ricardo, 619 F.2d 1124 (5th Cir.1980)
- United States v. Ricker, 670 F.2d 987 (11th Cir.1982)
- United States v. Rodgers, 150 U.S. 249, 14 S.Ct. 109, 37 L.Ed. 1071 (1893)
- United States v. Rodriguez, 182 F.Supp. 479 (S.D.Cal.1960)
- United States v. Ross, 439 F.2d 1355 (9th Cir.1971)
- United States v. Sampol, 636 F.2d 621 (D.C.Cir.1980)
- United States v. Schutte, 610 F.2d 698 (10th Cir.1979)
- United States v. Sepulveda, 115 F.3d 882 (11th Cir.1997)
- United States v. Smith, 18 U.S. 153, 5 L.Ed. 57 (1820)
- United States v. Tallmadge, 829 F.2d 767 (9th Cir.1987)
- United States v. Thomas, 893 F.2d 1066 (9th Cir.1990)
- United States v. Turpin, 117 F.3d 678 (1997)
- United States v. Vasquez-Valesco, 15 F.3d 833 (9th Cir.1994)
- United States v. Walczak, 783 F.2d 852 (9th Cir.1986)
- United States v. Wells, 519 U.S. 482, 117 S.Ct. 921, 137 L.Ed.2d 107 (1997)
- United States v. West Indies Transport Inc., 127 F.3d 299 (3rd Cir.1997)
- United States v. Whitlock, 663 F.2d 1094 (D.C.Cir.1980)
- United States v. Wiltberger, 18 U.S. 76, 5 L.Ed. 37, 5 Wheat. 76, 95 (1820)
- United States v. Wright-Barker, 784 F.2d 161 (3rd Cir.1986)
- United States v. X-Citement Video, Inc., 513 U.S. 64, 115 S.Ct. 464, 130 L. Ed.2d 372 (1994)
- United States v. Yannott, 42 F.3d 999 (6th Cir.1994)

- United States v. Young, 936 F.2d 1050 (9th Cir.1991)
- United States v. Yunis, 681 F.Supp. 896 (D.D.C.1988)
- United States v. Yunis, 924 F.2d 1086 (D.C.Cir.1991)
- Vacco v. Quill, 521 U.S. 793, 117 S.Ct. 2293, 138 L.Ed.2d 834 (1997)
- Vantandillo, (1815) 4 M. & S. 73, 105 Eng. Rep. 762
- Vaughan, (1769) 4 Burr. 2494, 98 E.R. 308
- Vaux, (1613) 1 Blustrode 197, 80 Eng. Rep. 885
- Walker, (1989) 90 Cr. App. Rep. 226, [1990] Crim. L.R. 44
- Wallis v. Duke of Portland, (1797) 3 Ves. 494
- Walt v. State, 727 A.2d 836 (Del.1999)
- Warren v. United States, 659 F.2d 183 (1981)
- Weaver v. Graham, 450 U.S. 24, 101 S.Ct. 960, 67 L.Ed.2d 17 (1981)
- West Rand Central Gold Mining Co. Ltd., [1905] 2 K.B. 391
- Whitesides v. State, 79 Tenn. 474 (1883)
- Williams v. United States, 327 U.S. 711, 66 S.Ct. 778, 90 L.Ed. 962 (1946)
- Winters v. New York, 333 U.S. 507, 68 S.Ct. 665, 92 L.Ed. 840 (1948)
- Winters v. New York, 333 U.S. 507, 68 S.Ct. 665, 92 L.Ed. 840 (1948)
- Woolmington v. Director of Public Prosecutions, [1935] All E.R. 1, [1935] A.C. 462, [1935] 104 L.J.K.B. 433, [1935] 153 L.T. 232, [1935] 51 T.L.R. 446, [1935] 79 Sol. Jo. 401, [1935] 25 Cr. App. Rep. 72, [1935] 30 Cox C.C. 234
- Wright v. Superior Court, 15 Cal.4th 521, 63 Cal.Rptr.2d 322, 936 P.2d 101 (1997)
- Wylie, [1976] 2 N.Z.L.R. 167
- Y.B. Hill. 19 Hen. VI, f. 62, pl.1 (1431)
- Y.B. I Edw. IV, Mich. pl. 13 (1460)
- Y.B. Mich. 1 Hen. VII, f. 2, pl.2 (1485)
- Y.B. Mich. 11 Hen. VII, f. 11, pl.35 (1496)
- Y.B. Mich. 3 Hen. VII, f. 15, pl.30 (1488)
- Y.B. Trin. 20 Hen. VII, f.2, pl.4 (1505)
- Yakus v. United States, 321 U.S. 414, 64 S.Ct. 660, 88 L.Ed. 834 (1944)
- Yu Cong Eng v. Trinidad, 271 U.S. 500, 46 S.Ct. 619, 70 L.Ed. 1059 (1926)
- Zakrasek v. State, 197 Ind. 249, 150 N.E. 615 (1926)

German Cases

- BGH[1] 2, 194
- BGH 2, 317
- BGH 3, 105
- BGH 3, 259
- BGH 4, 1

[1]Bundesgerichtshof.

- BGH 4, 80
- BGH 5, 111
- BGH 5, 129
- BGH 6, 359
- BGH 7, 234
- BGH 7, 256
- BGH 8, 137
- BGH 9, 164
- BGH 9, 358
- BGH 10, 63
- BGH 10, 375
- BGH 11, 117
- BGH 12, 379
- BGH 13, 135
- BGH 14, 116
- BGH 15, 332
- BGH 16, 155
- BGH 17, 87
- BGH 18, 136
- BGH 20, 22
- BGH 20, 342
- BGH 21, 18
- BGH 22, 223
- BGH 23, 40
- BGH 27, 30
- BGH 29, 129
- BGH 30, 1
- BGH 33, 244
- BGH 34, 63
- BGH 35, 347
- BGH NStZ 1983, 268
- BGH NStZ 1992, 535
- BGH St 2, 300
- BGH St 4, 379
- BGH St 18, 12
- BGH St 20, 22
- BGH St 26, 288
- BGH St 30, 285
- BGH St 35, 390
- BGH VRS 65, 127
- BVerfG[2] NJW 1990, 1103
- BVerfG NStZ 1994, 480

[2]Bundesverfassungsgericht.

- BVerfGE 19, 342
- BVerfGE 24, 33
- BVerfGE 25, 269
- BVerfGE 25, 269
- BVerfGE 26, 41
- BVerfGE 26, 42
- BVerfGE 35, 382
- BVerfGE 37, 207
- BVerfGE 39, 1
- BVerfGE 39, 155
- BVerfGE 45, 187
- BVerfGE 48, 48
- BVerfGE 57, 250
- BVerfGE 61, 126
- BVerfGE 65, 76
- BVerfGE 71, 108
- BVerfGE 73, 206
- BVerfGE 88, 203
- RG[3] 32, 165
- RG 36, 402
- RG 53, 189
- RG 68, 65
- VRS[4] 60, 313

European Cases

- Brumarescu v. Romania, (2001) 33 E.H.R.R. 35
- C.R. v. United Kingdom, (1995) 21 E.H.R.R. 363
- Case 106/77 Amministrazione delle Finanze dello Stato v. Simmenthal SpA, [1978] E.C.R. 629, [1978] 3 C.M.L.R. 263
- Case 6/64 Costa v. E.N.E.L., [1964] E.C.R. 585, [1964] 3 C.M.L.R. 425
- Case 11/70 Internationale Handelsgesellschaft v. Einfuhr und Varratsstelle füd Futtermittel, [1970] E.C.R. 1125, [1972] C.M.L.R. 255
- Kokkinakis v. Greece, (1993) 17 E.H.R.R. 397
- SW and CR v. United Kingdom, (1995) 21 E.H.R.R. 363
- Case 26/62 Van Gend en Loos v. Netherlands Inland Revenue Administration, [1963] E.C.R. 1, [1963] C.M.L.R. 105
- Wünsche Handelsgesellschaft v. Germany, [1987] 3 C.M.L.R. 225

[3]Reichsgericht.

[4]Verkehrsrechts-Sammlung.

International Cases

- Anglo-Norwegian Fisheries, [1951] I.C.J. Rep. 116, 160
- Asylum Case, [1950] I.C.J. Rep. 266
- Corfu Channel, [1949] I.C.J. Rep. 1
- Land and Maritime Boundary between Cameroon and Nigeria, [1998] I.C.J. Rep. 28
- North Sea Continental Shelf Cases, [1969] I.C.J. Rep. 3, 44
- Rights of Passage over Indian Territory Case, [1960] I.C.J. Rep. 6

Bibliography

Abraham Abramovsky, *Extraterritorial Jurisdiction: The United States Unwarranted Attempt to Alter International Law in United States v. Yunis*, 15 Yale J. Int'l L. 121 (1990)

Norman Abrams, *Interpreting the Criminal Code Ordinance, 1936 – The Untapped Well*, 7 Isr. L. R. 25 (1972)

Ralph W. Aigler, *Legislation in Vague or General Terms*, 21 Mich. L. Rev. 831 (1923)

Edgar H. Ailes, *Substance and Procedure in the Conflict of Laws*, 39 Mich. L. Rev. 392 (1941)

Michael Akehurst, *Jurisdiction in International Law*, 46 British Yearbook of International Law 145 (1972)

Larry Alexander, *Are Procedural Rights Derivate Substantive Rights?*, 17 Law and Philosophy 19 (1998)

Peter Alldridge, *Making Crimianl Law Known*, Criminal Law Theory – Doctrines of the General Part 103 (Stephen Shute and A. P. Simester eds., 2005)

Kumaralingam Amirthalingam, *Mens Rea and Mistake of Law in Criminal Cases: A Lesson from South Africa*, 18 U.N.S.W.L.J. 428 (1995)

Jos Andenaes, *Determinism and Criminal Law*, 47 J. Crim. L. Criminology & Police Sci. 406 (1957)

John D. Appel, *Law as a Social Science in the Undergraduate Curriculum*, 10 J. Legal Educ. 485 (1958)

Gunther Arzt, *Ignorance or Mistake of Law*, 24 Am. J. Comp. L. 646 (1976)

Gunther Arzt, *The Problem of Mistake of Law*, 1986 BYU L. Rev. 711 (1986)

Andrew Ashworth, *Interpreting Criminal Statutes: A Crisis of Legality?*, 107 L.Q.R. 419 (1991)

Andrew Ashworth and Meredith Blake, *The Presumption of Innocence in English Criminal Law*, [1996] Crim. L. R. 306 (1996)

Andrew Ashworth, *Testing Fidelity to Legal Values: Official Involvement and Criminal Justice*, 63 Mod. L. Rev. 663 (2000)

Andrew Ashworth, *Is the Criminal Law a Lost Cause?*, 116 L.Q.R. 225 (2000)

Andrew Ashworth, Human Rights, Serious Crime and Criminal Procedure (2002)

Andrew Ashworth, Principles of Criminal Law (5th ed., 2006)

John Austin, The Province of Jurisprudence Determined (1832, 2000)

Mark Warren Bailey, *Early Legal Education in the United States: Natural Law Theory and Law as a Moral Science*, 48 J. Legal Educ. 311 (1998)

Thomas G. Barnes, *Star Chamber Mythology*, 5 Am. J. Legal. Hist. 1 (1961)

Thomas G. Barnes, *Due Process and Slow Process in the Late Elizibethan-Early Stuart Star Chamber*, 6 Am. J. Legal. Hist. 221 (1962)

Edouard Bartin, Principes de Droit International Privé I (1930)

Cherif M. Bassiouni, *Universal Jurisdiction for International Crimes: Historical Perspectives and Contemporary Practice*, 42 Va. J. Int'l L. 81, 88 (2001)

Robert Batey, *Vagueness and the Construction of Criminal Statutes – Balancing Acts*, 5 Va. J. Soc. Pol'y & L. 1 (1997)
Bernard W. Bell, *Legislative History without Legislative Intent: The Public Justification Approach to Statutory Interpretation*, 60 Ohio St. L. J. 1 (1999)
Jeremy Bentham, A Comment on The Commentaries: A Criticism of William Blackstone's Commentaries on the Laws of England 80 (1776, C.W. Everett ed., 1928)
Jeremy Bentham, Theory of Legislation (1975)
Norman Bentwich, *The Criminal Code of Palestine*, 83 L.J. 390 (1937)
Frances F. Berdan, The Aztecs of Central Mexico: An Imperial Society (2nd ed., 2005)
Harold J. Berman, Law and Revolution: The Formation of the Western Legal Tradition (1983)
Harold J. Berman, Faith and Order: The Reconciliation of Law and Religion (1993)
Harold J. Berman and Charles J. Reid Jr., *Roman Law in Europe and the Jus Commune: A Historical Overview with Emphasis on the New Legal Science of the Sixteenth Century*, 20 Syracuse J. Int'l L. & Com. 1 (1994)
James B. Blackburn, *Solicitation to Crimes*, 40 W.Va. L. Rev. 135 (1934)
Christopher L. Blakesley, *A Conceptual Framework for Extradition and Jurisdiction over Extra-territorial Crimes*, 1984 Utah L. Rev. 685 (1984)
Yehuda Z. Blum, *The Missing Reversioner: Reflections on the Status of Judea and Samaria*, 3 Isr. L. Rev. 279 (1968)
John J. Bonsignore, *Law as a Hard Science: On the Madness in Method*, 2 ALSA F. 49 (1977)
Gary B. Born, *A Reappraisal of the Extraterritorial Reach of U.S. Law*, 24 Law & Pol'y Int'l Bus. 1 (1992)
Henry de Bracton, De Legibus et Consuetudinibus Angliae (1260; G. E. Woodbine ed., S. E. Thorne trans., 1968–1977)
Curtis A. Bradley, *Universal Jurisdiction and U.S. Law*, 2001 U. Chi. Legal F. 323 (2001)
John Brewer and John Styles, An Ungovernable People: The English and Their Law in the Seventeenth and Eighteenth Centuries (1980)
Martin Broszat, Der Staat Hitlers – Grundlegung und Entwicklung seiner inneren Verfassung (1969)
Bartram S. Brown, *The Evolving Concept of Universal Jurisdiction*, 35 New Eng. L. Rev. 383 (2001)
George D. Brown, *Constitutionalizing the Federal Criminal Law Debate: Morrison, Jones and the ABA*, 2001 U. Ill. L. Rev. 983 (2001)
Lowell H. Brown, *Extraterritorial Jurisdiction Under the 1998 Amendments to the Foreign Corrupt Practices Act: Does the Government's Reach Exceed Its Grasp?*, 26 N.C. J. Int'l L. & Com. Reg. 239 (2001)
Ian Brownlie, Principles of International Law (4th ed., 1990)
Lynn R. Campbell, *Law as a Social Science*, 9 Dalhousie L. J. 404 (1984)
William C. Canby, American Indian Law in a Nutshell (3rd ed., 1998)
Russell Christopher, *Does Attempted Murder Deserve Greater Punishment than Murder – Moral Luck and the Duty to Prevent Harm*, 18 Notre Dame J.L. Ethics & Pub. Pol'y 419 (2004)
Helmut Coing, Europäisces Privatrecht, Band II: 19 Jahrhundert: Überblick Über die Entwicklung des Privatrechts in den ehemals gemeinrechtlichen Ländern (1989)
Sir Edward Coke, Institutions of the Laws of England – Third Part (6th ed., 1681, 1817, 2001)
Rex A. Collings Jr., *Unconstitutional Uncertainty – An Appraisal*, 40 Cornell L. Q. 195 (1955)
Lawrence Collins, Dicey and Morris The Conflict of Laws I (13th ed., 2000)
Lawrence Collins, Dicey and Morris The Conflict of Laws II (13th ed., 2000)
Michele Cotton. *A Foolish Consistency: Keeping Determinism out of the Criminal Law*, 15 B. U. Pub. Int. L. J. 5 (2006)
Theodore W. Cousens, *Agreement as an Element in Conspiracy*, 23 Va. L. Rev. 898 (1937)
James Crawford, The Creation of States in International Law (1979)
Homer D. Crotty, *The History of Insanity as a Defence to Crime in English Common Law*, 12 Cal. L. Rev. 105 (1924)

John W. Curran, *Solicitation: A Substantive Crime*, 17 Minn. L. Rev. 499 (1933)
Ian Dennis, *The Critical Condition of Criminal Law*, 50 Current Legal Problems 213 (1997)
Reed F. Dickerson, The Interpretation and Application of Statutes (1975)
Paul R. Dimond and Gene Sperling, *Of Cultural Determinism and the Limits of Law*, 83 Mich. L. Rev. 1065 (1985)
William S. Dodge, *Understanding the Presumption Against Extraterritoriality*, 16 Berkeley J. Int'l L. 85 (1998)
Veronica M. Dougherty, *Absurdity and the Limits of Literalism: Defining the Absurd Result Principle in Statutory Interpretation*, 44 Am. U. L. Rev. 127 (1994)
Markus Dirk Dubber, *The Possession Paradigm: The Special Part and the Police Power Model of the Criminal Process*, Defining Crimes – Essays on the Special Part of the Criminal Law 91 (Robin Antony Duff and Stuart P. Green eds., 2005)
Antony Robin Duff, Criminal Attempts (1996)
Robin Antony Duff, *Criminalizing Endangerment*, Defining Crimes – Essays on the Special Part of the Criminal Law 43 (Robin Antony Duff and Stuart P. Green eds., 2005)
Antony Robin Duff, *Rule-Violations and Wrongdoings*, Criminal Law Theory – Doctrines of the General Part 47 (Stephen Shute and A. P. Simester eds., 2005)
Antony Robin Duff, *Strict Liability, Legal Presumptions, and the Presumption of Innocence*, Appraising Strict Liability 125 (A. P. Simester ed., 2005, 2007)
Ronald Dworkin, Taking Rights Seriously (1977)
Ronald Dworkin, A Matter of Principle (1985)
Elizabeth Edinger, *Mistake of Law – Bona Fide Diligent Effort to Ascertain and Comply with the Law*, 10 U. Brit. Colum. L. Rev. 320 (1976)
Jerome B. Elkind, *Impossibility in Criminal Attempts: A Theorist's Headache*, 54 Va. L. Rev. 20 (1968)
Arnold N. Enker, *Impossibility in Criminal Attempts – Legality and Legal Process*, 53 Minn. L. Rev. 665 (1969)
Albin Eser, *The Principle of 'Harm' in the Concept of Crime – A Comparative Analysis of the Criminally Protected Legal Interests*, 4 Duq. U. L. R. 345 (1966)
David L. Faigman, *To Have and Have Not: Assessing the Value of Social Science to the Law as Science and Policy*, 38 Emory L. J. 1005 (1989)
John D. Falconbridge, Selected Essays on the Conflict of Laws (2nd ed., 1954)
Lindsay Farmer, Criminal Law, Tradition and Legal Order (1997)
Michael A. Fitts, Can Ignorance Be Bliss? Imperfect Information as a Positive Influence in Political Institutions, 88 Mich. L. Rev. 917 (1990)
Barry Fitzpatrick, The House of Lords: Its Parliamentary and Judicial Roles (Brice Dickson and Paul Carmichael eds., 1999)
George P. Fletcher, Basic Concepts of Criminal Law (1998)
George P. Fletcher, The Grammar of Criminal Law – American, Comparative and International, Volume One: Foundations (2007)
Michel Foucault, Discipline and Punish (1979)
Morris D. Forkosch, *Determinism and the Law*, 60 Ky. L. J. 350 (1952)
Sir John Fortescue, De Laudibus Legum Angliae (1470, trans. Gregor, 1874)
Nigel Foster, German Legal System & Laws (2nd ed., 1996)
Nigel Foster and Satish Sule, German Legal System and Laws (3rd ed., 2002, 2007)
Sam E. Fowler, *Criminal Attempt Conspiracy and Solicitation under the Criminal Code Reform Bill of 1978*, 47 Geo. Wash. L. Rev. 550 (1979)
Ernst Freund, *The Use of Indefinite Terms in Statutes*, 30 Yale L. J. 437 (1921)
David D. Friedman, *Impossibility, Subjective Probability, and Punishment for Attempts*, 20 J. Legal Stud. 179 (1991)
Lon L. Fuller, The Morality of Law (1964)
Leona Christine Gabel, Benefit of Clergy in England in the Later Middle Ages (1928, 1969)

Geoff Gilbert, *Crimes sans Frontiers: Jurisdictional Problems in English Law*, 63 British Yearbook of International Law 415 (1992)
P.R. Glazebrook, *How Old Do You Think She Was?*, [2001] C.L.J. 26, 30 (2001)
George W. Goble, *Law as a Science*, 9 Ind. L. J. 294 (1934)
Gino Gorla and Luigi Moccia, *A "Revisiting" of the Comparison Between "Continental Law" and "English Law" (16th to 19th Centuries)*, 2 J. of L. Hist. 143 (1981)
Philip Gosse, The History of Piracy (1932, 1968)
Richard L. Gray, *Eliminating the (Absurd) Distinction between Malum in se and Malum Prohibitum Crimes*, 73 Wash. U. L. Q. 1369 (1995)
Stuart P. Green, *Why It's a Crime to Tear the Tag Off a Mattress: Overcriminalization and the Moral Content of Regulatory Offenses*, 46 Emory L. J. 1533 (1997)
Stuart P. Green, *What's Wrong With Bribery*, Defining Crimes – Essays on the Special Part of the Criminal Law 143 (Antony Robin Duff and Stuart P. Green eds., 2005)
Stuart P. Green, *Six Senses of Strict Liability: A Plea for Formalism*, Appraising Strict Liability 1 (A. P. Simester ed., 2005, 2007)
Thomas Andrew Green, Verdict According to Conscience (1985)
John Hagan, Victims Before the Law – The Organizational Domination of Criminal Law (1983)
Malvina Halberstam, *Terrorism on the High Seas: The Achille Lauro, Piracy and the IMO Convention on Maritime Safety*, 82 Am. J. Int'l L. 269 (1988)
Matthew Hale, Historia Placitorum Coronae (1736) [Matthew Hale, History of the Pleas of the Crown (1736)]
Jerome Hall, Theft, Law and Society (1935)
Jerome Hall, *Ignorance and Mistake in Criminal Law*, 33 Ind. L. J. 1 (1957)
Jerome Hall, General Principles of Criminal Law (2nd ed., 1960, 2005)
Livingston Hall, *Strict or Liberal Construction of Penal Statutes*, 48 Harv. L. Rev. 748 (1935)
Livingston Hall and Selig J. Seligman, *Mistake of Law and Mens Rea*, 8 U. Chi. L. Rev. 641 (1941)
Gabriel Hallevy, *Victim's Complicity in Criminal Law*, 2 Int'l J. of Punishment & Sentencing 72 (2006)
Gabriel Hallevy, *The Impact of Defense Arguments Based on the Cultural Difference of the Accused in the Criminal Law of Immigrant Countries and Societies*, 5 J. of Migration & Refugee Issues 13 (2009)
Gabriel Hallevy, *The Defense Attorney as Mediator in Plea Bargains*, 9 Pepp. Disp. Resol. L. J. 495 (2009)
Gabriel Hallevy, *Is ADR (Alternative Dispute Resolution) Philosophy Relevant to Criminal Justice? – Plea Bargains as Mediation Process between the Accused and the Prosecution*, 5 Or. L. Rev. 1 (2009)
Gabriel Hallevy, *Rethinking the Legitimacy of Anglo-American High Courts' Judicial Review of Determining Factual Findings in Courts of the First Instance in Criminal Cases*, 5 High Ct. Q. Rev. 20 (2009)
Gabriel Hallevy, *The Recidivist Wants to Be Punished – Punishment as an Incentive to Re-offend*, 5 Int'l J. of Punishment & Sentencing 124 (2010)
Henry M. Hart Jr., *The Aims of the Criminal Law*, 23 Law & Contemp. Probs. 414 (1958)
Herbert L. A. Hart, *Legal Positivism and the Separation of Law and Morals*, 71 Harv. L. Rev. 593 (1958)
Herbert L. A. Hart, Punishment and Responsibility: Essays in the Philosophy of Law (1968)
Stephen W. Hawking, A Brief History of Time (1989)
Douglas Hay, Property, *Authority and the Criminal Law*, Albion's Fatal Tree (1977)
Edward Heath, *How Federal Judges Use Legislative History*, 25 J. Legis. 95 (1999)
Richard H. Helmholz, Roman Canon Law in Reformation England (1990)
John L. Hill, *Freedom, Determinism, and the Externalization of Responsibility in the Law: A Philosophical Analysis*, 76 Geo. L. J. 2045 (1988)
Michael Hirst, Jurisdiction and the Ambit of the Criminal Law (2003)
Walter Harrison Hitchler, *The Physical Element of Crime*, 39 Dick. L. Rev. 95 (1934)

Walter Harrison Hitchler, *Solicitations*, 41 Dick. L. Rev. 225 (1937)
Thomas Hobbs, Leviathan (1651, 1967)
Charles B. Hochman, *The Supreme Court and the Constitutionality of Retroactive Legislation*, 73 Harv. L. Rev. 692 (1960)
Oliver W. Holmes, The Common Law (1881, 1923)
Jessica Holroyd, *Incitement – A Tale of Three Agents*, 65 J. Crim. L. 515 (2001)
Jeremy Horder, *Strict Liability, Statutory Construction and the Spirit of Liberty*, 118 Law Q. Rev. 458 (2002)
Barbara Hudson, *Pushing the Poor: a Critique of the Dominance of Legal Reasoning in Penal Policy and Practice*, Penal Theory and Practice 302 (Robin Antony Duff ed., 1994)
William Hudson, *Treatise of the Court of Star Chamber*, 2 Hargrave Collectanea Juridica 8 (1882)
Douglas Husak and Andrew von Hirsch, *Culpability and Mistake of Law*, in Action and Value in Criminal Law 157 (Stephen Shute, John Gardner and Jeremy Horder eds., 2003)
Douglas Husak, *Strict Liability, Justice, and Proportionality*, Appraising Strict Liability 81 (A. P. Simester ed., 2005, 2007)
R. M. Jackson, *Common Law Misdemeanors*, 6 Camb. L. J. 193 (1936–1938)
Louis L. Jaffe, Judicial Control of Administrative Action (1965)
Nils Jareborg, *Criminal Attempts and Moral Luck*, 27 Isr. L. Rev. 213 (1993)
Robert Jennings and Arthur Watts, Oppenheim's International Law (9th ed., 1996)
Hans-Heinrich Jescheck und Thomas Weigend, Lehrbuch des Strafrechts – Allgemeiner Teil (5 Auf., 1996)
Sanford H. Kadish, *The Criminal Law and the Luck of the Draw*, 84 J. Crim. L. &. Criminology 679 (1994)
Franz Kahn, *Gesetzeskollisionen: Ein Beitrag zur Lehre des internationalen Privatrechts*, 30 Jhering's Jahrbücher für die Dogmatik des Heutigen Römischen Privatrechts 1 (1891, 1928)
Leo Kats, *Why the Successful Assassin is More Wicked than the Unsuccessful One*, 88 Cal. L. Rev. 791 (2000)
Arthur Kaufmann, *Subsidiaritätsprinzip und Strafrecht*, Grundfragen der gesamten Strafrechtswissenschaft, Festschrift für Henkel (1974)
A.W.G. Kean, *The History of the Criminal Liability of Children*, 53 L. Q. Rev. 364 (1937)
Edwin R. Keedy, *Ignorance and Mistake in the Criminal Law*, 22 Harv. L. Rev. 75 (1909)
Anthony John Patrick Kenny, Freewill and Responsibility (1978)
Nancy Jean King, *The American Criminal Jury*, World Jury Systems 93 (Neil Vidmar ed., 2000, 2003)
Larry Kramer, *Vestiges of Beale: Extraterritorial Application of American Law*, 1991 Sup. Ct. Rev. 179 (1991)
Volker Krey, Deutsches Strafrecht Allgemeiner Teil, Teil I: Grundlagen (2002)
Nicola Lacey, Celia Wells and Oliver Quick, Reconstructing Criminal Law (3rd ed., 2003, 2006)
Anthony LaCroix, *Attempted Online Child Enticement: Not Impossible, but Not That Simple*, 5 Dartmouth L.J. 97 (2007)
Wayne R. LaFave, Criminal Law (4th ed., 2003)
John Laurence, A History of Capital Punishment (1932, 1960)
Robert A. Leflar, *Mistake of Law in Arkansas*, 3 Law Sch. Bull. 28 (1932)
Gerald Leonard, *Rape, Murder, and Formalism: What Happens if We Define Mistake of Law*, 72 U. Colo. L. Rev. 507 (2001)
René Lévy, *Crime, the Judicial System, and Punishment in Modern France*, Crime History and Histories of Crime – Studies in the Historiography of Crime and Criminal Justice in Modern History 87 (1996)
David Lewis, *The Punishment that Leaves Something to Chance*, 18 Philosophy and Public Affairs 53 (1989)
Thomas P. Lewis, *The Sit-In Cases: Great Expectations*, 1963 Supreme Court Rev. 101 (1963)
W. D. Lewis, *The Law of England Considered as a Science*, 10 L. Rev. & Q. J. Brit. & Foreign Jurisprudence 23 (1849)

Wayne A. Logan, *The Ex Post Facto Clause and the Jurisprudence of Punishment*, 35 Am. Crim. L. Rev. 1261 (1998)
Frank Pakenham Longford, History of the House of Lords (1999)
Ernest G. Lorenzen, *The Qualification, Classification, or Characterization Problem in The Conflict of Laws*, 50 Yale L. J. 743 (1940)
Ernest G. Lorenzen, Selected Articles on the Conflict of Laws (1947)
Neil MacCormick, Legal Reasoning and Legal Theory (1978)
Andrej Malec, *Legal Reasoning and Logic*, 5 Studies in Logic, Grammar and Rhetoric 97 (2002)
John F. Manning, *Putting Legislative History to a Vote: A Response to Professor Siegel*, 53 Vand. L. Rev. 1529 (2000)
Paul Marcus, *Conspiracy: The Criminal Agreement in Theory and in Practice*, 65 Geo. L. J. 925 (1977)
Geoffrey Marston, *Mens Rea and Mistake of Law*, 8 U. W. Austl. L. Rev. 459 (1968)
Geoffrey Marston, *Contemporaneity of Act and Intention*, 86 Law Q. Rev. 208 (1970)
Breck P. McAllister, *Ex Post Facto Laws in the Supreme Court of the United States*, 15 Cal. L. Rev. 269 (1927)
Fiona McKay, Universal Jurisdiction in Europe (1999)
J. F. McMahon, *Legal Aspects of Outer Space*, 38 British Yearbook of International Law 339 (1962)
John Henry Merryman, The Civil Law Tradition: An Introduction to the Legal Systems of Western Europe and Latin America (1969)
Athy Poulos-Mobilia, *Ignorance or Mistake of Law – Will the Memory Ever Fade*, 62 St. John's L. Rev. 114 (1988)
Michael Moore, Act and Crime: The Philosophy of Action and Its Implications for Criminal Law (1993)
Michael S. Moore, *Plain Meaning and Linguistics – A Case Study*, 73 Wash. U. L. Q. 1253 (1995)
Joseph E. Murphy, *The Duty of the Government to Make the Law Known*, 51 Ford. L. Rev. 255 (1982)
Alan Norrie, Crime, Reason and History – A Critical Introduction to Criminal Law (2nd ed., 2006)
Note, *Criminal Conspiracy*, 72 Harv. L. Rev. 920 (1958–1959)
Note, *The Distinction between Mala Prohibita and Mala in se in Criminal Law*, 30 Colum. L. Rev. 74 (1930)
Note, *Today's Law and Yesterday's Crime: Retroactive Application of Ameliorative Criminal Legislation*, 121 U. Pa. L. Rev. 120 (1972)
Robert Nozick, Anarchy, State, and Utopia (1974)
Daniel Patrick O'Connel, International Law (2nd ed., 1970)
Vernon G. Owen Jr., *Mistake of Law – Reliance upon Advice of Public Official*, 2 W. Res. L. Rev. 91 (1950)
Kenneth Pennington, The Prince and the Law, 1200–1600: Sovereignty and Rights in the Western Legal Tradition (1993)
Rollin M. Perkins, *Ignorance and Mistake in Criminal Law*, 88 U. Pa. L. Rev. 35 (1940)
Ellen S. Podgor, *International Computer Fraud: A Paradigm for Limiting National Jurisdiction*, 35 U.C. Davis L. Rev. 267 (2002)
Herbert Pope, *The English Common Law in the United States*, 24 Harv. L. Rev. 6 (1911)
George L. Priest, *Social Science: Theory and Legal Education: The Law School As University*, 33 J. Legal Educ. 437 (1983)
Charles Radding, The Origins of Medieval Jurisprudence: Pavia and Bologna, 850–1150 (1988)
Leon Radzinowicz and J. W. Cecil Turner, The Modern Approach to Criminal Law (1948)
Kenneth C. Randall, *Universal Jurisdiction under International Law*, 66 Tex. L. Rev. 785 (1988)
Hastings Rashdall, The Universities of Europe in the Middle Ages (1935)
John Rawls, A Theory of Justice (revised ed., 1971, 1999)
Joseph Raz, The Authority of Law (1979)
Joseph Raz, The Morality of Freedom (1986)

Michael W. Reisman, *The Concepts and Functions of Soft Law in International Politics*, Essays in Honour of Judge Taslim Olawale Elias 135 (Bello and San eds., 1992)
Olivia F. Robinson, The Criminal Law of Ancient Rome (1995)
Paul H. Robinson, *Some Doubts About Argument by Hypothetical*, 88 Cal. L. Rev. 813 (2000)
Joseph H. Rodriguez, Laura M. LeWinn and Michael L. Perlin, *The Insanity Defense Under Siege: Legislative Assaults and Legal Rejoinders*, 14 Rutgers L. J. 397 (1983)
Charles H. Rose III, *Criminal Conspiracy and the Military Commissions Act: Two Minds That May Never Meet*, 13 ILSA J. Int'l & Comp. L. 321 (2007)
Stephen F. Ross, *The Limited Relevance of Plain Meaning*, 73 Wash. U. L. Q. 1057 (1995)
Bernd Rüthers, Rechtstheorie (1999)
John William Salmond, On Jurisprudence (Glanville Williams ed., 11th ed., 1957)
Mauro-Rubino Sammartano and C. G. J. Morse, Public Policy in Transnational Relationships (1992)
Friedrich Karl von Savigny, System des Heutigen Römischen Rechts (1840–1849)
Francis B. Sayre, *Criminal Conspiracy*, 35 Harv. L. Rev. 393 (1922)
Joseph Schacht, An Introduction to Islamic Law (1964, 1998)
Walter V. Schaefer, *The Control of 'Sunbursts': Techniques of Prospective Overruling*, 42 N.Y.U. L. Rev. 631 (1967)
Heribert Schumann, *Criminal Law*, Introduction to German Law (2nd ed., Mathias Reimann and Joachim Zekoll eds., 2005)
Edmund H. Schwenk, *The Administrative Crime, Its Creation and Punishment by Administrative Agencies*, 42 Mich. L. Rev. 51 (1943)
Benjamin B. Sendor, *Crime as Communication: An Interpretive Theory of the Insanity Defense and the Mental Elements of Crime*, 74 Geo. L. J. 1371, 1380 (1986)
Malcolm N. Shaw, International Law (4th ed., 1997)
Ian Shrank, *Determinism and the Law of Consent – A Reformulation of Individual Accountability for Choices Made without Free Will*, 12 Suffolk U. L. Rev. 796 (1978)
Jonathan R. Siegel, *The Use of Legislative History in a System of Seperated Powers*, 53 Vand. L. Rev. 1457 (2000)
Norman J. Singer, Sutherland on Statutory Construction (5th ed., 1992)
A.T.H. Smith, *Judicial Lawmaking in the Criminal Law*, 100 L. Q. Rev. 46 (1984)
A. T. H. Smith, *Error and Mistake of Law in Anglo-American Criminal Law*, 14 Anglo-Am. L. Rev. 3 (1985)
John R. Spencer and Antje Pedain, *Approaches to Strict and Constructive Liability in Continental Criminal Law*, *in* Appraising Strict Liability 237 (A. P. Simester ed., 2005)
Marcia Speziale, *Langdell's Concept of Law as Science: The Beginning of Anti-Formalism in American Legal Theory*, 5 Vt. L. Rev. 1 (1980)
William Teulon Swan Stallybrass, *Public Mischief*, 49 L. Q. Rev. 183 (1933)
Peter Stein, Roman Law and English Jurisprudence: Yesterday and Today (1969)
David A. Strauss, *Why Plain Meaning?*, 72 Notre Dame L. Rev. 1565 (1997)
James Fitzjames Stephen, A History of the Criminal Law of England (1883, 1964)
Donald Stuart, *The Actus Reus in Attempts*, [1970] Crim. L.R. 505 (1970)
Edwin H. Sutherland and Donald R. Cressey, Criminology (4th ed., 1970)
Mark Thornton, *Attempting the Impossible (Again)*, 25 Crim. L. Q. 294 (1983)
Stephen C. Todd, The Shape of Athenian Law (1995)
Michael L. Travers, *Mistake of Law in Mala Prohibita Crimes*, 62 U. Chi. L. Rev. 1301 (1995)
Frank Tuerkheimer, *Globalization of U.S. Law Enforcement: Does The Constitution Come Along?*, 39 Houston L. Rev. 307 (2002)
J. W. Cecil Turner, *Attempts to Commit Crimes*, 5 Cambridge L. J. 230 (1933)
Franco Venturi, Utopia and Reform in the Enlightenment (1971)
Adrian Vermeule, *Veil of Ignorance Rules in Constitutional Law*, 111 Yale L. J. 399 (2001)
Russ VerSteeg, Early Mesopotamian Law (2000)
Joseph Vining, Legal Identity (1978)

Raphael M. Walden, *Customary International Law: A Jurisprudential Analysis*, 13 Isr. L. Rev. 86, 97 (1978)

Edwin C. Walker, *Mistake of Law Defense Based on Reasonable Reliance on Apparent Authority*, 14 Wake Forest L. Rev. 136 (1978)

Henri A. Wassenbergh, Principles of Outer Space in Hindsight (1991)

Geoffrey R. Watson, *Offenders Abroad: The Case for Nationality-Based Criminal Jurisdiction*, 17 Yale J. Int'l L. 41 (1992)

Geoffrey R. Watson, *The Passive Personality Principle*, 28 Tex. Int'l L. J. 1 (1993)

Duncan Watts, Tories, Unionists and Conservatives, 1814–1915 (2nd ed., 2002)

Herbert Wechsler, William Kenneth Jones and Harold L. Korn, *The Treatment of Inchoate Crimes in the Model Penal Code of the American Law Institute: Attempt, Solicitation, and Conspiracy*, 61 Colum. L. Rev. 571 (1961)

Mark A. Weisburd, *Due Process Limits on Federal Extraterritorial Legislation*, 35 Colum. J. Transnat'l L. 379 (1997)

Peter Westen, *Impossibility Attempts: A Speculative Thesis*, 5 Ohio St. J. Crim. L. 523 (2008)

Walter Wheeler Cook, *Act, Intention, and Motive in Criminal Law*, 26 Yale L. J. 645 (1917)

A. R. White, *The Identity and Time of the* Actus Reus, [1977] Crim. L. Rev. 148 (1977)

George Wilfred Stumberg, *Mistake of Law in Texas Criminal Cases*, 15 Tex. L. Rev. 28 (1937)

Glanville Williams, Criminal Law: The General Part (2nd ed., 1961)

Glanville Williams, *The Draft Code and Reliance upon Official Statements*, 9 Legal Stud. 177 (1989)

Cal Winslow, *Sussex Smugglers*, Albion's Fatal Tree: Crime and Society in Eighteenth-Century England (1975)

Jonathan Wolff, Robert Nozick: Property, Justice and Minimal State (1981)

Frederick Woodbridge, *Physical and Mental Infancy in the Criminal Law*, 87 U. Pa. L. Rev. 426 (1939)

John J. Yeager, *Effect of Impossibility on Criminal Attempts*, 31 Ky. L. J. 270 (1943)

Raymond Youngs, *Mistake of Law in Germany – Opening up Pandora's Box*, 64 J. Crim. L. 339 (2000)

Bruce Zagaris and Julia Padierna Peralta, *Mexico-United States Extradition and Alternatives: From Fugitive Slaves to Drug Traffickers – 150 Years and beyond the Rio Grande's Winding Courses*, 12 Am. U. J. Int'l L. & Pol'y 519 (1997)

Nick Zimmerman, *Attempted Stalking: An Attempt-to-Almost-Attempt-to-Act*, 20 N. Ill. U. L. Rev. 219 (2000)

Benjamin C. Zipursky, *Two Dimensions of Responsibility in Crime, Tort, and Moral Luck*, 9 Theoretical Inq. L. 97 (2008)

Index

FSC
www.fsc.org
MIX
Papier | Fördert
gute Waldnutzung
FSC® C083411

Kolibri 360 GmbH
Ferdinand-Jühlke-Straße 7
99095 Erfurt, Deutschland
produktsicherheit@kolibri360.de